TREATING SEXUALLY ABUSED BOYS

TREATING SEXUALLY ABUSED BOYS

A Practical Guide for Therapists and Counselors

Lisa Camino

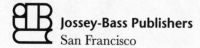
Jossey-Bass Publishers
San Francisco

Jossey-Bass books and products are available through most bookstores. To contact Jossey-Bass directly, call (888) 378-2537, fax to (800) 605-2665, or visit our website at www.josseybass.com.

Substantial discounts on bulk quantities of Jossey-Bass books are available to corporations, professional associations, and other organizations. For details and discount information, contact the special sales department at Jossey-Bass.

 Manufactured in the United States of America on Lyons Falls Turin Book. This paper is acid-free and 100 percent totally chlorine-free.

Library of Congress Cataloging-in-Publication Data

Camino, Lisa, date.
    Treating sexually abused boys: a practical guide for therapists and counselors / Lisa Camino. — 1st ed.
        p.   cm.
    Includes bibliographical references and index.
    ISBN 0-7879-4793-8 (alk. paper)
    1. Male sexual abuse victims—Rehabilitation.   2. Sexually abused children—Rehabilitation.
    3. Child psychology.   4. Adolescent psychotherapy   I. Title.
    RJ507.S49C36   1999
    618.92'85836'0081—dc21   99-16647

FIRST EDITION
PB Printing   10 9 8 7 6 5 4 3 2

CONTENTS

This book is dedicated with much love and many thanks to

My parents, Vella and Carroll Berryman, who gave the unconditional love, nurturing, and encouragement that made it possible for me to work with abused children.

My husband, J. Bruce Camino, who never let me forget my purpose in writing this book and the importance of completing it.

My sons, Kevin and Brandon, whose births clarified all my reasons for writing this book. May every child in your generation enjoy life free from abuse and full of liberty.

PREFACE

It is my belief that every person who reads this book shares my goal of stopping child abuse. I hope you also share my conviction that providing early and effective intervention for molested boys is an essential step in meeting that goal. Ten years ago, two coworkers and I were asked to expand a sexual abuse treatment program to include boys. At that time we were able to find only one book on the subject. Also, when we looked for detailed, structured activities to use in therapy with boys, we found none.

We did manage to find and consult with some professionals who had worked with molested children of both sexes, but what they said about therapy with boys gave us pause. We were warned to expect problems with sexual talk and behavior during sessions. We were cautioned that abused boys would exhibit rage and, therefore, that we needed to be prepared to use verbal and physical techniques for managing aggression. It was suggested that we not use play therapy except as a reward for good behavior. We were even advised not to offer refreshments (although these same professionals offered refreshments to girls) because boys might make a mess or behave inappropriately with the food.

At that point we took a long, hard look at our options: we could wait until other professionals published information on the "right" way to provide therapy for boys, or we could proceed on our own by taking risks, making mistakes, and applying what we learned. We decided to proceed. After carefully considering the available information we had on the subject, we developed our own approach.

We started with group therapy but soon discovered that the group setting is not the best alternative for all boys. We added individual therapy and discovered that the same treatment approach that we used in groups was also effective in individual work.

We based our work in both individual and group settings on the theme of *empowerment*. This theme is explained in detail in Chapter One, and it is woven into the subsequent chapters in Part One as well as the structured activities in Part Two. When a boy begins therapy, he generally feels helpless, fearful, and vulnerable; sexual abuse has robbed him of his personal power.

During therapy, we consciously avoid the word *victim* in describing a client. When a boy hears himself described in this way, he begins to perceive himself as a victim. That self-image then reinforces dependent and helpless behaviors on his part.

The goal in therapy is to help every abused boy break free of the image of himself as a victim and to regain his personal power in positive ways. This process involves separating the trauma he has experienced from who he is as a person. It also involves equipping each boy with the knowledge and skills he needs in order to choose how he will respond to circumstances and other people. It is my hope that helping boys make the transition from victimization to personal empowerment will be as rewarding for you as it is for me.

Acknowledgments

First I want to thank my clients—all the boys who accepted the challenge of therapy and persisted with it. I am grateful to them for their hard work in therapy and for educating me about the issues they face as a result of sexual abuse.

I also want to thank Kathy Schurkman and Tim Bynum, MFCC, who were my coleaders when I began doing group therapy for sexually abused boys, and Andrew Brett, MFCC, who joined our team a little further into the process. We learned together and enjoyed every step of our learning process. Their encouragement and support of this book are very much appreciated.

Many thanks also go to Debra Holland, Ph.D., MFCC, for her willingness to read this manuscript and offer constructive feedback.

August 1999   Lisa Camino
Buena Park, California

TREATING SEXUALLY ABUSED BOYS

PART ONE

A THERAPEUTIC APPROACH BASED ON EMPOWERMENT

CHAPTER ONE

INTRODUCTION

Chapter One acquaints you with this book, its format, and its contents. It also gives you the basic and essential information you will need in order to fulfill your role as a therapist working with sexually abused boys.

This Book and Its Intended Audience

Treating Sexually Abused Boys offers options for both individual and group therapy for sexually abused boys ages seven through eighteen. It presents an overview of clinical information, a specific clinical approach that has been used successfully with this challenging population, and fifty group activities based on that approach (many of which can be adapted for use with an individual child).

Contents

Part One, which consists of Chapters One through Six, concentrates on the therapeutic approach that my colleagues and I use in our work with sexually abused boys. This first chapter not only describes your responsibilities as a therapist but also explains the important relationship between a boy's reactions to sexual abuse and the impact of the conditioning messages he receives early in life. Chapter Two explains how to complete a thorough initial assessment of a potential client and how to prepare the boy for entering abuse-specific therapy.

Chapter Three describes how to work with a sexually abused boy in individual therapy and how to determine when individual therapy is the appropriate choice for a child. It offers sample cases (with names and certain details changed to protect confidentiality) to illustrate the complexity and uniqueness of each child's situation. Although this chapter discusses the specific approach that my colleagues and I use, it is neither possible nor appropriate to conduct every session as though you were following a recipe (start with this theme, use this approach, then follow with this intervention). What is addressed in each session and how it is addressed must be determined by your continual assessment of the boy's needs, problems, priorities, and choices.

Chapter Four covers how to conduct therapy in a group setting. It consists of guidelines for developing a therapy group and for determining when a group approach is more appropriate for a child than individual therapy.

Chapter Five presents information on working with parents and other significant adults, such as guardians and teachers. Chapter Six offers ways to handle problems and difficult situations that occur when working with sexually abused boys. These suggestions are intended not only to help you in working through certain situations but also to stimulate your own creativity in developing interventions.

Part Two offers fifty structured activities. The introductory information that precedes them explains why structured activities are an important part of therapy, how the activities are formatted, and how to use them. The activities are designed to target specific therapy goals for sexually abused boys. Although they are written as group designs, most can be adapted for use in individual therapy. The overriding themes of these activities are (1) restoring empowerment to the children, (2) offering them the opportunity to express all of their feelings with regard to the abuse they have experienced, and (3) giving them a chance to explore their concerns about sexuality and to learn from that process.

It is impossible to predict how a particular group will respond to a given activity. Although I have described common participant reactions to each of the activities in Part Two, these reactions are based exclusively on my own experiences and those of my colleagues. You will need to assess both the process of the entire group and the response of each boy on an ongoing basis, and then plan accordingly.

The Appendix describes nine therapeutic interventions that can be used to educate sexually abused boys and to develop their skills in such areas as communicating, exploring and expressing their feelings, and making decisions. These interventions include such techniques as art therapy, games, puppets, and tension busters. The Resources section comprises several lists of books and articles that are highly recommended as sources of background information on abuse-related topics.

Your Background as Therapist

In writing this book, I have assumed that you are either a practicing therapist or a graduate student who currently works with sexually abused boys or is preparing to do so. To use the materials in this book effectively, you need to have a solid background of training in the following areas:

- Child and adolescent development
- Group therapy process and skills
- Child abuse and neglect
- Psychiatric diagnosis
- Play therapy theory and skills
- Crisis intervention, including the management of aggressive behaviors and suicidal symptoms

Meeting a Potential Client

Your first meeting with an abused boy may be similar to the following scenario:

As the boy and his mother enter your office, you greet them and introduce yourself. Your referral sheet indicates that the boy, Danny, is eleven years old and was referred to you by his family doctor because of behavioral problems at home and school.

Danny sits in the chair farthest from you and his mother and looks at the floor. His mother, who appears tired and somewhat anxious, confirms that the family doctor has recommended counseling. You explain that what you will be doing during this first session will later enable you to determine whether therapy is needed and, if so, what the process and treatment plan will be.

When you ask Danny if he understands and if he has any questions, he again looks at the floor and shrugs. Despite your efforts to involve him during this first interview, he responds minimally and demonstrates no observable response to hearing his mother's description of his behavioral problems. She relates that he has been fighting at school, that he is defiant with teachers, and that his grades have dropped drastically. The fighting and defiance are so severe, she says, that he has been suspended several times.

His mother further states that at home Danny stays in his room and that he awakens with nightmares at least three nights a week. He has also been reluctant to participate in activities that he used to enjoy and excel in, especially soccer and karate.

You learn that Danny's family consists of a father who has his own profitable business, a mother who is a homemaker, a teenaged brother, and a younger sister. In answer to your inquiry, Danny's mother tells you that no one in the family has a history of mental health difficulties. When you ask for more details about Danny's symptoms and when they began, his mother says that she cannot identify any event that triggered his new behaviors.

At the end of the session, you explain that you will need to gather additional information before deciding on the course and focus of therapy. When you ask Danny how he feels about returning to talk to you, he tells you that there is nothing wrong with him and that he has nothing to discuss. Before they leave, however, Danny's mother asks to speak to you privately.

When Danny is gone, his mother informs you that one of his soccer teammates has reported being sexually abused by their coach and his wife. During an interview with the police, the teammate said that the same two individuals not only molested Danny as well but also took pornographic pictures of the two boys together. When Danny was subsequently interviewed by the police, he denied any form of abuse. The police indicated that there would be no prosecution unless they gathered additional evidence to take to court.

Danny's mother says that his father does not believe Danny could have been sexually abused and refuses to discuss the matter further. However, the father has recently withdrawn from the family by working even longer hours than usual. Danny's mother also shares that her husband told her before they were married that a neighbor "bothered him" when he was young. At the time, she did not understand what he meant or why he told her, but now she is wondering if he was referring to molestation.

The mother begins to cry and tells you that she does not know what to do to help her son or her husband. She says that Danny is very angry now and that he does not seem to trust anyone. She asks if you can help Danny.

Although your first meeting with a potential client may vary somewhat from this scenario, Danny's case does present some common themes related to the sexual abuse of boys. In order to work with boys like Danny, you need to develop an understanding of these themes and become sensitive to the reality of this abuse.

Sexual Abuse of Boys

Over the last twenty-five years there has been increasing awareness of the prevalence of sexual abuse of children. As our recognition of the problem has grown, so has our understanding that both sexes experience such abuse. Like substance abuse and domestic violence, the sexual abuse of boys in particular seems like a new problem only because public awareness of it is relatively recent. It is now estimated that between 2 and 5 percent of the male population experiences childhood sexual abuse (Watkins & Bentovim, 1992). However, only a small percentage of those abused report the abusive incidents, and of that percentage only a small number of boys receive adequate mental health treatment.

Danny, like most boys, has been influenced since birth by conditioning messages about appropriate male roles and behavior. When you examine these messages and become aware of their impact, Danny's denial of abuse is understandable.

Messages About Self-Reliance

Through the words and actions of others, boys are taught very early that they need to be strong, powerful, in control of themselves, fearless, self-reliant, and able to handle problems on their own. When sexual abuse occurs, a boy often interprets the experience as a failure to meet these gender-specific expectations.

To many people—not just young boys but adults of both sexes as well—a boy who admits being molested also admits weakness, passivity, inability to take care of himself, lack of control, and behaving "like a girl." Frequently, a boy believes that if he discloses molestation, he will be viewed by others as an inadequate male, as a failure, or as a homosexual because he was unable to prevent or stop the abuse.

Messages About the Stigma of Abuse

Some messages evoke fears related to the stigma of abuse. The disclosure of abuse carries the risk that others will believe the boy is lying, will reject him, will minimize the harm he has experienced, or will assume he will become an offender himself (James & Nasjleti, 1983). Often the boy also knows that if he discloses, he may have to contend with threats, bribes, and coercion from the offender. In addition, many boys are reluctant to disclose because of the potential disruption and pain their families may experience.

Messages About Male Sexuality

Common messages about sexuality can interfere with a boy's recognition that a sexual experience may be abusive (Dimock, 1988). Boys generally believe that they are supposed to enjoy any type of sexual behavior or activity. Therefore, a molested boy often struggles with the notion that he has been abused.

Messages About Expressing Feelings

Strong societal norms suggest that some feelings are unacceptable for boys and men to express. Vulnerability, helplessness, and fear are only a few of these feelings. For many boys, acknowledging their abuse and the resulting unacceptable feelings creates an overwhelming sense of shame.

Empowerment: The Foundation of Recovery

Sexual abuse causes children to feel powerless, and the negative impact of that powerlessness on behavior has been noted by many experts (Porter, Blick, & Sgroi, 1982; Rogers & Terry, 1984; Finkelhor & Browne, 1985). The specific difficulties that arise depend on such factors as the child's preabuse strengths and overall functioning, the details of the abuse, and the response of the child's family or support system when the abuse becomes known. In general, however, if a boy does not resolve his feelings of powerlessness, he faces one of two consequences: (1) he will continue to see himself as a helpless victim with very few behavioral options, or (2) he will try to regain power by controlling others through aggressive or abusive behaviors.

Consequently, the primary goals of the therapeutic approach presented in this book are to help sexually abused boys (1) reduce their feelings of powerlessness and (2) differentiate between negative and positive uses of power. During therapy, boys are taught that exerting power and control over one's own behavior is positive and desirable, whereas exerting power and control over another person is not.

Your Responsibilities as a Therapist

Accepting the role of therapist to sexually abused boys entails assuming a number of responsibilities. These responsibilities, which are described in the remainder of this chapter, are as follows:

- Promoting empowerment
- Setting aside assumptions
- Creating a safe environment in which a boy can acknowledge abuse
- Recognizing and reacting to clues about abuse
- Identifying abuse as an underlying dynamic
- Offering options for treatment
- Establishing and maintaining trust
- Facilitating a boy's acceptance of help

Promoting Empowerment

You can help a boy regain empowerment in the following ways:

- By building his sense of responsibility and accountability
- By developing his understanding of his power and its limitations
- By equipping him with knowledge and skills

Building Responsibility and Accountability. To rebuild his sense of power and control, a boy needs to recognize when choices are available, choose an alternative, and follow through on that alternative. By implementing his own decisions, a boy develops competence and judgment. The more a boy practices making choices and accepting accountability for those choices, the more powerful he feels. Please note that before you can help a boy build a sense of responsibility and accountability, you may need to assist him in resolving feelings of guilt about the abuse, as these feelings interfere with appropriately assuming responsibility.

As a therapist, you must assist in the process of building responsibility and accountability by emphasizing choices and decision making at every stage of therapy. Clearly communicate your expectation that the boy will make choices during therapy rather than blame others for his problems; explain that blaming others only makes him helpless. Involve the boy in all of the following:

- Setting up the assessment appointment
- Developing the rules that the two of you will follow during treatment
- Planning his treatment
- Determining the extent and type of his participation in each session
- Deciding when to leave therapy

Also encourage the boy to make choices in the important realms of his life outside therapy: at school, in the family, in relationships, in reacting to feelings, and in behavior.

Emphasize that after he has acted on a decision, the boy must evaluate the effectiveness of that decision. Explain that every choice involves consequences and that he is accountable for the consequences that follow his choices. If one of his choices does not result in the desired outcome, use the safety of the therapy environment to explore what happened, what other choices he might have made, and what he might do in the future in similar situations. Be sure to stress that something valuable can be learned from every choice.

Another way in which you can teach and reinforce personal accountability is by consistently demonstrating responsible behavior. Always watch what you say to ensure that it conveys responsibility; never talk in terms of blaming others or outside circumstances, and never make excuses. Authority tends to be threatening for a sexually abused boy, so you need to remember that part of your responsibility is to correct his image of authority figures. You can provide a positive image by giving support, setting limits firmly and gently, demonstrating respect for the boy's personal boundaries, and showing that you believe what he tells you.

Developing an Understanding of Power and Its Limitations. You must help a sexually abused boy recognize that one of the limitations of his power is that he is a child and that children often cannot control situations. He must clearly understand that he is not responsible for the choices made by others—particularly by the person who molested him.

He also must understand that in many situations, even difficult ones, he does have the ability to make choices and decisions about his own behavior. Point out that he can exercise power in the following ways:

- By choosing whether to develop his own ideas or to accept the ideas of others
- By choosing whether to take action
- By choosing whether to follow through on a decision he has made
- By choosing whether to express himself in a situation (as opposed to saying nothing and simply hoping that people will figure out what he wants)
- By choosing whether to tell someone his thoughts and feelings or to keep them to himself
- By choosing what he eats and how he exercises
- By choosing to control his own thoughts in such a way that the negative impact of other people's actions is lessened

You will be helping the boy develop an internal locus of control—an essential component of personal empowerment. The attitude on his part that you are striving for can be described in this way: "I can make choices and decisions for myself to feel in control; I'm no longer powerless."

Equipping a Boy with Knowledge and Skills. Equipping a boy with knowledge and skills increases his sense of competence, confidence, and personal power. The use of knowledge and skills helps him recognize more options in situations, thereby alleviating his feelings of helplessness. When you engage him in therapeutic activities that require him to rehearse, role-play, and practice new skills, he will increase his ability to use these skills in daily life.

In addition to the skills related to decision making and assuming responsibility that were discussed earlier, each boy needs to acquire knowledge that will help him deal with the issue of sexually abusive behavior toward others. My colleagues and I believe that addressing this issue directly is important. Boys of all ages, as well as their parents, fear that a sexually abused boy is destined to molest others.

As a therapist you need to emphasize to both the boy and his parents that future abuse on the boy's part is not a foregone conclusion; *the majority of sexually abused children do not become abusers.* Explain that the perpetration of sexual abuse is the result of a variety of factors and that being abused in childhood is only one such factor. Do not minimize their concerns, but explain that intervening at this point—thoroughly discussing the issue with the child and the parents, working through the child's trauma in therapy, and restoring his sense of empowerment—can help prevent abusive behavior on the child's part. Following are two quotations from the literature that you may want to share:

> We do not yet know all the factors (biological, psychological and social) that need to occur, in what combinations or relationship to each other, at what critical points in development, with what intensities, and in what contexts, for the outcome to be the development of a proclivity towards sexual molestation or assault. However, work with identified abusers has indicated the presence of two major types of risk factors in the etiology of erotic interests toward children or inclinations to assault others sexually: biological flaws and unresolved sexual trauma [Groth & Oliveri, 1989, pp. 316–317].

> A high incidence of sexual victimization appears to be a common early life event for identified sexual offenders. There are no data, however, to indicate that all or most male victims of sexual abuse become sexual offenders themselves [Johanek, 1988, p. 104].

My colleagues and I believe that all molested boys need to be involved in therapeutic strategies designed to prevent the development of sexually abusive behavior. Others who have written on the subject share this belief. Ballester and Pierre (1995), for example, stress the importance of early intervention in halting the abuse cycle; they suggest educating abused boys about power, self-control, and responsibility. Ryan (1989) states that the prevention of abusive behavior requires therapeutic work in the following areas:

• Denial and minimization
• Guilt and accountability
• Power and control
• Anger and retaliation
• Fantasies and reinforcement
• Secrets and confidentiality
• Empathy

In both individual and group therapy, you must discuss these topics. You also need to provide each boy with opportunities to experience that being powerful does *not* mean controlling others.

Setting Aside Assumptions

It is important to remember that there is no "typical" profile of an abused boy. To emphasize this point, I have purposely not included in Danny's case many of the psychosocial factors that may put a child at risk for sexual abuse. Although it is true that his father may have been molested, Danny was not emotionally troubled before the abuse, not lacking attention or affection, not poorly supervised or neglected, not from a family with a low socioeconomic status, and not exposed to substance abuse or domestic violence.

Sexual abuse can happen to any male child, regardless of age, size, race, ethnicity, cultural background, family socioeconomic circumstances, religion, personality, or physical appearance. Consequently, in working with any boy—regardless of whether or not he has been referred to you because of sexual abuse—never assume that he has not been molested; using age-appropriate vocabulary, always inquire about the possibility of abuse.

In addition, you must set aside any assumptions regarding a boy's specific problems, his potential responses to treatment, or his capacity for recovery. You must believe that no matter how horrible his experiences have been or how much damage he has suffered, he will benefit from therapy. Any feelings of hopelessness on your part will limit your ability to help and will discourage creativity in your efforts on his behalf. Also, if a boy senses from you anything less than a wholehearted belief in his ability to benefit from therapeutic intervention, his own belief in recovery will be diminished.

Creating a Safe Environment

When you work with a sexually abused boy, you must help him overcome the conditioning messages he has received to an extent that allows him to acknowledge abuse. This means that you must establish a safe environment in which the boy can develop the skill and comfort necessary to talk openly and to listen to your direct questions about sexual abuse. To create safety, you need to convey unconditional acceptance and communicate in the boy's own terminology.

Conveying Unconditional Acceptance. It is your responsibility to ensure that you convey a consistent message of unconditional acceptance of the boy and recognition of his problem. The child must know that you believe him and accept him, no matter what has happened to him. Any expressions of frustration, impatience, or intolerance on your part will place additional pressure on the child. Keep in mind that when, how, where, and with whom he talks about the abuse must be his choice; if he feels forced into disclosure, even more of his personal power and control will be eroded.

Communicating in a Boy's Own Terms. It is not useful to ask a question like "Have you ever been sexually abused or molested?" Generally such a question results in denial; boys often do not know what the terms *abused* and *molested* mean, and many have had sexual experiences that they do not perceive as abusive.

Instead, you must find out what terms the boy uses for genitals and sexual behaviors and communicate with him in those terms. If you are uncomfortable with saying graphic words such as *pussy, dick,* or *butthole,* the child will sense your discomfort, feel that there is something wrong, and decide that it is not safe to disclose. Any expression of your personal feelings in reaction to a boy's comment may be construed as disbelief or rejection (Summit, 1983). In addition, if you wait for a disclosure to be shared spontaneously, the boy may interpret your behavior as unwillingness or inability to hear what has happened to him.

There needs to be an effective balance in exploring this area. Pressuring a child involves asking about sexual abuse repeatedly, focusing sessions solely on this area, suggesting that he must tell, and disregarding any other therapeutic needs he may have. A sensitive therapist will instead do the following:

- Ask directly and gently about sexually abusive experiences. If he denies any abuse, accept this as his answer for now.
- Focus on building trust, rapport, and safety in his relationship with you.
- Address the problems or feelings that he identifies as important to him.
- When a related topic comes up in therapy, use this as an opportunity to educate the child about molestation and about children's possible feelings and behaviors.
- Share your own experiences with other molested boys.
- Continue to ask about sexual abuse experiences. If you suspect he has been victimized, ask once a month (if you see the child every week).

Recognizing and Reacting to Clues About Abuse

When you are talking with a boy who denies that he has been sexually abused but you believe that he has been, trust your intuition. Watch and listen for clues. For example, when the topic of abuse is addressed, the child may react in a number of ways:

- By expressing his denial in a very tentative manner
- By exhibiting discomfort, agitation, or restlessness

- By changing the subject
- By avoiding eye contact
- By beginning to talk in response to a question from you, then stopping himself
- By talking about a "friend's" situation

In addition, the boy may test his relationship with you by exhibiting hostile or aggressive behavior or by maintaining an extended silence. Your reactions to such behavior give him a way to assess your levels of comfort and patience.

When you pick up on a clue, you can handle the situation in several different ways. You can share with the child what you are observing, or you can drop the subject for the moment and plan to bring it up at a more opportune time. Another alternative is to explore the possibility of abuse through some kind of activity. For example, you might read a therapeutic book with the child, play an abuse-prevention game, or use puppets or dolls to help him achieve the distance and safety he needs in order to disclose (see the Appendix).

Identifying Abuse as an Underlying Dynamic

In Danny's case, the family doctor had referred Danny for therapy because of the boy's behavioral problems at home and at school. This situation emphasizes an important point: boys whose sexual abuse history has not yet been discovered are often identified as needing help with such problems as running away, aggression, and noncompliance (Urquiza & Capra, 1990). In addition, many do not appear overtly angry but instead exhibit symptoms of anxiety or depression.

Hunter (1990) suggests that therapists who work with troubled boys need to address not only the presenting symptoms but also the possibility that sexual abuse is the underlying dynamic. How a boy reacts to sexual abuse is determined by many factors: his personality strengths, the support he receives from his family, the identity of the perpetrator, the duration of the abuse, the severity of the abuse, whether force was used, and what happened following disclosure.

Offering Treatment Options

When you offer a boy treatment options (generally either individual or group therapy) instead of just one approach, you are more likely to be successful in engaging him and keeping him in therapy. Faced with only one approach, a boy may either refuse to try therapy or experience less benefit from therapy than is possible.

Individual therapy offers several advantages. When individual therapy is begun immediately after it is learned that a boy has been molested, you can focus your interventions on that crisis. Thus, you may be able to prevent the development of long-standing abuse, and you can assist the child in quickly developing coping skills. When a boy's anxiety is particularly high or his behavior involves severe acting out, individual therapy is a good option. (Refer to Chapter Three for a detailed discussion of individual therapy.)

Group therapy also offers advantages. It can reduce the stigma, the need for secrecy, and the overwhelming isolation that an abused boy often feels. A group also provides opportunities for the child to learn and practice social skills and to develop and strengthen peer relationships. (A detailed discussion of group therapy appears in Chapter Four. In addition, Part Two offers fifty activities designed primarily—although not exclusively—for use with groups.)

Regardless of whether you or the child and the parent choose individual therapy or group therapy, you need to involve at least one parent in the boy's treatment (see Chapter Five). Sometimes particular circumstances make intensive parental involvement essential, such as when the child's abuse reminds a parent of his or her own abuse, as in Danny's case.

Establishing and Maintaining Trust

When a boy is molested, his sense of betrayal can be profound—especially when the offender is someone he knows. Danny, for example, may believe that the only way to avoid further betrayal is to trust no one. The therapeutic relationship you share with an abused boy offers you an opportunity to provide that child with a powerful, corrective experience in rebuilding trust. An abused boy needs to regain not only his trust in protective adults but also in himself.

Understand that building trust can be a slow process. However, there are a number of things that you can do to help a boy rebuild a sense of security and trust in his world. In fact, you can start during the first interview. Give the boy as much choice as possible about his involvement in therapy; emphasize that both you and the parent must hear and acknowledge his choices.

Throughout your relationship with the boy, be careful to keep your word; never make any promises that you cannot personally guarantee. Also be consistent in both words and actions, and make sure that you do not send a different message from what you say.

Convey respect toward the boy at all times, but set limits on any behaviors that are unacceptable, and consistently enforce those limits. Always believe what the boy says about the sexual abuse and express your acceptance of any feelings he has about what happened. If he asks you to share your own feelings, do so honestly. Always give him accurate information, even about unpleasant things he may not like hearing.

Honor the agreements about confidentiality that you make with the boy. Explain to him that you must adhere to any legal requirements regarding such issues as the reporting of suicidal risk; the documentation of further abuse; and recommendations or reports to outside agencies such as schools, probation officers, courts, or child protective services. Emphasize, though, that whenever you must comply with such requirements, you will apprise him that you are doing so.

You may find that other professionals who work with the boy—teachers, for example—ask you for reports about his progress and your recommendations for him. Let the boy know that you will review with him any such reports before you submit them. When you go over the reports with him, listen carefully to his questions and feedback. If he does not agree with you, encourage him to write down his own opinions so that they can be attached to the report. This approach not only builds trust but also lets the boy know that you regard his ideas as important.

If circumstances necessitate breaking another type of agreement, you and the boy must renegotiate that agreement before you take any action. It can be all too easy for a therapist to overlook seemingly small details: beginning sessions on time, conducting all sessions on the same day of the week and in the same place, bringing a snack item that the boy has requested. But these details are not small to the child, and your overlooking them can lead to an erosion of trust.

Facilitating a Boy's Acceptance of Help

One of the most widely documented facts in the literature on male sexual abuse is boys' reluctance to acknowledge that being abused has caused problems for them. As a therapist of a sexually abused boy, you will need to find out whether there is anything at all that he wants to be different in his life and then work with him on accepting the help he needs.

You can facilitate the boy's acceptance of help by offering treatment options (either individual or group therapy) whenever possible. Although you need to make it clear that the boy has permission to refuse either kind of treatment, you also need to talk about treatment as a positive choice, a chance to make changes for the better.

Often a boy sees the possibility of change as frightening, overwhelming, or threatening. Consequently, you will want to emphasize what he can learn through therapy. In a group setting, for example, a boy can learn that he is not alone in the experience of abuse, that his feelings are understandable, and that there are safe ways to express those emotions. He can also learn how other boys have handled the problems they have experienced. Explain that although sexual abuse is the focus of the group, the boys will be discussing many other topics and issues of interest. In almost every case, a boy becomes less resistant to therapy when he feels that he is in control of his own participation.

In some instances, individual therapy may be the preferred modality or at least a good alternative while a boy is waiting for a group to begin. Under these circumstances you might want to suggest that the boy think of individual therapy as a form of tutoring; this analogy can be useful in helping him accept the value of individual therapy. Emphasize that a therapy session is a special time set aside every week just for him so that he can receive some extra support and assistance from an attentive adult. Let him know that his input is important and that you and he will work together to determine which areas he addresses in therapy and what he does during sessions.

Conclusion

This introductory chapter has offered an overview of this book, a discussion of some of the issues faced by boys who have experienced sexual abuse, and a summary of the responsibilities you will need to assume in your efforts to help these children. Subsequent chapters will deal with these and related topics in greater detail.

CHAPTER TWO

COMPLETING AN INITIAL ASSESSMENT

This chapter describes how to complete an initial assessment of a boy who is considering therapy or is about to enter therapy. The assessment process is primarily one of exchanging information so that all parties acting on the child's behalf can learn as much as possible about the boy, his case, and his options for therapy. Those parties include you, the child, his parent or another adult who has legal responsibility for him (referred to as "the parent" throughout this book), and any agents or officers of the court who may be involved, such as an assigned social worker or probation officer.

It is strongly recommended that you conduct a thorough assessment of every boy who comes to you as a potential client before you decide which treatment option you will recommend. Completing the assessment process will increase the child's chances of success in therapy, regardless of whether you use an individual or a group approach.

The initial assessment serves several purposes:

- It gives you a chance to *gather information* that is essential to therapy (information about the child, his family, the sexual abuse he has experienced, his current functioning, his symptomatology, and so on).
- It offers you an opportunity to *prepare the child for therapy* by thoroughly explaining the process and ascertaining whether he is willing to give it a try.

- It helps you *identify and remove or lessen the impact of obstacles* that might interfere with the child's therapy.
- It allows you and the child to *determine whether individual or group therapy would be better* for him, assuming that both options are available. (See Chapters Three and Four for the criteria governing the use of these options.)
- It allows you to *determine whether the child truly needs therapy and whether you are the best person to provide it.*

You will base this last decision on several factors: (1) your own criteria for admitting a child into therapy, (2) the requirements of the child's insurance company (or another party or agency that will be paying for the therapy), and (3) whether the child's overall ability to function indicates that he would or would not be able to complete therapy. (If you decide that you cannot or will not provide therapy for a child, you need to give him and the parent information about other resources that might be more appropriate.)

The initial assessment is conducted in two phases:

- Phase One consists of an interview with the person who has referred the child for therapy (a social worker or another therapist, for example).
- Phase Two consists of an assessment session during which you meet first with the parent and the boy together, then with the parent separately, next with the child separately, and finally with both parties together again to close the session.

Phase One: Interview with the Referring Party

Before the assessment session, it is preferable to gather as much information as possible about the sexual abuse from the person who referred the boy to you. When the parent is not the referring party, the information you need can easily be gathered by phone or in person. The referring person may be a social worker who is monitoring the family due to court intervention, a therapist who is already working with the child, or a school counselor. If the boy is a dependent of the court, the supervising social worker will already know much about the child and will have access to court records containing detailed information. If the boy is a ward of the court and is being monitored by the juvenile justice system, his probation officer is likely to be a good source of information.

If the parent is the referring party, you will need to explore whether he or she is comfortable with giving you specific details about the sexual abuse. If the parent appears resistant or is unable to provide the necessary information, these are your options:

- Ask the parent again during the assessment session, when he or she has gotten to know you somewhat.
- Ask the child during the assessment session.
- Determine whether there is anyone else connected with the child who could provide more thorough information; ask the parent for permission to contact that person and then follow through.

You need answers to the following questions, which cover a wide range of topics. (Although the questions have been numbered for your convenience and related questions appear together, you may ask these questions in a different order if the circumstances warrant doing so.) Be sure to document all of the responses you obtain.

1. *When and how was the abuse disclosed or discovered?* Did the boy tell as a result of his own choice, or was the abuse discovered in some other way (for example, through another child's or a witness's disclosure)? Boys who did not decide to tell are likely to feel more angry and powerless than those who decided to tell.

2. *If disclosure was the boy's decision, was there anything specific that motivated him to tell?* Motivators might be such factors as the involvement of a sibling or the escalation of violence on the part of the perpetrator.

3. *If the boy disclosed, whom did he tell?* This information gives you an idea of the people in his support system and the quality of his relationships with parental figures.

4. *When, how frequently, and for what period of time did the molestation occur?* You need to gather as many details as possible, in view of the fact that time frame, duration, and frequency affect the degree of impact on the child.

Although there are many factors that determine how traumatized a child becomes, in general the boy who is molested more frequently and over a longer period tends to experience more residual trauma than the boy who experiences less frequent abuse over a shorter period. (Nightly abuse for six years, for example, tends to produce more severe trauma than abuse once a year for five years.)

In addition, if multiple perpetrators were named, find out when each had access to the boy. If the parent is an accurate historian, he or she may be able to designate each specific period of abuse. Also try to determine the approximate age of the child when the molestation began and when it stopped, regardless of whether there were multiple perpetrators. All of this information will give you some idea of how the boy's emotional development has been affected.

5. *Who has been identified as the offender, and what is the relationship of that person to the boy?* If the offender was previously known to the child (a family member or a friend of the family, for example), there is a greater likelihood of impaired trust

issues and family disruption. Also, if multiple known offenders were involved, the boy probably has been molested over a longer period, resulting in more extensive trauma to him than if the circumstances were different.

Make sure that you document each offender's full name as well as his or her relationship to the child. Additional disclosures frequently occur during the course of treatment, so maintaining a complete record on the child is essential. You also need to assess future risk to the child by clarifying whether he still has any contact with the perpetrator(s).

6. *What event or circumstances caused the abuse to stop?* For example, did the abuse stop when the boy told someone, when the offender moved away, or as a result of some other specific occurrence?

7. *Was the abuse disclosed recently or some time ago?* If the abuse was recently disclosed, the boy is probably still experiencing crisis issues. This is particularly true when intrafamilial sexual abuse has occurred and the family is currently involved with the judicial or child protective system.

8. *If the abuse was discovered some time ago, what has happened to the boy since the discovery?* For example, he might have been removed from the home, had previous treatment failures, or been involved in court proceedings against the offender. It is also possible that his parents were resistant to treatment or that they minimized the sexual abuse for an extended period.

9. *If the abuse was discovered years ago and there has been no treatment, why is the boy being referred at this time?* It is important to determine why treatment was not pursued earlier. Because the same reasons often resurface and become problematic again, promptly identifying these reasons helps you address them in a timely manner. For example, a parent may believe that the best way to help the boy is to forget about the abuse and move on. If you do not uncover and openly discuss this belief, the parent may remove the child from treatment as soon as there is any improvement in his symptoms.

10. *What were the responses of significant adults when the abuse was disclosed?* One significant factor in a boy's recovery from sexual abuse is the responses of important adults in his life, especially those of parents (or parental figures). You may want to add other, more specific questions: Was the boy believed? Was he given support? Did anyone get angry with him? Was he blamed for the abuse or for any resulting family disruption? Has either parent taken sides with the offender?

11. *What actions were taken as a result of disclosure?* Was the perpetrator arrested? Were the family members separated from one another? Answers to such questions are critical in gauging the degree of stress that the child has had to cope with since the disclosure.

When the molester was a parent, you may find that the child has been separated from the offender but is still living with the other parent. It is highly stressful for the boy when the custodial parent wants the offender to return to the home. Or you may find that the boy has been removed from the home, due to the non-offending parent's inability or unwillingness to provide adequate protection. A child who has been separated from one or both parents has to deal with issues and stressors related to loss and abandonment as well as those related to the abuse.

When there are multiple current stressors (such as placement in foster care, the arrest of a parent, or the family's move to a different area as a result of disclosure), these stressors must be addressed as priorities in therapy. The boy will need to feel some relief from stress before he can work effectively on his abuse-related problems. Also, you need to be aware that major changes like those mentioned in this discussion generally cause the child to feel significant guilt or to blame himself.

12. *Is the boy currently involved with the legal system?* Such involvement might include any of the following situations or circumstances:

- Court supervision of the family (when the child has been neglected or abused by a family member)
- A court requirement that the child testify against the offender
- The child's own violation of the law, which might be virtually anything (from truancy to molesting others, for example)

If the answer to the question is yes, you need to follow with other questions: What are the court requirements for the family and the boy? Is a department of child protective services involved? If so, what is the name of the social worker assigned to the case? Has the boy committed any offenses for which he is on probation or parole? If so, what is the name of his probation or parole officer?

Ask the parent to sign a release of information so that you can contact a representative of the legal system (usually the assigned social worker or the probation or parole officer) for further information. Your objectives are as follows:

- To obtain any information that the parent could not or would not provide
- To ask for details on the legal requirements connected with the case
- To learn whether there are any pending court appearances for the offender
- To find out whether and when the boy needs to appear or testify in court

If the offender was a parent, for instance, you need to find out what specific requirements have been established for monitoring or reunifying the family. (Sometimes the court representative will give you a copy of these requirements; if not, you will at least be able to speak with someone about them.) Be aware that many families enter treatment only when a court-mandated deadline is rapidly approaching.

Consequently, you need to find out immediately whether there are legal issues involved so that you can contact a court representative as soon as possible.

Everyone connected with the case—including you, the child, the parent, and the offender, among others—must comply with any requests from the court or its representatives. Be aware that all courts closely scrutinize compliance. You might be asked to provide written or oral information concerning your evaluation of the child, a description of the course of treatment you have planned for him, any recommendations regarding his situation, or all of these. You may even be summoned to testify in court.

You also have an obligation to report any noncompliance with court-ordered treatment. Suppose, for example, that the child misses an appointment with you and neither he nor the parent gets in touch with you. If that appointment was part of the therapy ordered by the court, you must report the noncompliance to a court representative. Another example might involve a situation in which the court has stipulated that the boy have no contact with the offender. Suppose the child tells you that the offender was included in his birthday celebration. You are required to report this incident to your contact.

13. *Has a medical exam taken place?* If so, what were the findings? A medical exam to verify sexual abuse can create additional trauma for the boy, and you will need to address this trauma immediately and directly.

For example, if a sexually transmitted disease has been diagnosed, an older boy in particular may experience pervasive shame and a feeling of being "damaged." In therapy you will need to reassure and educate the boy so that he assumes responsibility for taking care of himself and following all medical recommendations.

The results of a medical exam may also alert you to a boy's denial or minimization of the abuse. For example, he may disclose only fondling or oral copulation, but his exam may suggest that anal penetration has occurred.

In addition, older boys have varying degrees of knowledge about HIV and AIDS, so you will need to explore the ramifications of obtaining an HIV test. If test results show that the boy has been exposed to HIV, it is strongly recommended that you refer the boy to additional counseling aimed at assisting him in coping with a chronic illness.

14. *What information about the specific sexual acts involved has been provided by the boy and other sources?* It is very important to have accurate baseline information about the manner in which the boy has been abused. In addition to asking about sexual activity, you need to inquire about other exposure to adult sexual behavior (being forced to observe adults engaged in sexual activity, for example), prostitution, pornography, and sexual acts with other children.

Ask the parent about any investigative interviews that have been conducted by the police or by child protective services. Generally you will find that the nature of the abuse has been addressed in such interviews. You must be prepared to inform the police or child protective services if the boy later discloses sexual acts in addition to those previously reported. Also, you need to be aware that in cases involving penetration, the court's response tends to be stronger than it would be otherwise.

15. *Were any other children in the family involved?* If so, what is their disposition? The involvement of siblings is often devastating for a boy. In many cases a boy will submit to molestation, thinking that by doing so he is protecting others from abuse. When he discovers that he was lied to and siblings were also molested, he often feels enraged as well as betrayed and guilty.

If siblings have been molested together, especially when they have been sexual with each other at the direction of the offender, it is important to ensure that all of them receive therapy. In addition, if the siblings subsequently engage in any sexual behavior, immediate intervention is indicated. You may want to consider sessions with all the children and their therapists involved. The children need to be able to talk openly with each other about their "shared secret."

When a sibling is the offender, you need to assess the adequacy of current supervision and protection. In this case the parents' awareness of the sexual activity is critical. If the parents deny, minimize, or ignore sexual behavior between siblings, they may inadvertently set up situations in which molestation can recur.

Sometimes you will find that the disposition for one child is different from that for another. (For example, one child may have been removed from the home, whereas the other has not.) If so, you need to find out why.

16. *Are there any indicators of physical force or violence in addition to the sexual abuse?* Sometimes an offender uses physical force or violence rather than (or in addition to) seduction, games, bribery, coercion, or threats. When a boy has experienced violence in addition to molestation, his sense of powerlessness and fear tends to be greater; as boys generally do not easily express powerlessness and fear, the boy may express high levels of anger instead.

In addition, you need to be aware that if a boy has been disciplined at home through physical means, he may see the offender's violence toward him as nothing unusual. Therefore, it is possible that no one but the child knows about the violence yet.

17. *Has the offender acknowledged that he committed sexual abuse and accepted responsibility for doing so?* Follow with other questions: Is the offender incarcerated or in treatment of any kind? Has the offender spoken directly to the child? If so, what did he or she say? It is helpful to learn as much as possible about the offender's reaction to the discovery or disclosure of the molestation. If the offender apologizes to the child and acknowledges full responsibility for the abuse, the child will benefit greatly, and therapy will be more effective.

Phase Two: Assessment Session

As mentioned previously, you will be conducting the assessment session with both the child and parent in attendance. Before they arrive, examine your office carefully and objectively to determine whether it is comfortable and nonthreatening for boys of all ages as well as for adults. First impressions are important—especially the boy's. His observations and feelings about this initial assessment are critical elements in establishing a relationship with you.

If you are concerned about any inadequacies in the setting, address them before the session. Also plan to conduct the session in a manner consistent with the primary objective of treating a sexually abused boy: *restoring his sense of empowerment.* As much as possible during the session, emphasize that your therapy approach involves having the child make his own decisions whenever possible. In this way you can help facilitate a positive response to therapy on the child's part.

Meeting with the Child and Parent Together

The first part of the assessment session, when you meet with the boy and parent together, will be the first time the boy has been to your office. It may also be the first time for the parent. For both parent and child, this may even be their first contact with a therapist.

Most people in this situation have no idea what to expect, and they feel a certain degree of anxiety. To alleviate some of this anxiety, you need to begin by addressing the purpose of the assessment session. Explain that this meeting will consist of an information exchange; it is not a therapy session and will not include psychological testing or assessment for the purpose of prescribing medication. State that during the first part of the meeting the three of you will be talking together; during the next part you will be talking with the parent alone; then you will be talking with the child alone; and at the close of the session the three of you will again meet together briefly.

Next provide some basic information about the alternatives of individual and group therapy, unless both are not available (see Chapters Three and Four). Then elicit and answer any questions the child and parent might have. Your purpose at this point is twofold: (1) to provide enough information so that the child and parent can make informed decisions about whether and how to proceed with therapy and (2) to let the child and parent know what to expect so that during therapy there will be no surprises.

State that during the session, you will be asking both of them a number of questions concerning the child, the abuse, and related topics. Explain that this information will help you plan and execute an effective therapy experience for the child.

Explain that you need information about the child's current functioning for two reasons: (1) so that you can determine how to help him and (2) so that at the conclusion of therapy you will be able to evaluate whether the therapy experience was helpful.

Clarify that you will be discussing a number of symptoms that are characteristic of sexually abused children and that for each symptom you will ask several questions:

• Has the symptom occurred only recently, or has it been going on for a long time? How frequent is it?
• Is it perceived as mild, moderate, or severe?
• Are there any patterns associated with the symptom? (For example, does a particular symptom show up only after a parent has visited?)

State that you want both the child and the parent to respond to each question, as you want to gather as much detail as possible. Also clarify that it is all right for them to have different opinions about something. Ask if they have questions about the process before you begin. You may need to give examples of symptoms from the following lists before you begin asking about each symptom on the list.

Symptoms Related to Blaming Oneself

• Guilt
• Ambivalence or confusion about offender
• Denial of incidents
• Impaired ability to trust
• Unusual protectiveness toward a nonoffending parent or others involved in the aftermath and effects of the abuse

Symptoms Related to Anxiety

• Regressed behavior
• Physical restlessness
• Sudden, unusual, or multiple fears
• Unusual shyness
• Nightmares
• Sleep disturbances
• Generalized fears relating to the offender
• Withdrawal or isolation

- Unusual or excessive need for reassurance
- Intrusive, recurring thoughts
- Nail biting
- Hyperalertness (startles easily)

Symptoms Related to Depression

- Sad mood
- Crying easily, often, or with no clear cause
- Irritability
- Suicidal statements, gestures, or attempts
- Dangerous or risky behaviors
- Low self-esteem
- Excessive self-criticism
- Hopelessness
- Sleep disturbance
- Passivity
- Marked change in appetite, with resulting weight change
- Low energy level
- Complaints of illness without any physical basis, or stress-related illness

Symptoms Related to Anger

- Temper outbursts
- Running away
- Aggression toward others
- Destruction of property
- Noncompliance with rules, authority, or both
- Verbal abuse or excessive profanity

Symptoms Related to Impaired Sexuality

- Seductiveness
- Sexually explicit conversation
- Persistent or age-inappropriate sexual behavior with others
- Excessive or public masturbation
- Concerns or confusion about sexual identity
- Compulsive sexual activity

Other Behavioral Symptoms

- Recurrent words or behaviors that suggest helplessness, powerlessness, or both
- References to self as different or damaged

- Pseudomature behavior in dress, talk, or behavior
- Unusual concern about food and eating habits
- Bingeing or purging
- Excessive exercise
- Wetting or soiling
- Labile mood
- Frequent use of denial (of reality, of feelings, and so on)
- Impaired social relationships
- Dissociative symptoms ("spacing out," being inattentive, demonstrating excessive use of imagination or fantasy play)
- Impairment in school functioning
- Substance use

After the child and parent have answered all questions with regard to each of these symptoms, tell the boy that you want to meet separately with the parent to ask about the boy's health, school, family, and so on. Explain that after you have spoken with the parent, you will be meeting with the boy alone. Then take him to the waiting room, where he can play on his own or interact with other children. (Make sure that the room is a comfortable environment for the child and is equipped with toys and games appropriate for a boy of his age.)

Meeting with the Parent Alone

Your objectives in meeting with the parent alone are as follows:

- To educate the parent further concerning therapy-related issues, including the parent's role in therapy
- To obtain more information about the child, the abuse, the ramifications of the abuse, and so on
- To identify obstacles to therapy and the underlying fears associated with those obstacles

Educating the Parent. Explain to the parent that your goal with the child during this first contact is to give him information about therapy, allay his fears, and enlist his cooperation in attending therapy. Emphasize that this is very different from an interrogation about the circumstances of the molestation. State that you need as complete a background on the child as possible, including information on any current or past therapy. At this point ask the parent to sign a release of information so that you can obtain the necessary information from past therapists and others as well.

This is a good time to explain the confidentiality of therapy and discuss its importance with the parent. Explain that regardless of whether the child is undergoing individual therapy or is a member of a therapy group, what is discussed in therapy stays in that room, with the following exceptions:

- As the boy's therapist, you must supply information demanded by the court or a representative of the court.
- You will supply information in response to a request from another therapist, but only if the parent gives written permission.
- You must report any noncompliance with court-ordered treatment (such as missing a session, if the session is part of a court mandate).
- You are required by law to report to the court and to the police any abuse or neglect that you discover.
- You will let the parent know if the boy expresses suicidal or homicidal feelings.

Clarify that it is permissible for the parent to ask the child what he learned in therapy, what he liked, and whether there is anything he would like the parent to know. This approach communicates the parent's interest in and support for the child; it also allows the child to be in control of what and how much he shares. However, you need to stress that it is not advisable for the parent to ask the child to divulge what he discussed in therapy.

You also need to remind the parent that the child has the options of individual and group therapy (unless one or the other is not available or is inappropriate for the child). Explain that the child will be choosing an approach later, with your help.

Obtaining Information. If you do not already have answers to the questions covered under the heading "Phase One: Interview with Referring Party" earlier in this chapter, you need to obtain them at this point. In addition, you need to ask the parent for as much information as he or she can recall on the following topics:

- The child's medical history
- Family history and how the child functions within the family
- School history and how the child functions at school
- Previous psychiatric history for the child and for all family members (especially current therapy)
- The quality and number of the child's peer relationships
- The child's strengths and limitations

Identifying Obstacles and Underlying Fears. Subtle and not-so-subtle obstacles to therapy will become apparent as you talk with the parent. Addressing these obstacles as soon as you are aware of them enables you to plan interventions aimed at removing them or lessening their impact. If obstacles are not addressed, the child's experience in therapy may be sabotaged.

Be prepared for some resistance from the parent, the child, or both. (Parental resistance to treatment can be especially high when incest has occurred.) Resistance on the part of the parent is commonly expressed in the form of problems that seem to be excellent justification for not following through with treatment. The most common obstacles that parents identify are lack of transportation, lack of money to pay for the therapy, and interference with school and extracurricular activities. You can help the parent identify alternatives for dealing with these obstacles; the parent who has choices is empowered to overcome feelings of helplessness and hopelessness.

There is another benefit to this process: the parent who models positive problem-solving behaviors teaches the child an important skill that he can use in recovering from abuse. The boy learns that for virtually every problem that seems insurmountable, there are alternative solutions available if he chooses to look for them and is willing to consider compromise.

Lack of Transportation. Parents commonly cite such difficulties as having no car, having only one car in a two-parent household when the other parent needs it for work, having no money for gasoline, being unable to negotiate time off from work in order to drive the boy, and having recurrent mechanical breakdowns. You can help solve a transportation problem by introducing the parent to a problem-solving process in which you help the parent generate alternatives and then choose the best one.

You may find that your community has some kind of program or grant to assist with transportation, so doing some research could pay off. For example, in my county, a certain amount of child-abuse funding is used to pay the salary of a transportation aide, who transports children to and from their group therapy sessions. When a boy has transportation problems and is involved with either dependency court or juvenile court, you need to contact the person who supervises his case to learn whether there are any transportation options that the court sponsors to ensure compliance with court-ordered plans. For example, supplemental funding sources may be available to pay a relative to transport the child or to allow the child to use public transportation.

Also consider asking the parent for written permission to contact the boy's school about transportation possibilities. When therapy is scheduled during school hours or immediately after school, there may be school transportation available to the boy. School options are definitely important to consider when the child is receiving special education services or is having significant behavioral problems in the classroom. In addition, older boys may consider taking a bus, and some parents who live close to your office may be willing to send their children in a taxi.

For boys in group therapy, you might consider encouraging parents to exchange phone numbers and create a car pool. When you are providing specialized group therapy for molested boys, schools or social service agencies may be amenable to providing transportation to therapy for their clients who need it.

Another possibility is to consider scheduling sessions in the early evening, when most parents are off work and therefore able to transport their children to and from therapy. Weekend sessions may also work if you have a flexible schedule.

Lack of Money. You can lead the parent through a problem-solving process that addresses finances. Again, this process can be empowering for the parent. It can also be therapeutic if the parent is feeling helpless, hopeless, angry, or victimized by "the system."

If you offer both individual and group therapy, you can point out that the group approach costs less than individual therapy. Depending on your particular treatment setting or organizational affiliation, you may consider adjusting your fees—especially those for group therapy—on the basis of parents' ability to pay. For example, you may be able to offer a reduced fee for several boys in a group if the other members are paying a full fee.

When you are able to help in generating a number of funding sources, such as those in the following list, the chances are that the parent will at least attempt to choose one that is appropriate for the family's needs. Note that the details of these options vary depending on the area in which you practice. They are offered here to demonstrate that many choices exist for those who are willing to pursue them.

- Medicaid
- State victim or witness funding
- School-based mental health funding for children who receive special education services
- Department of Public Social Services or Department of Juvenile Probation funds (if the boy is a dependent or ward of the court system)
- Private health insurance
- Petitioning to use money from a child's trust fund or savings account
- Requesting financial assistance from relatives
- Asking the offender to pay for therapy or suing to recover the cost of treatment
- Taking out a personal loan

If you are able to see that finances are being used only as an excuse for avoiding therapy, you will need to address the parent's feelings and gently confront him or her about financial concerns. Explain that therapy can have a significant positive impact on a boy, not only in terms of his present functioning but also in terms of his future. Also emphasize that treatment resources specifically for sexually abused boys are scarce, so this is an opportunity that may not be readily available again.

Interference with School or Other Activities. Often a parent's motivation for bringing up concerns about interference with school, Boy Scouts, music lessons, baseball practice, or other activities stems from a desire to minimize the disruption of the boy's normal activities. This desire to minimize disruption is common after the discovery of sexual abuse. Another common but unconscious motivation is that the parent wants to keep the child (and himself or herself) extremely busy in an effort to block out thoughts of the molestation. You need to use a gentle approach to point out that whereas the first motivation is a healthy one, the second generally is not.

Another consideration is that school staff members may be reluctant to have a boy miss any school time on a regular basis in order to attend therapy. If the parent is willing to sign a release of information, you can call the teacher, counselor, psychologist, or principal (or all these people, if necessary) to solve the problem while the parent is present in your office. This approach has several advantages:

- It allows the parent to observe and learn about the process of problem solving on the child's behalf.
- If there is some kind of action that needs to be taken with the parent's involvement, such as scheduling a meeting, it can be done immediately.
- It allows you to determine the reality of a parent's story. (Sometimes parents say that they do not want their children to miss school when they are actually resistant to treatment.)

Ask the parent to identify specifically what problems the child is having in the academic, social, or behavioral arenas. Then explain how therapy can address those problems, either directly or indirectly. Following are some examples of problems that may result from conditions related to molestation:

- The child's inattentiveness or "spacing out" may be related to dissociative episodes.
- Sleeping in class may be caused by nightmares, insomnia, or interrupted sleep.
- Aggressiveness is frequently caused by the boy's inability to ventilate his anger about the molestation in a safe manner.

When you are able to show school staff members that you want to work cooperatively with them, that you and they share the same goals for the child, and that you can explain how therapy will benefit the child in terms of his behavior in the school environment, their reluctance will be greatly lessened. Also, if the parent has already told the school about the molestation, you can use your contact with school staff members as an opportunity to give them information about two important issues: (1) the behavioral dynamics of abused children and (2) how the school can effectively manage these behaviors.

Many parents are reluctant to disclose their children's abuse to teachers. Regardless of the reasons for a parent's reluctance, you need to respect his or her choice not to share information.

When therapy is likely to affect extracurricular activities, a solution can be as simple as scheduling piano lessons for a different day of the week or explaining to the soccer coach why it is necessary for the child to leave practice early on the day therapy is held. In the case of inflexibility on the part of someone like a soccer coach or a music instructor, either you or the parent may be able to discuss the problem with someone higher in the organization's administration.

If all these efforts fail, it may be necessary for the parent to decide which is more important to the boy right now—therapy or the extracurricular activity. A helpful activity to do with a parent is to list all the negatives and positives about each possible decision before he or she makes a final choice. As tempting as it may be to insist that a parent carry out the decision you feel is best for the child, do not do so. It is important for the parent to be responsible for both the decision and its consequences.

Addressing Fears. Even the best problem-solving methods will not help remove obstacles to therapy if the parent's underlying fears are not addressed and resolved. Usually parental fears are connected to a real or potential loss, such as loss of control, loss of privacy, or loss of the important parental role as the only person in whom the child will confide. Sometimes a parent fears learning about the details of the child's abuse, because those details make the situation more real. Other parents feel shame about the molestation, and they fear that others will come to know about the abuse.

You may find that as you assist the parent in solving problems related to the obstacles initially identified, new obstacles appear as if by magic; then the parent uses these new obstacles to justify not allowing the child to participate in therapy at this time. When your attempts at problem solving are continually met with "Yes, but . . ." responses, recognize that the most critical issue is the parent's resistance, which is attributable to some kind of fear.

A parent's fears, which may be either conscious or unconscious, often represent the biggest obstacle to therapy. Whereas many parents welcome treatment opportunities for their children, others feel threatened, defensive, ashamed, or angry. Keep in mind that much of the fear may be generated by their mistrust of "the system" (including mental health services, child protective services, and the legal system), misinformation, or both. Often the simple act on your part of correcting inaccurate information can lessen a parent's fear enough that he or she can allow the child to enter treatment.

The following are some of the more common parental fears. Included are suggestions for dealing with those fears. In some cases you may be able to address the fear directly.

1. *"I will have no control over the decision to go ahead with therapy."* Parents frequently feel that this decision is out of their control. Those who are currently involved with child protective services may have been ordered to put their boys in therapy. As mentioned elsewhere in this book, parents as well as children may have strong reactions to being ordered to seek treatment; some react with extreme anger, others with passive resignation, and still others with behavior that sabotages the therapy.

In working with a parent in this situation, you might want to point out that there are two related issues that can be looked at separately: (1) getting help for the child and (2) being required by "the system" to do certain things or to make specific changes. On the one hand, if the parent does not believe in the benefits of therapy, does not believe that the boy was molested, blames the boy for family disruption, or has other fears about therapy, then each of these issues needs to be addressed separately. On the other hand, a parent's primary source of resistance may be solely that an outside party is telling him or her what to do. Often, too, the parent receives an ultimatum along with the edict: you must comply, or your child may be removed from your care. In these situations, you must identify, hear, and validate the parent's resentment and fear of loss of control. Acknowledge that you can empathize with the parent's discomfort about feeling helpless and powerless, but also point out that the parent can be either a positive or a negative model for the child in coping with these feelings.

Ask for the parent's view of the best or quickest way to regain a sense of control. During the ensuing discussion you can help the parent evaluate the accuracy of his or her view. For example, when the parent acts on his or her resentment and fear by purposely not complying with a social worker's recommendations, the result will likely be an extension of the amount of time that the family must be supervised by the court. Thus, through noncompliance the parent receives more of the very thing that he or she hoped to be rid of. Through this type of discussion, a parent eventually becomes aware that in the long run he or she will regain control sooner by complying with the court requirements. To make this example more vivid, you can suggest to the parent that feeling powerless for six months is certainly more tolerable than feeling powerless for a year or more.

2. *"I will be seen as a 'bad' parent."* Parents often fear what their children will say about them. As discussed previously, you need to clearly explain confidentiality and its exceptions to the parent during the assessment session. Stress that after the child enters therapy you will discuss with the parent any issues regarding the child's safety or protection.

Let the parent know that if the child discloses additional abuse, you are obligated to report that abuse to child protective services and the police. Also state that if the child makes suicidal or homicidal statements, you will notify the parent as well as any person potentially in danger.

If the court is involved in the child's case, you need to let the parent know that you may be asked to report on the child's progress in therapy and on what issues are typically covered; you may even be asked to testify in court.

Often a parent is concerned that others may view him or her as a "bad parent" simply because the child has been sexually abused and regardless of the perpetrator's identity. It is important to discuss the parent's fear of your judging him or her based on information you are given by the child. You might ask the parent, "What is the worst thing the child could say about you?" Once this information is out in the open and the parent can see your nonjudgmental response, he or she may begin to relax a bit. You can also remind the parent that your emphasis is on helping the child recover, not on judging the quality of parenting he has received. It is a good idea to let the parent know that if concerns develop about the way the child has been parented, you will address them directly with the parent and make any necessary recommendations at that time. Finally, you can emphasize that many kinds of assistance are available to the parent if he or she wants to improve parenting skills (for example, stress-management training, financial assistance, parenting skills courses, and individual therapy).

3. *"Talking about the molestation will only make things worse."* Parents frequently fear that talking about the molestation will exacerbate the situation. Ask where this belief comes from. What exactly does the parent believe will get worse? Does this fear come from previous experiences with therapy? Has a friend indoctrinated the parent by saying that bad results are inevitable? Does the family have a cultural or religious norm that suggests problems need to be handled within the family and not with outsiders? You might be able to alleviate this particular fear by educating the parent on the facts about the sexual abuse of boys (see Chapter One) and by correcting any misinformation.

You might want to add that some of the boy's behaviors may worsen initially in the course of therapy, as the child begins to deal with painful issues. It is possible that the child will focus his anger on the parent when he realizes that he was not protected from abuse. In addition, a depressed child who is working through losses and is able to share anger may eventually start demonstrating his feelings through acting-out behaviors. However, the goal for therapy is not only short-term improvement but also healing and recovery over the long term.

The parent may need to hear some of the potential—*not inevitable*—long-term outcomes for children if the sexual abuse is not adequately resolved. If so, go ahead and share this information (see Chapter One). Then emphasize that current knowledge supports the belief that talking about the molestation in a supportive therapeutic environment will help the child, both in the present and in the future. Explain that therapy is not only a healing intervention but also one that can prevent the child from developing additional problems when he is older.

This is an appropriate time to explore whether the parent was molested as a child. Perhaps no one has ever asked the parent about this possibility; therefore, the parent may believe that the abuse has had no impact on his or her present life. The parent may have no knowledge of the resources available to adult survivors of child sexual abuse.

If you find that the parent was sexually abused, the family will undergo a double crisis. The parent may be overwhelmed by his or her own memories and unresolved issues in addition to the discovery of the child's abuse. Usually you need to plan to spend more time with this parent; it takes several contacts to provide information, establish rapport, and reduce fears so that the parent can follow through on a therapy referral. The parent may or may not be able to accept the suggestion that by taking care of personal needs he or she will be better able to support the child in his recovery.

Meeting with the Child Alone

The following are your goals in meeting with the child alone:

- To establish rapport and to begin rebuilding the child's sense of empowerment
- To obtain more information about the abuse and the child's reactions to it
- To evaluate the boy's resistance to and fears about therapy
- To encourage a decision about whether and how to proceed with therapy

Establishing Rapport and Rebuilding Empowerment. To set the stage for a positive therapy experience, from the outset you want to work on establishing rapport with the child and rebuilding his sense of empowerment. Strive to accomplish the following:

- Helping him feel safe in therapy so that he can be open and honest with you
- Developing his trust in both you and the therapy process
- Validating all of the feelings he expresses
- Defusing any anger, fear, or confusion he exhibits
- Expressing your confidence in his ability to recover from the abuse

The first thing to do is explain your main reasons for meeting with the child alone: to get to know him, to answer any questions he may have, and to tell him more about therapy so that he knows what to expect. Then you need to give the child age-appropriate definitions of the terms *sexual abuse* and *molestation* so that he understands them adequately and so that the two of you share the same definitions when you discuss these matters.

This meeting is your first opportunity to emphasize how important it is for him to exercise power responsibly by making his own decisions. Consequently, the next thing you need to do is ask whether he was told that he *must* come to the assessment session. It is important that he participate in therapy because he chooses to, not because he was forced to. If you discover that the child was compelled to attend, let him know that you disagree with this approach and tell him why. Explain about empowerment and the need for him to make his own decisions whenever possible. Let him know that you will also review this information with the person who insisted that he come, so that you can advocate for the boy's active involvement in the decision about therapy.

Also, throughout the meeting you need to pay close attention to signs of powerlessness or of using power inappropriately:

- Does he appear inflexible or unwilling to compromise?
- How does he respond to your setting limits and to the limits themselves?
- Does he "take over" your office, trying to show you that he is in charge?
- Does he repeatedly tell you what to do?
- Does he act passively or have difficulty initiating things on his own?
- Is he indecisive or ineffective?
- Does he give up easily?
- Does he attempt to use coercion, manipulation, or bribery in any manner?

To evaluate his use of power as well as to build rapport, you need to encourage him to talk about anything he feels comfortable with. As you will have gathered some background information on him by this time, you can ask about things that he is likely to be enthusiastic to share. After you have asked him several questions, you can also invite him to question you on any topic he chooses.

If he cannot or will not share much spontaneously, try asking more structured questions or inviting him to draw or play.

Obtaining Information About the Abuse. One of your purposes in obtaining information about the abuse directly from the boy is to assess whether he is able to discuss it and to listen to others as they talk about it. Depending on the child, you can use a variety of approaches. Sometimes very general questions are enough to help him share. In other situations, you will find that a boy opens up readily if you suggest various feelings and reactions that may occur when a child is asked to talk about abuse. Other children prefer to respond to specific and detailed questions.

If the boy has been interviewed previously either by child protective services or by the police, ask him what he disliked about those contacts and then make your interview different. If he wants to know why you are asking certain questions, tell him that you can help him more effectively in therapy when you know what he has experienced.

Much of what you do to elicit information will be dictated by the child's responses. For example, if he shares that being in a room with closed doors is scary for him, take him to a different area where he can see other people but still have some privacy. Also, regardless of how comfortable or resistant he appears, you need to emphasize that the choice about sharing is up to him.

The following are specific topics to address during this meeting with the child:

- How he feels about attending the assessment session and being interviewed by you
- How he feels about having to comply with conditions imposed by the court and about the potential consequences for noncompliance (if applicable)
- Why he thinks the abuse happened to him (If he cannot answer, note that you need to explore this issue further during therapy; do not make direct suggestions about what the abuse might mean.)
- What he would like to change by coming to therapy (Young boys and those with no previous experience in therapy might not be able to respond to this topic; however, you need to determine whether what the child wants is unlikely to be achieved through abuse-specific therapy and, if so, be forthright in telling him.)

Evaluating Resistance and Fears. As is the case in meeting with the parent alone—and throughout the assessment session, for that matter—you need to observe and listen carefully in order to identify any resistance to therapy or fears about it that need to be overcome in order for therapy to be useful. The boy may fear any of the following in connection with individual or group therapy:

- Experiencing strong emotions
- Being judged by others
- Incurring retribution (probably from the offender) for disclosing the abuse
- Being perceived as damaged because of what happened to him
- Being interrogated about the details of the molestation

Most children with impaired trust find it difficult to view taking a risk, such as entering group therapy, in a positive light.

In interviewing the child, remember that talking about the abuse itself is generally the hardest part of disclosure. It may trigger feelings of shame, humiliation, anger, and embarrassment. Also keep in mind that prior questioning by other child-abuse professionals may have felt like an interrogation and, therefore, felt very threatening. If you need to clarify or gather additional details about the abuse, emphasize that the child controls what he shares and how much he shares. Try to give him as many options as possible to help him feel in control of this difficult discussion.

Encouraging a Decision About Whether and How to Proceed with Therapy. If you offer group therapy as an alternative to individual therapy and the child meets the criteria for group therapy (see Chapter Four), then you will probably want to recommend it to the boy at this time. Describe how the group approach works (as described in Chapter Four) and then provide details about the group that you have planned for him. (It is possible that you will not know all the details at this point, in which case you just share what information you have and explain that more will come later.) If you are recommending individual therapy, describe the group option only briefly so that he knows it exists.

Following are some examples of details the boy needs if he is to join a group:

- What day of the week the group will meet (Most groups meet once a week.)
- What time each group session will begin and what time it will end
- Approximately how many boys will be attending
- The name of the cotherapist (unless you will be working without one) and some details about the cotherapist
- If the group is limited to a particular life span, how long that life span will be
- A brief description of the kinds of activities the child can expect during group sessions (see Chapter Four and Part Two)

Next provide a description of individual therapy (see Chapter Three). If you are recommending group therapy, just give a brief introduction; but if you are recommending individual therapy for this child, give more details, such as what he can expect and what kinds of activities might be used during therapy.

Be direct with the child about the range of activities and possible experiences covered in therapy. He needs to know the realities: that some things will be fun, some things difficult; that he probably will experience a lot of emotions; and that sometimes he will remember more than is comfortable. Stress the positive outcomes and let him know that most boys who have participated in this therapy approach have described it afterward as a positive experience.

If the child has a history of therapy, ask what aspects he enjoyed as well as what aspects he disliked. If his previous experience was negative, emphasize how your therapy differs. Later, when you are planning his therapy sessions, be sure to review the elements he disliked so that you can avoid them. If his previous experience was a positive one, find out what he liked about it; in later planning you can consider incorporating some of those positive characteristics into your own therapy with him.

After you have explained both the individual and group approaches and ascertained what the boy may like or dislike about therapy, introduce him to your rules concerning therapy. The following three rules—which apply to all sessions, individual or group—emphasize safety, boundaries, and standards for acceptable behavior. Review them carefully with the boy to ensure that expectations are clear.

Rule 1: What is discussed must be kept confidential. Explain confidentiality in detail (see Chapter One) and the expectation that what the group members discuss is not shared with anyone outside the group. Also inform the boy about the nonnegotiable exceptions to confidentiality (also covered under "Educating the Parent" in this chapter):

- As the boy's therapist you must supply information demanded by the court or a representative of the court.
- You will supply information in response to a request from another therapist, but only if the parent gives written permission.
- You must report any noncompliance with court-ordered treatment (such as missing a session, if the session is part of a court mandate).
- You are required by law to report to the court and to the police any abuse or neglect that you discover.
- You are obligated to inform a parent if the boy expresses suicidal or homicidal feelings.

You will generally find that you spend more time explaining and discussing confidentiality than you do on any of the other rules. Boys are frequently concerned about what their parents might be told, what could be written in a report submitted to the court, or what other boys might say about them outside the group setting.

Rule 2: Substance abuse will result in reevaluation. The second rule that is non-negotiable and explained as such covers substance abuse. You need to inform all boys ages ten and older that coming to a therapy session under the influence of any substance will automatically result in a reevaluation of their treatment needs. It is important to explain that this rule is intended to ensure safety, not to punish. The treatment program described in this book is designed to enhance a boy's power through increasing self-control and making positive choices for himself. Consequently, you need to stress that someone using drugs or alcohol cannot practice self-control or benefit from therapy. In some cases you may even find that a substance-abuse assessment and subsequent treatment may be necessary before a boy resumes therapy for the sexual abuse he experienced.

Rule 3: Do not put your hands on another person, for any reason. Physically aggressive behavior and any sexual behavior are unacceptable; depending on the severity of such behavior, the boy may be immediately suspended from therapy. Each boy is told that angry feelings are understandable, that therapy will provide an opportunity to work out disagreements in appropriate ways, and that there are safe ways to express strong feelings. However, in therapy, as in "real life," there are consequences for behavior that is hurtful to another person. This limitation of physical contact helps ensure a therapy environment that feels safe to all boys.

Prior to ending the meeting, let the boy know which treatment option you recommend for him. Ask him if he will agree to attend either group or individual sessions. If the boy seems reluctant, ask if he is willing to sign a four- to six-week contract to attend. Explain that if he chooses not to continue at the end of this period, then all he has to do is inform you.

If you are unsure about whether the boy will be able to cope with the group (for example, if he has severe behavioral problems or a history of multiple treatment failures) but you think it would benefit him to try, encourage him to sign a four- to six-week contract. If for any reason he does not want to continue after this period, then other treatment alternatives can be explored. Also explain that you and your cotherapist may also decide at the end of the contract period that a different type of therapy would be more beneficial. (This option allows you to give a child a chance, with the possibility of removing him from the group after observing his participation for a while.)

If the child needs more time to think about his decision, make an agreement to contact him on a day of his choice in the near future. If he refuses to consider even a four-week trial, make sure that he is aware of any potential consequences of refusal. For example, if the court has mandated therapy, the boy could incur problems as a result of noncompliance. Also explain that if he decides on the group approach later, he may have to wait for another group to begin.

You can also develop a contract with a boy who needs individual therapy but is reluctant to commit to it. If he is willing to try even a few sessions—and you can make those sessions nonthreatening, with an emphasis on building rapport—you have a better chance of gaining his cooperation to remain.

If the boy does decide to go ahead with individual or group therapy—regardless of whether he chooses the four-week option—you need to have him sign a contract stating what he has agreed to do. In the contract, be sure to list the particulars of the therapy sessions: where you and the child will meet, on what days, at what times, and so on. Exhibit 2.1 shows an example of a contract.

Closing the Assessment Session

Before you close the session, ask the parent to return. In the presence of the boy, explain what he has decided to do about pursuing therapy and which option he chose. If he decided not to participate at this time, emphasize to the parent why his choice needs to be respected: forcing an abused child to attend therapy is never appropriate, as it replicates the dynamics of abuse and makes the child feel that he is not in control and that no one listens to him.

If there is concern due to court involvement (for example, if the court has mandated group therapy but the child refuses, or if you feel that the child must

---

EXHIBIT 2.1. EXAMPLE OF A THERAPY CONTRACT.

Date: March 27, 1999

I, Robert Rearden, agree to attend group therapy with Maureen Smith every Wednesday from 3:00 to 4:30 P.M. at the Roseville Therapy Center, starting April 1 and ending April 29. At the end of these four weeks, I understand that I will meet with Maureen Smith to discuss whether I want to continue and whether this is the best choice for me.

Child's signature _____

Witness _____

---

undergo individual therapy instead), volunteer to write a letter explaining the child's decision, the rationale for supporting his decision, and your recommendation for future action. Often a child who refuses group therapy at first is willing to try it later.

If the child has accepted your recommendation, share the details with the parent and make plans for starting therapy. After eliciting and answering any questions, close the session.

Conclusion

The initial assessment is a critical part of therapy. By giving and receiving information about a potential client and options for therapy, you prepare all parties—yourself, the child, and the parent—for the process that is about to take place. Even if the child decides not to enter therapy and you never see him again, he will benefit from the information you gave him and the concern and caring you showed.

If the boy has not yet decided to continue, you will need to follow up later by contacting him on the agreed-on date, learning his decision, and creating a contract as necessary. If the child has already committed to therapy, you can begin making plans to work with him. Chapters Three and Four will tell you what you need to know about individual and group therapy.

CHAPTER THREE

INDIVIDUAL THERAPY

This chapter deals with individual (one-on-one) therapy with a sexually abused boy. It describes the situations that warrant individual rather than group therapy, actions you can take to increase a boy's chances for success in individual therapy, a sample session format, and ways to address the problem behaviors that the boy has adopted in an effort to cope with abuse.

Determining When to Use Individual Therapy

Individual therapy is the preferred treatment modality for some sexually abused boys and in specific situations. The following sections describe the situations in which you will want to work with a boy one-on-one instead of in a group setting.

Molestation Is Suspected but Not Disclosed

Group therapy is not recommended when molestation is suspected but the boy has not disclosed it. Molestation may be suspected, for example, when the boy has undergone a medical examination and the results strongly indicate sexual abuse, when another child discloses that the boy has been molested (probably by the same offender), or when the boy exhibits behavioral indicators of abuse. (See "Addressing Problem Behaviors" later in this chapter.)

The Offender Was a Stranger

When a boy has been abused by a stranger rather than someone known to him, individual therapy is more appropriate than the group option. Assault by a stranger results in the development of issues that are uncommon in cases of assault by someone known, and these issues require special attention for which an individual setting is more suitable. In addition, some of the issues commonly addressed when the offender was someone close to the child do not apply when the perpetrator was a stranger.

For example, the child may have a strong perception of being "damaged" because of injuries he may have incurred or sexually transmitted diseases he may have contracted. Also, if the molestation included physical violence or force, he may be experiencing fear or anger, or questioning why he was chosen. In contrast, the issues of betrayal, mistrust, and ambivalence about the perpetrator, which are common when the boy knows the perpetrator, are typically not experienced after assault by a stranger.

It has not yet been determined whether an assault by a stranger tends to be more or less traumatic to the child than ongoing abuse by a known perpetrator. This matter needs further research.

The Boy Is Resistant to Group Therapy

When a boy meets your criteria for group therapy but is resistant to your recommendation, individual therapy gives him an alternative. If he agrees to come to individual sessions, you can explore his fears and reluctance about group therapy while you work with him on resolving his specific problems. In this way he receives the necessary intervention even if he decides never to join a group.

The Boy Has Been Assaulted by a Group

Individual therapy is more effective than the group approach when a boy has been abused by a group of perpetrators. Although he may not be able to verbalize the anxiety he feels about the prospect of being in a group, you need to be aware that placing him in a group is likely to trigger multiple problem behaviors.

The Boy Has a Thought Disorder or Developmental Disability

A group atmosphere usually is too stressful, overwhelming, or frustrating for a boy who has a thought disorder or developmental disability. When such a condition exists, a very different and highly individualized treatment approach is required.

You will need to use simplified concepts, a gradual approach to exploring the trauma of the abuse, and interventions aimed at correcting the child's problem behaviors rather than exploring his feelings or insights about the abuse. If the child is exhibiting psychotic symptoms, you will need to ensure that he has been thoroughly evaluated and medically treated for these symptoms before you attempt any therapeutic work.

The Group Approach Is Not an Option

Individual work may be your only available treatment approach in certain situations, such as the following:

- When you do not have enough boys in the same age range to form a group
- When other therapists or administrators in your professional practice do not support the group approach
- When you feel that you need more experience in working with molested boys before attempting to use the group approach

Increasing the Likelihood of Success in Individual Therapy

You can increase a boy's chances for success in individual therapy in a number of ways:

- By creating an environment that feels safe to the boy
- By allowing the boy to decide about disclosure on his own (avoiding any behavior that may be construed as pressure to disclose)
- By identifying the boy's strengths and interests and incorporating them into your therapeutic approach
- By offering hope to the boy
- By working with the boy to develop a contract concerning his attendance at therapy sessions

Creating a Safe Environment

Keep in mind that the therapy setting may feel highly threatening to the boy. From his point of view, the sessions take place in a closed room, where he is alone with a stranger; they also involve talking about confidential matters that he probably thinks of as "secrets." In addition, if you are the same gender as the perpetrator, that fact alone may create additional anxiety for him. You need to be prepared to explore with the boy what you can do to help him feel safer in the therapy setting.

Examine the room in which you conduct individual sessions. Ask yourself whether it appears welcoming and comforting from a boy's perspective. The room needs to include materials that immediately engage a child's attention, such as a toy shelf, books for children, games, puppets, stuffed animals, a sandbox or sand tray with accompanying items, a dollhouse, and a readily accessible drawing surface such as a chalkboard or dry-erase board. Different types of cardboard and wooden building blocks are often a young boy's first choice. Art materials—paper, felt-tipped pens, crayons, colored pencils, stamps, a variety of stickers—are also attractive to children.

An informal setting that includes beanbags or large pillows helps a child feel at ease. Talking while sitting on the floor or at a child-size work table often feels more natural and comfortable than using a formal conversation area with chairs and couches. Color is also important to consider; you may choose either soothing colors, such as pastels, or bright, cheerful ones.

Plan to use the room to teach and reinforce boundaries. You need to tell each child what he can and cannot play with; he needs to learn what he can touch and explore and what is off-limits. However, you will want to keep items that are off-limits to a minimum—perhaps just your desk. You will probably want to avoid keeping any breakable or irreplaceable items in the room.

Allowing the Boy to Decide About Disclosure

If you pressure a boy to disclose, you will almost certainly guarantee his opposition to therapy. He will feel as if he is being interrogated, and he will not develop the feeling of safety that is necessary in order for him to disclose. From your first encounter with him, however, you do need to be on the lookout for possible obstacles to disclosure, and you need to try to remove those obstacles. After the obstacles have been removed and you and the boy have established trust in your relationship, he may choose to disclose, but this must be his choice.

Identifying Strengths and Interests

When you start therapy with a boy, identify his strengths and interests; determine which of those strengths and interests might facilitate and reinforce therapy, and figure out how you can incorporate them into your therapeutic approach. If the boy you are working with likes to read, for example, you might consider giving him books to read between sessions; they might be about abuse, certain problem behaviors that the boy is exhibiting, how other children have reacted to abuse, or other related topics. Then when the boy returns after reading the books, you can discuss them with him. Similarly, in the case of an insightful child who likes to write, you might ask him to maintain a journal so that he can capture his thoughts and ideas about the abuse; then during subsequent sessions you can encourage him to share his writings with you or to bring up issues related to what he has written.

Offering Hope

Hopelessness is common among molested boys, especially when they have undergone previous therapeutic experiences that did not specifically address the abuse and thus provided no relief from their overwhelming feelings and no improvement in their problem behaviors. Consequently, it is critical that you convey from the outset and throughout therapy that you are hopeful about the boy's future and that you expect therapy to help him grow and change.

Developing an Attendance Contract

It is wise to work with the boy to develop a contract specifying requirements for attending therapy sessions. For example, the two of you might agree to meet weekly for three months or for twelve sessions. Specifying attendance issues helps lessen the boy's resistance, especially when therapy has been mandated by the court and both parent and child feel angry about this requirement.

Sample Session Format

You will be organizing each therapy session around a boy's specific needs, his age, and your own style as a therapist. Similarly, the content of each session is unique and depends on such factors as how long the boy has been in treatment and which of his problems have been identified as most urgent. Taking these unique aspects of therapy into account, you may still find helpful the following sample format for a session of approximately one hour, particularly if you have had only minimal experience in working with children. This sample is not intended to be prescriptive. Feel free to draw on your own experiences, creativity, instincts, and insights in preparing for and conducting a session.

The sample format works well with boys who have had previous experience with therapy. If you are working with a boy who has not had previous experience, you will need to place greater emphasis on building rapport, mutually sharing information, and helping the child feel safe enough to explore therapy issues.

To build rapport, you need to ask about the boy's interests, hobbies, likes, and dislikes. Consider these questions:

- What do you like about school?
- Are you involved with any sports or clubs?
- What do you do on the weekends or during the summer when there is no school?
- What are your friends like?

It is easier to build a relationship with a child when you are familiar with currently popular toys, television shows, computer games, movies, musicians, and actors. These are topics that are easy and fun for boys to discuss; and when you demonstrate that you know something about what the child is interested in, he will feel encouraged to keep talking.

As therapy progresses and the child develops trust in you, he will begin to share more information. It is important to balance your requests for information with giving the child information.

Avoid constantly questioning the child, as this process may feel like an interrogation and is not conducive to building a relationship. Tell him specifically what you do to help boys like him: "John, what I do is talk and play with kids who have been hurt by someone or something. I want to help you understand what happened and who is responsible for what. I also want to help you get over being so sad and angry all the time."

You can also give information about what the two of you will be doing in sessions: "I know you've seen all the materials I keep in my office. Sometimes we will do art projects together; sometimes I will bring an activity to share with you; other times you will be free to choose what you would like to play with. What we will always be doing, though, is working together to help you feel better and learn some better ways of managing things."

Assessing the Current Situation

The first five to fifteen minutes of any session are spent assessing the boy's situation, following up on previous issues or assignments, and sharing the session agenda. Regularly starting sessions with a period of assessment and sharing fosters the child's feelings of security and trust. The verbal interaction required also helps him settle into the work of therapy and steers him away from immediately requesting a game or toy.

The results of this initial phase will let you know whether you can follow through with your plans for the session. As a result of the boy's sharing, for example, you may find that a crisis has arisen. If so, you must change your plans and deal with that crisis before you work on any other problems.

Following are two examples of the kinds of questions you might ask to ascertain the child's current situation:

> "Last week you were feeling pretty sad because your dad didn't show up to see you over the weekend. What happened this past weekend?"

> "I had a call from your mom, and she said that you had another fight at school and that the principal was getting pretty upset with you. What was it like to meet with the principal again?"

In questioning the boy, remember that you want him to feel that the two of you are working together, not that you are doing something to him. You also need to reinforce that what he shares and when he shares it are completely his choice. To encourage the child's openness, his sense of shared responsibility in working with you, and his feeling of empowerment and control with regard to sharing, you might say something like this: "I wonder if there is anything on your mind that you want to get some help with today. Remember that I may not be able to give you the best help possible if there's something I don't know about. My job is to help you whenever you feel ready to share about problems or feelings."

If you choose, you may even develop a ritual for assessing and sharing. Children find the consistency and structure of a ritual comforting. The following comments introduce rituals:

> "Let's start by making our lists for today. First we'll list all the good things that have happened since I last saw you. Then we'll make a list of any bad things that have happened."

> "Remember that we've been talking about how everyone has feelings and how there is nothing 'right' or 'wrong' about what we feel? Where do you think your anger is today, on our scale from zero to ten, where zero means no anger at all and ten means the most anger you've ever felt? Where on the scale would you put your worried feelings today?"

After you have assessed the boy's situation, you need to follow up on any issues or assignments from the previous session. Doing so not only reinforces the child's responsibility for active involvement in his therapy but also allows you to intervene with recommended changes if he is encountering obstacles in a particular course of action. Here is a comment, for example, designed to elicit information about progress on a previously agreed-on assignment: "This week you were going to practice shooting baskets outside to cool down whenever you felt like hitting your sister. Were you able to do that? How well did it work for you?"

Finally, you will want to share your agenda for the session. You may end up sharing an entirely different agenda from the one you originally planned, depending on any new information you have just received. Consequently, although planning a session in advance is important, you need to remain flexible enough to accommodate the boy's immediate needs: "We've known for a while that you have to go to court soon and tell what happened with your grandfather. To prepare you for this, I have an activity that I'd like us to do together. It's about finding different ways to solve problems. It's fun and easy; we get to do some role playing, and we can get some ideas about what to do in court next week."

Working on Problems

During the next thirty to forty minutes of the session, you will be working with the boy on problems that he is experiencing in connection with his molestation (see "Addressing Problem Behaviors" in this chapter). As mentioned previously, if a crisis has arisen, you will need to deal with that crisis before tackling any other problems.

When there is no crisis at hand, you might want to introduce the working phase by saying something like this: "We have about thirty minutes. Why don't you choose what we do for the first twenty minutes, and then I'll choose what we do for the next ten? If you don't like what I choose, you let me know, and we'll work it out together." Sometimes a boy chooses to engage in one activity for the entire time, whereas another might not be able to focus on a single activity for more than five to ten minutes before moving to something else.

Be sure to have available a range of age-appropriate materials for the boy to choose from as he addresses his problems. These materials might include toys, games, art supplies, books, and puppets. While you and the boy work, your primary responsibility is to help him rebuild his sense of empowerment. Consequently, during this phase you will need to watch for opportunities to point out alternatives and to encourage decision making on his part.

Wrapping Up

Be sure to allow five to ten minutes at the end of the session to bring closure to your time with the child. Choose a consistent ending ritual that gives him a positive experience and makes it easier for him to leave the session.

What is positive for one boy may not be for another, so you may need to experiment with several ritual endings before you find one that works. As is the case throughout therapy, you need to give the boy choices; be sure to ask which ritual he likes instead of simply imposing what you feel is the best option.

If you began the session with a ritual that the boy likes, you might want to repeat that ritual in a closing form. Here is an example: "Let's check your feelings again. When we started today, your anger was at seven on our scale of zero to ten, and your worry was at eight. Where is your anger now? Where are your worried feelings?"

Another way to end a session on a positive note is to give the boy a specific and genuine compliment about the progress he is making. Following are two examples:

> "I really appreciate it that you took a risk today in talking to me about your stepdad. I know it's not easy, especially because he threatened you."
>
> "Thank you for following my directions to help clean up. We made a game out of it so it would be more fun. Maybe we can share that idea with your mom. Do you want to tell her, or do you want me to tell her?"

Yet another idea is to end with a brief relaxation or guided-imagery activity. Teaching relaxation skills to a molested boy is an excellent way to enhance his overall coping ability, and incorporating these skills into a closing activity gives him an opportunity to practice regularly. Also, this approach to closure is especially helpful after highly emotional therapeutic work, when you will need to decrease the child's level of tension before he leaves. Here is one way to introduce an activity that combines relaxation with guided imagery: "Before you go, let's practice our belly breathing together. If you feel comfortable enough, you can close your eyes while you breathe. I'll take you on a little walk to the beach while your eyes are closed."

Addressing Problem Behaviors

The majority of your time in an individual session with a boy will be spent working on problem behaviors. In an effort to manage his feelings about being abused, every boy adopts coping behaviors, most of which cause problems in terms of his ability to function and interact with others effectively. The specific behaviors that a boy adopts are influenced by a variety of factors, such as his age, his personality, his family relationships, people's responses to the disclosure of the abuse, the factors involved in the abusive situation, and the boy's functioning before the abuse occurred. However, all behavioral problems result from one or more of the following three responses to abuse:

- Depression
- Denial or minimization
- Anger

By examining the boy's history and presenting problems, you can determine whether he is coping primarily through depressed behaviors, denying or minimizing behaviors, or angry behaviors. Once you have categorized the behaviors the boy is exhibiting, you can aim your efforts at helping the child replace them with effective strategies. (See Chapter Four for a discussion of the impact of the three types of behaviors on a group therapy setting.)

The following sections offer some general treatment guidelines and case examples for the three types of ineffective coping behaviors. Keep in mind, though, that all sexually abused boys—regardless of whether they are trying to cope through depression, through denial, or through anger—need to develop an understanding of certain dynamics associated with abuse:

- Why feelings of helplessness and powerlessness arise after sexual abuse
- How to recognize these feelings
- How to regain power and control in positive ways

Developing such understanding is critical in preventing victimizing behavior toward others.

Coping Through Depression

The experience of sexual abuse results in several different kinds of loss; some are readily apparent, whereas others are subtle and difficult to identify. These losses can be overwhelming to a child and can result in depression, helplessness, hopelessness, withdrawal, and a pessimistic view of life.

For the sexually abused male child who becomes depressed, that depression pervades all areas of his life. It interferes with all interactions—with family members, with teachers and classmates, and with friends. Irritability and sullenness are also common with depression. The boy who presents with these symptoms is attempting to cope with abuse by adopting this belief: "If I pretend not to care about anything and if I keep myself distant from people, then I won't be hurt again or lose anything else that is important to me." Similar symptoms may be seen in a boy who feels guilty and responsible for the molestation: he gives up all sense of control and becomes passive and helpless.

In individual therapy with a depressed boy, you will need to address the following issues:

1. *Are there other significant people in the boy's life who have responded to crises with symptoms of depression?* This issue is important for two reasons. First, if there is a family history of depression, psychiatric consultation and antidepressant medication might need to be considered early in the process of treating the child. Second, if a parent or caretaker has been depressed for extended periods, the boy may have learned only a limited number of effective coping skills from these role models. Thus, educating both the parent and the child on how to manage each depressive symptom will be a priority for treatment.

If at all possible, facilitate a referral for psychiatric treatment for the parent if you suspect or know that he or she is currently experiencing depression. The parent is likely to find it extremely difficult to be nurturing and supportive with the boy until that depression is alleviated. In the meantime, ascertain whether there are any other adults who can be available to nurture and support the boy.

2. *What benefits is the boy receiving from his depression?* Such benefits commonly stem from parental guilt feelings and can include extra attention, being allowed to stay home from school, getting treats when siblings do not, lack of discipline, and no follow-through when rules are broken. These benefits can reinforce depression and inhibit the boy's motivation to make necessary changes. Most of the time, a parent is unaware of this dynamic and certainly does not intend to reward depression. Clearly, then, the benefits the child receives must be identified so that the parent can learn to reinforce the child's positive efforts to cope and change.

3. *Does the boy understand the impact of sexual abuse on a person's self-esteem?* A boy who is molested commonly reacts with feelings of shame, humiliation, and helplessness. These feelings are destructive to his self-image. In therapy you need to help him determine what kinds of resources, experiences, and support he needs in order to feel better about himself.

One way you can fulfill this responsibility is to help him recognize his own unique strengths, abilities, and successes. Once he knows these, he can learn how to capitalize on them to build self-esteem over time.

It is important that the boy does not rely solely on external elements such as physical appearance or athletic prizes to validate himself. He needs to feel unconditional self-esteem. To foster this feeling, concentrate on pointing out options that are available to him and on reminding him that he is capable of making good choices for himself.

4. *What is the boy's potential for self-harm due to suicidal thoughts or feelings, anger, the desire for revenge, ongoing hopelessness, or guilt?* Remind the child that there is a difference between acknowledging his thoughts or feelings and choosing to act on them. If he feels that he cannot control his impulses, you must help him develop and

write down a feasible plan to impose control on himself. Explore the conditions that precipitate suicidal tendencies for him (such as feelings of helplessness or powerlessness) so that he can create new ways to cope with or change these conditions.

5. *Does the boy understand the connection between anger and depression?* An inability to acknowledge or express anger can result in profound depression. Anger is normal and natural; it only becomes harmful when people repress it, deny it, or become abusive in some manner. Let the boy know that there are many options available for releasing anger: talking it out, writing about it in a journal or a letter, crying, expressing it through artwork, engaging in physical exercise, screaming, and stating his needs assertively.

Help the boy identify what he fears will happen if he becomes openly angry. Figure out his family's rules and norms regarding anger. He may never have witnessed a healthy way of expressing anger that allows for resolution; instead, he may have seen only the extreme ends of the continuum, such as withdrawal or physical aggression.

6. *What losses has the boy experienced as a result of being abused?* He cannot even begin to address these losses until he recognizes exactly what they are. You must help him identify and accept the reality of each loss he has experienced. Explain that if he does not resolve his experiences of loss, eventually he will end up releasing his pent-up emotion in a way that may prove harmful to himself or others.

The boy needs to know that depression is a part of grieving and that grieving is a normal response to loss. He needs to accept that boys can and do cry and that crying is healthy. Educate him about the stages of grieving; make sure he understands that recovering from loss and the accompanying depression is a process that requires time and patience.

◆ ◆ ◆

Two examples of boys who entered therapy with depression as a coping strategy are presented in the following paragraphs. Identifying information has been changed in order to protect confidentiality.

Matthew

Matthew first entered individual therapy at the age of ten, one year after his disclosure of sexual abuse by his uncle, who was also his godparent. A solemn boy, Matthew expressed many complaints about physical pain and illness, held his anger inside, feared abduction and retribution, experienced nightmares, and felt intensely responsible for the molestation. His parents pursued criminal charges, and his extended family experienced extreme disruption as a result of these charges and the subsequent arrest and trial. When the jury found his uncle not guilty, Matthew blamed himself.

Kyle

Kyle was a quiet, intelligent sixteen-year-old whose father had molested him repeatedly over a five-year period. At the time he entered therapy, court supervision of the family was about to end, which meant that his father would be returning home to live with the family.

Kyle had very few friends, preferred to isolate himself, exhibited a sad demeanor, and showed no awareness of the anger he felt toward his parents. He demonstrated excitement about only one thing: his goal of becoming an architect. Although he was functioning adequately in a superficial sense (earning good grades in high school, maintaining a part-time job, and preparing to attend college), he manifested depressive symptoms that included low self-esteem, altered eating and sleeping habits, and a pessimistic and hopeless outlook. Also, his father's homosexuality raised Kyle's concerns and confusion about sexual-identity issues.

Coping Through Denial or Minimization

A boy who has learned to deny or minimize the impact of being molested generally receives reinforcement of this coping strategy from society. Most male children understand that society expects them to be strong, invincible, fearless, and devoid of "weak" emotions. Clearly, the expectation communicated involves a double standard: it is acceptable for girls to be fearful or passive, but it is definitely not acceptable for boys. When a boy of any age is molested, he often believes that he is the only one who has had this experience, because he has never heard of others who have been sexually abused. There are few role models for males of any age in recovering from sexual abuse.

Due to their own discomfort with the topic of sexual abuse, many parents, police officers, and investigative workers find it difficult to believe a boy's disclosure of molestation. As a result of their ignorance, they often minimize the severity of the consequences of molestation. Rarely is the child encouraged to talk about the experience or to identify his feelings about it. The result is the abused boy's powerful belief that if people know what has happened to him, he will not be accepted or will be viewed as abnormal.

Therefore, he works hard to hide any uncomfortable feelings and to present a facade that conveys the impression that everything is all right in his world. He may make jokes, deny any current or past problems related to the molestation, or reveal only portions of the abusive experience. The boy in denial typically says something like, "I have no problems, so why do I need therapy?" To engage him in the therapeutic process, you will need to find something that he does acknowledge is a problem.

In individual therapy with a boy who denies or minimizes the abuse he has experienced, you will need to address the following issues:

1. *What messages about the molestation does the boy receive from his father or another significant male adult?* Have he and his father talked about what happened to him? How did his father react when he found out? What did he say? Often a boy receives one or more of the following messages, either directly or indirectly, from his father:

- Stop talking about it.
- The abuse is insignificant.
- I cannot tolerate hearing about the abuse.
- It is your fault this happened.

Given such messages, it is not surprising that so many boys react to sexual abuse with denial and minimization. For some boys, a one-time conversation with their fathers or even a single comment is enough to convince them that denial is the best approach. Other boys are exposed to continual reminders to keep quiet, pressure to recant, or even threats. When this is the case, you must give a great deal of support to the child as he tries to change his patterns of coping. He needs to learn that it is safe to disclose in therapy even though it is not safe to do so at home.

2. *Has the boy seemingly succeeded in getting through difficult times in the past by using denial or minimization?* Explore any previous situations in which the child may have ignored a problem, avoided it, purposely not thought about it, or lied about it. Reassure him that at those times he did the best he could with the coping options available to him. But also let him know that there are alternative ways of coping that can have long-term, positive results instead of the merely temporary relief from emotional pain that denial or minimization usually provides.

3. *What is it about full disclosure that the boy fears?* Regardless of whether his fears are realistic, likely to come true, or irrational, they are real to him; in fact, they may be so overwhelming that he is immobilized. Your task is to guide and direct the boy in breaking down his fears into manageable pieces that he can confront. If you discover that his fears are being created or exacerbated by someone else, you need to contact and work with that person so that he or she can be a more positive influence on the child. Sometimes simply acknowledging fears gives the child enough impetus to begin talking more openly about the molestation.

4. *Do other family members use the coping strategy of denial or minimization?* The boy may be surrounded by family members who cope with problems through avoidance, denial, blaming, scapegoating, or minimizing rather than through open acknowledgment and taking appropriate responsibility. If this is the case, intervening with the family is important. If there is any role model for the boy who takes appropriate responsibility and confronts problems openly, you can encourage the boy to spend more time with this person so that he can be exposed to healthier behavior patterns.

◆ ◆ ◆

The following paragraphs offer examples of two boys who started therapy with denial or minimization as a coping strategy.

Robbie

Robbie was a thirteen-year-old dependent of the court who had recently been discharged from a group home into foster care. Previously he had lived a transient lifestyle with his mother, who was fourteen when he was born. She claimed that Robbie was the product of an incestuous relationship with her own father.

When Robbie was ten, his mother found pornographic pictures of him taken by her current husband and reported this to the police. Robbie stated that his stepfather had been abusing him sexually for five years. Subsequently the stepfather was imprisoned, and Robbie was placed in a group home. However, Robbie told his therapist that he could not remember why he was placed in the group home.

Court records revealed that Robbie had engaged in highly sexualized behavior with other children as well as animals. Psychological testing indicated that he was at high risk for continued impulsive behavior and that he had many fears about being victimized again.

Robbie presented as superficially compliant, but he wanted to observe rather than actively participate in therapy sessions. He said he could not trust anyone, and he tended to be guarded and manipulative when sharing the little information he chose to provide.

Jason

Jason was a young adolescent referred for therapy after he was caught fondling a much younger boy. In the course of a police interview, he disclosed that two different adolescents had sexually abused him when he was five and nine. Jason initially presented as remorseful about his actions, and he expressed the desire to be involved in therapy.

His father had left the family when Jason was six, and in the last year had unexplainably ceased all contact with his sons. Jason lived with his mother, her boyfriend, his grandmother, and a younger brother.

Jason consistently minimized his sexual abuse (which he referred to as "just playing around") and the need to address its effects on his life. Minimization and avoidance were also evident in problems he was experiencing at school, at home, and with peers.

A pervasive sexualized theme was apparent in Jason's life. Although he bragged about sexual activity and was suggestive in comments and gestures toward females, he saw this behavior as normal and not a problem in any way.

Coping Through Anger

A boy who has been sexually abused may use anger in an attempt to regain a sense of control and power. In working with a boy who is trying to cope in this way, you will need to help him recognize his angry feelings, understand why they are happening, and direct them appropriately and safely.

Some boys present as angry about everything and virtually all the time; they seem "mad at the world." Typical manifestations of this coping style include oppositional or defiant behavior, fighting, destructiveness, verbal or physical threatening, and sexualized behavior with peers or younger children. These boys are the most likely to be identified as needing treatment, as their behavior attracts a great deal of attention from adults.

The child who attempts to cope through anger is the most at risk for involvement with juvenile law enforcement and for significant problems at school. His parents and teachers are more likely to be invested in treatment than are those of boys who cope in other ways, as these adults are more obviously affected by behavior that is driven by anger.

When a boy is using anger as a coping strategy, you will need to address the following issues:

1. *What other emotion is the boy feeling when he manifests anger?* It is common for many boys to express anger in an attempt to obscure other feelings that they believe are unacceptable, such as worthlessness, sadness, loneliness, fear, or helplessness. Expressing anger is often a boy's attempt to reassert control when he is feeling powerless or out of control. You can create a positive environment for therapy with such a child by accepting and validating all of his feelings and by teaching him that all emotions are acceptable and normal.

2. *What is the payoff for the boy when he is overtly angry?* What positive rewards does he receive for this behavior? For example, his friends may let him have his way, his parents may give in rather than enforce limits, and his teachers may send him out of class so that he is released from the demands of schoolwork.

3. *Can the boy identify any patterns in the situations or feelings that tend to provoke angry behaviors on his part?* What factors contribute to his feelings of powerlessness? Can any typical progression be identified? It is important to consider such factors as the boy's overall stimulation level, the degree of structure in the situation, the time of day, and the actions of other people. When he begins to understand the reasons for his anger, he can also begin to see ways to control or influence that anger or at least his responses to it. Sexually abused boys often find that some of the things that make them angry include the following:

- People who somehow remind them of their offenders
- Authoritarian people who deny them choices and thereby evoke feelings of powerlessness
- Situations that offer either no structure or an extremely rigid one
- Demands made on them when they are tired

Many sexually abused males resist limits of any kind because they must feel in control at all times. Individual therapy can help them experience limits in a more positive light. The purpose of setting limits for such a child is to let him know what is expected of him and to provide external control until he demonstrates the ability to control behavior on his own. When you explain the purpose in this way, you can help reassure a boy who fears what might happen if he loses control or expresses anger openly.

4. *Does the boy understand that angry feelings are normal and natural rather than "bad"?* Anger is only a problem when it is expressed in a way that is hurtful to oneself or others. Boys need to learn that it is healthy to discuss anger in a positive way with the person who is the source of that anger, rather than to express anger in a negative way toward some other person who just happens to be a convenient target. Put in the child's terms, nothing good happens when he punches a peer because he is angry with his teacher for making him stay inside at recess.

5. *Does the boy accept the assertion that his anger needs to be redirected to nondestructive outlets?* Does he know the difference between hurtful and acceptable behaviors for expressing anger? In therapy you can help a boy discover actions he can take on his own to release his anger effectively. Such options might include screaming, writing in a journal, writing a letter, running or engaging in other physical activities that use a lot of energy, expressing himself in assertive words and behavior, talking it out, crying, creating works of art, or punching something inanimate like a pillow. Visualizing the person who has made him angry and saying everything he would like to can also be effective.

6. *Does the boy take responsibility for the consequences of his behavior?* The treatment process and atmosphere must make this expectation very clear. When a boy learns

to accept responsibility for his actions, his feelings of being victimized will be reduced. Blaming others and refusing to assume accountability will only prolong his role as a victim.

◆ ◆ ◆

Following are examples of two boys who began therapy with anger as a coping strategy.

Daniel

When Daniel began therapy, he was an eight-year-old dependent of the court and was living with his paternal grandmother. His father was dead, and his mother had lost all of her parental rights because she had neglected Daniel and physically and sexually abused him. Daniel was removed from her care when he was five, and he had been placed in two foster homes prior to coming to live with his grandmother. He had witnessed adult sexual behavior and had been molested not only by his mother but also by a number of her adult lovers.

Daniel was highly intelligent but did poorly in school due to his disruptiveness, his defiance toward adults, and his constant fighting with peers. He was easily provoked into intense anger; he had been caught setting fires, lying, stealing, and destroying property. He also frequently made homicidal threats. In addition, he demonstrated symptoms of depression: two attempts at suicide, frequent threats to harm himself, ongoing sleep disturbances, and frequent gorging on food until he was physically ill.

Thomas

Thomas entered therapy on a crisis basis; he was referred by his school district for aggressive and destructive behavior. He had been in a special education class due to a diagnosis of severe emotional disturbance. This class emphasized strict control, rigid adherence to rules, and swift punishment for all infractions.

From the time he was four until he was nine, Thomas had been both physically and sexually abused by an uncle. The same uncle also abused his older sister. When Thomas disclosed the molestation, he was first ostracized and then humiliated by his mother's family, while his sister received concern, support, and reassurances of safety. The family chose not to file charges against the uncle.

It was evident that Thomas's defiance and aggressive outbursts were attempts to maintain some degree of control in his life. Underneath his angry demeanor was an anxious and fearful boy, sorely in need of nurturing from the adults in his life.

Conclusion

This chapter has concentrated on individual therapy with sexually abused boys. It offered suggestions about when to use an individual rather than a group approach, what you can do to increase the likelihood of success in individual therapy, what a one-on-one session might look like, and how you can work with a child to replace problem behaviors with effective ones. The next chapter is a similar discussion of therapy conducted in a group setting.

CHAPTER FOUR

GROUP THERAPY

This chapter deals with group therapy. It covers issues such as determining when to use group therapy, planning a group, developing a base of potential members, recruiting group members, setting group goals, leading a group session, and preparing a child to leave group therapy.

Determining When to Use Group Therapy

As is the case with individual therapy (see "Determining When to Use Individual Therapy" in Chapter Three), certain requirements must be met before a child can enter group therapy. Although it can be extremely difficult to refuse a client whose situation does not qualify, my colleagues and I adhere to these criteria because by doing so we help ensure the best possible experience for all members of a group. We use four criteria:

1. The boy must have acknowledged that he was abused.
2. The offender must be someone known to the boy rather than a stranger.
3. The boy must be able and willing to join a group.
4. The boy's parent (or another adult who is responsible for him—referred to as "the parent" throughout this book) must agree to attend the assessment session.

These criteria are described in detail in the following sections. Determining whether a boy's case meets the first two is a simple process. The person who refers the child to you will be able to give you the necessary information. If the child has not acknowledged abuse or was molested by a stranger, you can then discuss other therapy options and referrals if needed. Determining whether the boy meets the last two criteria is somewhat more involved; but after you have completed the initial assessment, you will know whether the child qualifies.

Ordinarily you and the client will choose only one kind of therapy: either individual or group. However, on rare occasions you may need to use both with a child. For example, a group member may suddenly be faced with a crisis that warrants meeting with him outside his regular group session.

The Boy Has Disclosed Sexual Abuse

The first requirement is that the boy must have remembered the abuse, disclosed it, and named the perpetrator. This requirement lessens the chances that claims of "false-memory syndrome" (Whitfield, 1995) might be made.

In addition, my colleagues and I believe that this requirement protects the child from further damage: if a boy denies abuse and yet is placed in abuse-specific group therapy, the message he receives is "We do not hear you, and we do not believe you. We will do what we think is right even if you do not agree." The resulting pressure on the child might create an even greater feeling of disempowerment and inability to trust than he is already experiencing. (Please note, however, that other professionals do not necessarily share this belief; some believe that all a boy needs to feel safe enough to disclose in a group setting is to hear from other boys who have also been molested.)

The Boy Knows the Offender

The second requirement is that the perpetrator must be someone known to the child, not a stranger. The offender might be a family member, a friend of the family, a neighbor, a teacher, a coach, a baby-sitter, or the parent of a peer.

As discussed in Chapter Three, a boy who is assaulted by a stranger generally experiences problems different from those experienced when the molester is known. For example, if the offender was a stranger and physical force was used, the boy tends to have problems connected with questioning why he was chosen. He may feel damaged and fearful due to the injuries he received, and he may be concerned about contracting sexually transmitted diseases. When the boy knows the offender, certain other problems arise—betrayal, mistrust, and ambivalent feelings about the perpetrator—that are typically not experienced after assault by a stranger.

The Boy Is Able and Willing to Join a Group

The third requirement has to do with the child's ability and willingness to participate in a group. You can judge him to be capable of participating if there is evidence that he can get along with peers sufficiently to meet the demands of group involvement. After you have completed the initial assessment, you will know whether he is likely to participate appropriately.

In addition, my colleagues and I believe that a molested child must agree to join a therapy group of his own free will. If he is not given a choice, he will be further disempowered.

The Parent Agrees to Attend the Assessment Session

The fourth and final requirement concerns the parent's involvement in therapy. Some therapists who work with groups require each boy's parent to participate in a parallel treatment group (Mandell & Damon, 1989; Gil & Johnson, 1993); if a boy's parent cannot or will not participate, the child is not accepted in group therapy. At the other end of the continuum, some therapists believe in making group therapy available to a child even if his parent refuses any level of involvement.

Through experience, my colleagues and I have learned that a parent who has no commitment to or investment in a boy's treatment inevitably sabotages the child's progress in some way. The most common result is that the parent works against the therapist, rather than with him or her, thus diminishing the child's benefit from group therapy.

Consequently, we decided on a position somewhere between the two extremes on the continuum. We require a parent to attend the assessment session. If the parent cannot or will not come, we will not consider the boy for group therapy. (See Chapter Two for information about the parent's role in the initial assessment.) This contact provides a necessary foundation for further therapeutic work with the parent.

Planning a Group

Before you start working with a group, you will need to complete a number of planning tasks. Some involve researching various resources, and all of them involve making choices about what will best meet your needs and those of the group:

- Location
- Age range

- Number of participants
- Group's life span
- Start date
- Time required for each session
- Group activities
- Preparation for behavioral problems
- Cotherapist issues (*please note that working with a cotherapist is optional*)

Location

Your selection of a location for group sessions depends on what options are available and what the group members will need. For a group of younger boys (ages seven through eleven), you will need ready access to play items and a setting in which the boys can engage in some type of play therapy. For a group of older boys (ages twelve through eighteen), you will need a private, comfortable room without distractions in the setting. (For example, you do not want shelves full of toys.)

Age Range

In the early stages of your work with groups, you may not have many names of children. Consequently, you may not have different age ranges from which to choose. Also, even if you are not new to group therapy, you will probably find that you cannot predict the ages of children who are referred to you. My colleagues and I have led groups in the following age ranges:

- Eight and nine
- Eight through ten
- Nine through eleven
- Eleven through thirteen
- Twelve through fourteen
- Fifteen through eighteen

All of these age groupings have been successful. However, we have found that certain combinations of members at different school levels do not work effectively. For example, combining elementary school students with junior high students does not work, nor does combining junior high students with high school students.

Chronological age and grade level are not the only factors to consider. During each boy's initial assessment you must also evaluate his developmental maturity in order to determine an appropriate group for him. A boy who is immature for his age may function much better in a group of younger children than with boys his own age.

Number of Participants

The ideal number of participants is six to eight. However, you may find yourself constrained by the size of the only room available, by having fewer than six referrals from which to select, or by outside pressure (from referral sources or the administrator of the group program, for example) to accept more than eight boys. Waiting for the ideal number of participants, though, may result in a situation in which a child never receives the treatment he needs.

Be flexible and creative if your group turns out very different from what you anticipated. It is possible—though not ideal or even recommended—to work successfully with a group of eight twelve-year-olds who have a tendency to act out. It is also possible that a group of only four seventeen- and eighteen-year-olds can function successfully.

Group's Life Span

You need to decide whether the group will be ongoing or limited to a particular life span—typically six to nine months.

Time-Limited Group. A time-limited group is generally "closed," which means that new members are not added once the group has started. Therefore, you might want to consider starting a time-limited group with nine or ten members, in case one or two boys drop out.

With a time-limited group, you need to plan carefully so that the group can continue to meet during potentially stressful times (such as holidays or the beginning or end of the school year). Boys especially need the support of their fellow group members during these times.

You may find that the boys ask for an extension of the group beyond its agreed-on ending date. Older boys in particular often request additional group sessions. In this case you and the boys may negotiate with the parents and the cotherapist (if you have one) to continue the group—usually another eight weeks or so.

My colleagues and I have found it impossible to predict the individual boys' responses to a group, the parents' ability to support regular group attendance, and any other factors that might interfere with participation. The best you can do is plan with the information you have at the time and then remain flexible enough to help the group adapt when different circumstances arise.

The advantages of a time-limited group include the following:

- If you have limited funding sources, you are more likely to receive support for time-limited groups than for ongoing groups.
- Imposing a time limit makes group therapy a cost-effective treatment for clients, so their parents may find it easier to convince insurance companies to cover at least a portion of your fees.
- A time-limited group tends to be more focused on reaching specific goals and alleviating specific symptoms—another characteristic that is preferable from an insurance company's perspective.
- In general, the same boys start and end a group together. (Occasionally you will find that one or two members drop out early.) This continuity contributes to the boys' feelings of comfort and safety, allows them to develop trust in one another, and creates a sense of group cohesiveness.
- By informing the boys and their parents in advance that the group will have a limited life span and providing them with the approximate ending date, you can help lessen their resistance to the group.
- When the members know that their group has an ending date, they feel a sense of urgency to accomplish as much as possible within the available time frame.
- A period of six to nine months is long enough to cover a wide range of topics yet short enough that most potential members can commit to attendance.
- You and your cotherapist (if you have one) are likely to feel less anxiety about leading a group for the first time if you know that it will end at a certain point.
- Ending groups after a specified time allows you to evaluate the progress made during each group's life span, pinpoint problems, and change your plans accordingly for subsequent groups.

There are also disadvantages associated with a time-limited group:

- Absences become especially problematic, as the group moves quickly in order to deal with a variety of clinical issues. The boy who misses one or more sessions may find it very difficult to catch up with his peers. Also, due to the limited time frame, the group may address certain issues only once; consequently, the boy who misses a particular session may lose his opportunity to deal with an issue that is particularly relevant for him.
- Each child progresses at his own pace. It is not realistic to expect six to eight boys to be equally ready and willing at the same time to address certain difficult issues.
- When the members have developed strong connections and formed friendships among themselves, the ending of a group may be experienced as another significant loss in their lives.

- A previously agreed-on ending date may come at a time when one or more members are in crisis and therefore especially in need of the group's support.
- The time involved in planning and starting a new group can be substantial. My colleagues and I have found that each group requires at least forty hours of preparation and "start-up" time.
- A time-limited group may not allow severely abused boys to address issues in enough depth to resolve them adequately.

Ongoing Group. An ongoing group presents different planning issues, as it involves a continual process of ushering some members out (for example, due to completion of their therapeutic goals or due to a change in living situation) and others in.

The advantages of an ongoing group are as follows:

- Because the boys generally attend therapy for a longer period than they would with a typical time-limited group, important issues can be covered in greater depth.
- Absences from sessions are not as problematic as they are with a time-limited group, as most issues are addressed more than once.
- It is easier to individualize a boy's treatment when his participation is not limited to a particular time frame.
- The time demands are less intensive. The periods spent in start-up and closure, with their accompanying planning and evaluations, are less frequent.
- Members who have been attending the group for a while may model helpful behaviors for new boys who join (sharing information about abuse, giving and receiving feedback, following rules, and so on).

The following are some of the disadvantages of an ongoing group:

- There is no way to predict when openings will become available.
- You are repeatedly faced with saying good-bye to members and introducing others. If there is frequent turnover, closure and welcoming can overshadow the sexual abuse issues.
- The dynamics of a group can change dramatically with the addition of a new child; you and your cotherapist may need to make significant changes as a result.
- It can be more difficult to gain cooperation from a boy and his parent when the ending time for treatment is uncertain.

Start Date

Give yourself a substantial amount of time for the process of soliciting and screening potential group members. You will probably need to contact approximately twelve referrals in order to confirm six members for group participation. Some children will not fit your own criteria; some will not fit the criteria established by social workers or other people involved in their cases; and circumstances may not permit others to join a group. You can also anticipate resistance from some boys and their families, who will avoid the initial assessment in various ways, through failure to keep appointments, sudden illness, unavoidable conflicts, or lack of response to telephone messages.

Time Required for Each Session

The length of your group sessions will depend on a number of variables: your available time, how long your cotherapist (if you have one) can be present, room schedules, and transportation schedules. In general, the older the boy, the more able and willing he is to tolerate a longer group session. Eight- to twelve-year-olds function well with a seventy-five-minute session each week, young adolescents with ninety minutes, and older adolescents with two hours.

Group Activities

The activities in Part Two are especially useful in group therapy sessions with sexually abused boys. You can incorporate other kinds of components as well, such as art therapy, movies, guest speakers, books, role plays, celebrations and outings, play therapy, and therapeutic games (see the Appendix for details). Both younger children and adolescents demonstrate more interest in attending groups when you let them know during the initial assessment that they will be participating in a variety of activities and when you describe those activities in some detail. You will create very little interest in and motivation for your group if you discuss therapy with the child as only "a place to talk about the abuse." The prospect of verbal interaction sounds threatening, especially as many molested children are told (directly or indirectly) never to talk about their abuse.

It is consistent with the theme of empowerment to encourage the boys to identify and bring up problem areas during a group session as they arise, rather than to wait for a peer or group leader to do so. When these problems come up, you will find numerous alternatives that address them among the activities in Part Two.

Preparation for Behavioral Problems

Planning ahead for behavioral problems is essential. The topic of sexual abuse precipitates anxiety, anger, and other feelings that are often demonstrated in a wide range of disruptive behaviors. It is possible for group issues to trigger aggressive behavior toward peers, the therapist, or property.

In addition, sexualized behavior is common in boys' groups and may be either overt or subtle. This includes sexualized conversation, masturbation, touching peers without permission, and making direct sexual overtures. The most common disruptive behavior is refusal to abide by group rules or to follow instructions. These boys need to regain their sense of personal power and control, and testing the rules is one way in which they can assess their power with you and among their fellow group members.

These behaviors are more problematic in a group setting because of the presence of peers and your need to manage and contain the group as a whole. One member's acting out can precipitate similar behaviors on the part of the other boys. Even the most skilled and experienced group therapist will be challenged by the dynamics in these kinds of groups. This is one of the main reasons that my colleagues and I strongly recommend using a cotherapist.

When problems arise, give the boys as many options as possible to regain control on their own before you step in. If you are working with a cotherapist, the two of you need to decide together on some simple signals to use to initiate the following behavioral interventions when verbal interventions are not working. They are listed in order from least to most restrictive:

- Change the members' seating arrangements.
- Sit between two disruptive individuals or beside one boy who is having difficulty.
- Remove an item from a child to reduce the possibility of harm.
- Take a child out of the room and have him engage in a physical alternative to aggression (hitting a punching bag, running, throwing a ball against the wall) or quiet time.
- Remove all group members from the room except the child who is having difficulties, so that attention paid to the behavior is reduced.
- Use physical restraint (which involves specific techniques for managing aggressive behaviors and requires specialized training).

Chapter Six includes additional suggestions of ways to manage problem behaviors.

Cotherapist Issues

Working with a cotherapist is not essential, but it is highly recommended if you are just beginning to lead groups of sexually abused boys. You will want someone who is as committed to the group's welfare and progress as you are. This commitment is essential, given the importance of trust issues with children who have been abused.

Working with a Cotherapist of the Opposite Sex. Having a cotherapist of the opposite sex offers several advantages:

1. *You can gain a better understanding of the boys' family dynamics.* Although the family systems of the group members will take every possible form, it is likely that two therapists of the opposite sex will come to represent "mom" and "dad" to each boy. Each boy's reactions to each cotherapist and to the cotherapists' interactions can provide insight into the child's relationship with his own parents and the dynamics within his family. Thus, you will be more likely to understand the problems of each individual child and to intervene effectively.

2. *The boys are able to act out family situations.* Exploring the issue of transference with the boys often leads them to realize that they tend to act out their individual family situations in the group. For example, when a boy has been sexually abused by a father figure, the male group leader will often become the focus for that boy's rage. The boy is probably not able to express that rage toward the father figure, but he may come to understand it and deal with it when transference occurs.

3. *Disruption in the group can be reduced.* It is common to see much greater opposition to a female therapist than to a male therapist. When there is both a male and female therapist, the boys are less likely to disrupt the group's work.

4. *You are representative of both sexes as offenders.* You will find that most groups are made up of boys molested by both male and female offenders; for each boy to feel safe in the group setting, he is likely to need an adult of the gender opposite that of his abuser. When there is only one therapist, the members who were molested by someone of the therapist's sex may experience anxiety around the therapist, and too much anxiety typically triggers disruptive behavior.

5. *You provide positive role modeling.* Having two therapists of the opposite sex allows for positive role modeling of teamwork, communication, and respect between men and women. The boys will be closely observing you and your cotherapist at all times. You can use your interactions with your cotherapist both in the group setting and during breaks—when you talk about the group process and address any potential problems—to model appropriate behavior. The boys will see how you and your cotherapist talk to each other, whether it is OK for the two of you to disagree, how you express feelings to each other, and how the two of you resolve your differences. For many of the boys, therapy sessions may be their only

consistent exposure to healthy female-male interactions. You can use the opportunity to show that men and women can share power.

6. *You can more easily deal with sex education.* Cotherapists of the opposite sex tend to be more effective than one therapist in educating the boys about sex and eliciting their questions.

Sharing Responsibilities with a Cotherapist. A cotherapist makes it possible to share the responsibilities of group leadership, including facilitating the group, setting limits, observing the boys as they interact, and providing individual intervention if necessary. Having an additional point of view also has advantages: the two of you together can develop more strategies for effectively managing the group, give each other feedback about interventions and group dynamics, and support each other in the demanding task of leading a group.

Selecting a Cotherapist. You need to meet with a potential cotherapist prior to making a decision about working with him or her. Share your expectations, strengths, weaknesses, and personal goals for group leadership so that you will know whether the two of you have beliefs and styles that will be complementary. Your understanding of these issues ahead of time helps you support each other effectively and encourages you to discuss potential problem areas before they arise. For example, if both of you feel more comfortable with the supportive role rather than with that of managing the group, you will need to work out your role relationships in advance.

Developing a Base of Potential Members

The way in which you obtain referrals of potential group members will vary, depending on your personal preferences as well as the resources available in your area. Here are some ideas on how to develop referral sources:

• Make phone calls to colleagues, therapists, and members of your professional community whom you know personally. Let them know of your intention to offer therapy for molested boys and ask them to spread the word. When you reach out to others in this way, you will need to act as a strong advocate for treating sexually abused boys, as many people do not realize how widespread and critical the problem is.

• If you are working in an agency setting, inform your coworkers about your plans and ask for their support in referring clients to you. For example, you can make announcements during staff meetings and in the materials given to new employees during orientation.

• Notify people who, by virtue of their work, come into contact with sexually abused boys: members of the department of social services, police officers, probation officers, parole officers, hospitals, urgent-care facilities, teachers, and school counselors.

• Obtain mailing lists of local therapists who work with children and families. (Contact professional journals and organizations, or ask your colleagues for ideas about other sources.) Write a cover letter introducing yourself, describing your experience and credentials, and announcing your intention to treat sexually abused boys. Mail the letter along with a flyer or brochure to each person on the list.

• Ask local governmental and charitable agencies if they have lists of children who were sexually abused and who are waiting for group therapy. Some county agencies, for example, maintain such lists and will allow therapists to use them. If you succeed in obtaining such a list, you might want to start your group work with those boys who have been waiting the longest.

• Seek opportunities to speak in public about the sexual abuse of boys. Inform your audiences about treatment resources that are available for boys.

Recruiting Group Members

When you are ready to start meeting with prospective group members and their parents, you will need to communicate clearly why and how your group will benefit the boy. Keep in mind that many of the boys referred will have been through individual therapy, hospitalization, or family treatment with minimal improvement. Here are some benefits of group therapy that you can discuss:

• Group therapy lessens isolation and the sense of being different.
• A boy can recognize that others share his feelings and problems.
• Group treatment may be less threatening and scary than the intimacy of individual therapy.
• A boy's denial is often lessened when he observes in group therapy that he has choices other than refusing to talk. He is likely to see his peers sharing about abuse even if they were told not to or were threatened with harm. He will also see that disclosing secrets can have a positive outcome, such as feeling relief or preventing others from being victimized. The interactions he observes will show him that some of his fears ("People will laugh at me" or "I must be gay if this happened to me") are unlikely to become reality.

- A boy can receive more and different kinds of support from peers in a group setting.
- Group therapy provides the opportunity for monitored peer interactions and the development of new friendships.
- A boy can gain self-esteem through helping others.
- Peer feedback may be more influential in guiding personal change than opinions from adults.
- Group therapy provides practice in developing improved social skills.
- Group therapy with peers allows a child to observe others in the process of overcoming sexual abuse and resolving related problems; thus, he becomes hopeful (Yalom, 1985).

After you have evaluated each member and obtained his agreement to participate, you need to work with him to establish a treatment plan, which identifies a maximum of three presenting problems that are the priorities for his treatment. Keep the problem areas specific and individualized. It is important for each boy to know the problems on his treatment plan at all times, so that you and he are working together in a collaborative manner to resolve problems.

Setting Group Goals

At the start of each new group, you need to post therapeutic goals for the group, share them with the group members, and engage the members in a group activity of revising or adding to them as the members see fit. Once goals have been discussed and established, you will want to keep them posted in clear sight in the group room, so that both you and the boys will be continually reminded of them. Being able to refer to the posted goals will help get the boys back on track when they start to wander from the group's purpose: healing from sexual abuse.

There are two kinds of goals that must be set: (1) general group goals, which apply to all groups of boys in a particular age range, and (2) individual goals, which each member sets for himself.

General Group Goals

At the first group session, you may want to post the general goals in the form of positive "I" statements, as though they were already accomplished. These goals represent areas that are essential to cover in the group, regardless of the boys' specific situations. My colleagues and I derived these goals from Ryan's issues for sexually abused children and offenders (1989).

Group Goals for Boys Ages Seven Through Eleven. Following are the issues that are relevant for boys ages seven through eleven and the group therapy goals associated with those issues. Each goal is stated as an "I" message so that a boy can read positive statements every time he comes to a group session.

Issue: Secrets and confidentiality
Goal: I know the difference between fun secrets (which are OK to keep) and tricky secrets (which are not OK to keep, because someone could get hurt).

Issue: Denial and minimization
Goal: I can talk about what happened to me without leaving out anything.

Issue: Empathy
Goal: I can talk about feelings, and I can listen to others when they talk about their feelings.

Issue: Guilt and accountability
Goals: I know that being molested was not my fault.
I know that some touching might feel good to me, but it is still never OK for a bigger person to touch kids' private parts.

Issue: Fantasies and revenge
Goal: I know that being molested does not make me homosexual or gay.

Issue: Power and control
Goals: I know that kids have rights and can say "no."
I know someone who will give me help, and I know how to ask for help when I need it.
My behavior is up to me.

Issue: Anger and retaliation
Goals: I know that kids who have been molested might think about hurting others, and I know ways to keep myself from doing that.
When I am angry I can talk it out instead of acting it out.

Group Goals for Boys Ages Twelve Through Eighteen. The specific issues that are relevant for boys ages twelve through eighteen and the group therapy goals associated with those issues are as follows. Again, each goal is stated as a positive "I" message.

Issue: Secrets and confidentiality
Goal: I can share completely all secrets about the abuse.

Issue: Denial and minimization
Goal: I am able and willing to talk about being molested in terms of the details and the effects on me.

Issue: Empathy
Goal: When I get in touch with my own feelings, I can better understand the feelings of others.

Issue: Guilt and accountability
Goals: I know I am not responsible for the molestation.
I can separate things for which I *am* responsible from the things for which I *am not* responsible.

Issue: Fantasies and revenge
Goals: I know that acts or words of revenge are hurtful, not helpful, to me.
I can talk about fantasies and any related feelings without acting on them.

Issue: Power and control
Goals: I am in control of my behavior, and I am responsible for my choices and their consequences.
I recognize when I am feeling powerless, and I have positive ways to regain a sense of being in control.

Issue: Anger and retaliation
Goals: I know that kids who have been molested might think about hurting others, and I have a plan to keep myself from doing that.
I can express my anger safely.

Individual Goals

In addition to setting group goals that emphasize clinical issues that are important for all of the members, you need to ask each boy to create one or more goals to address in his own therapy. In this way, you make goal setting a collaborative effort, which increases each boy's sense of ownership of the group goals and willingness to examine tough issues.

Following are some examples of goals that were developed by members of actual groups. Each goal represents one boy's perspective on improving in a specific area (shown in italics):

- *Accepting negative feelings as natural and normal:* "I know it's OK to have both positive and negative feelings about people in my life." This goal is often important for boys who have been molested by family members or other people with whom they have close relationships.
- *Self-esteem:* "I can say that I like myself and mean it."
- *Ability to trust people:* "I know whom I can trust in my life, and I develop trust slowly with new people."
- *Forming healthy relationships:* "I know what is most important for me to have and to give in my personal relationships."

Leading a Group Session

In determining how you will run a group session, you need to strive for balance between structure and flexibility. Structure is important in that it provides the group members with a predictable and consistent routine, which facilitates a safe therapeutic environment and reduces anxiety. However, too much structure may not allow you or the members to respond appropriately to various circumstances that might arise. The right amount of structure

- Meets the unique needs of your group
- Accommodates your leadership style
- Accommodates the style of your cotherapist (if you have one)
- Incorporates input from the members
- Is flexible enough that you can "switch gears" when necessary

The structure described in the following paragraphs, which my colleagues and I use, is offered to illustrate one way of conducting a group and to spark your own ideas. Feel free to duplicate certain elements or to design an entirely different structure of your own.

Group Session for Boys Ages Seven Through Eleven

Establishing Rules and Correcting Problematic Behavior. Boys ages seven through eleven benefit from a consistent group routine, with clear expectations and limits set for their behavior. When you make sure the boys understand these limits right from the beginning of a new group, you are less likely to spend a lot of time in behavior management.

You and the members will work together at the beginning of the group to establish group rules. Be sure to emphasize that you need everyone's cooperation, participation, and personal responsibility. Because many young boys perceive rules negatively, you will need to discuss the concept of rules as guidelines to make the group run smoothly.

Generally the rules that you and the members establish will govern only behavior that disrupts the group or poses some kind of danger; any proposed rule is included only if it will benefit all the members and assist in an effective therapy process. In this way you can keep rules to a minimum so that the group atmosphere is not rigidly controlling.

The following are suggestions for correcting problematic behavior when it occurs:

1. *Five-minute time-out.* Explain that a five-minute time-out outside the group room may be used to help a member gain control of unacceptable behavior.

2. *Suspension from group.* Suspension for a specific time period may be necessary when a member's behavior compromises his own safety or that of others (for example, assaulting someone in the group or running away from the group while on an outing).

3. *Behavior modification.* For groups with a preponderance of members whose behavior disrupts the group, my colleagues and I use a behavior modification system. We choose a maximum of three areas of behavior (rules) to address at one time. For example, we might choose (1) following directions the first time, (2) listening without interrupting, and (3) no hands-on behavior. Each child's name is written on a large posted chart. Every week, each child can earn a star for each rule he follows while participating in the group, meaning that he can earn up to three stars each time the group meets.

Here is how the system is used in practice: you assign a group goal for the boys to work toward together, such as 150 stars. Then you ask the boys to brainstorm to come up with the reward for the group when this goal is achieved. You might offer such enticements as an outing for pizza, going to play miniature golf, or a group session playing video games. Peer pressure to conform to the group rules becomes an important factor, and seeing the stars add up provides continued motivation to work toward the desired group goal. After each group goal is achieved, you and the group members together decide whether the same areas need additional work or whether the group as a whole needs to target some different areas for improvement.

When the group members' needs for rules are particularly diverse, you may find it necessary to institute an individual behavior modification system. One approach is to encourage the boys to evaluate one another and work cooperatively to change problematic behaviors. Another is to have the boys help one another identify one personal target behavior—one that is seen as essential to the boy's progress in therapy. The following are examples of target behaviors:

- I make no physical or verbal threats.
- I stay focused on the topic.
- I share about my problems.
- I take responsibility for myself.

These behavioral changes must not be assigned to a child without his input: each boy's target behavior has to be something he wants to change. When the boy does well with his own target area throughout a group session, you give him a small item (a sticker or small toy, for example) as a reward.

Structuring a Session. The most effective group structure for boys ages seven through eleven consists of three phases.

Phase 1: Sharing and Discussion Time. During the first phase, you check in with each member, inviting him to share anything he wants. Then you identify a clear focus for the session. Consistently give positive reinforcement for those boys who, instead of maintaining secrecy or denial, accept responsibility to share problems at the start of the group time.

Phase 2: Structured Therapeutic Activity. The second phase of the session consists of conducting a structured therapeutic activity designed to address molestation issues (see Part Two). Keep in mind when you are preparing for a group session that each group has its own unique personalities and needs. Similarly, some group members will have suffered a severe degree of trauma from their abuse, whereas others will be traumatized to a lesser degree. You need to be aware that an activity or intervention used successfully with one group will not necessarily be successful with another group. Consequently, you need to have at least two therapeutic activities prepared at the start of each session; thus you will have another option available if your first choice does not go well.

Also, even though you will have prepared activities, you need to be flexible. For example, during the first part of the session, one of the members may share that he has experienced an acute problem or crisis that requires your immediate attention. In such an event, you need to switch gears and intervene in a way that helps not only the child with the problem but also the other group members as they strive to meet their goals.

For example, if a child is facing an upcoming court appearance and possible confrontation with his offender, he may be experiencing great anxiety and fear. In this situation you have two choices: (1) alter the selected activity to incorporate this crisis (and perhaps similar ones faced by other group members) or (2) change the focus of the session to address the crisis. The other members will almost always receive something valuable from the process of addressing one member's crisis. Discussing such issues as preparing for court, exploring the fears that the experience evokes, and explaining such symptoms as flashbacks and nightmares can be helpful for the entire group.

Occasionally you will find that one group member clearly wants to avoid the therapeutic activity or discussion for the day and requests play or outside time instead. When this occurs, the boy's avoidance needs to be gently confronted so that he can be helped to identify and cope with uncomfortable feelings.

Phase 3: Wind-Down. The wind-down is a period of relaxation during which you encourage calmness and then review the group process and plan for the upcoming week. If you do not structure this wind-down time, the boys will routinely be returning home exhibiting feelings and behaviors that parents may not understand or be prepared for.

Due to their high energy level, boys in this age group may need some outside activities during the wind-down period that allow them to release their emotions and energy before going home. If time outdoors is not possible, you can substitute unstructured playtime in a playroom setting. You need to explain to the boys that this time is for relaxation and discharging excess energy, again keeping them focused on the overall purpose of the group.

Group Session for Boys Ages Twelve Through Fourteen

My colleagues and I experimented with various formats and concluded that adolescents benefit most from a minimally structured group process in which the cotherapists and the group members share equal responsibility for bringing up therapy issues and current concerns. As our groups are closed and time limited, this structure is established after a six-week introductory period that is highly controlled by the cotherapists. This introductory period is used to clarify group focus and purpose, develop a sense of cohesiveness and rapport, and establish group rules and goals.

Structuring a Session. With boys ages twelve through fourteen, we use a structure consisting of alternating a therapist-initiated discussion or activity one week with an open sharing time the following week. Again, make sure to prepare two activities for each activity session, in case the first one you try does not work as anticipated.

You will find that waiting for the group members to address certain thera-peutic issues is ineffective. Instead, you need to use a direct approach, in which you initiate discussion or activities on the difficult topics related to abuse. When you initiate a subject, the boys know it is safe to explore it.

Although you do need to bring up topics, you also need to emphasize con-tinually that it is each boy's choice to participate in treatment activities, respond to questions, do homework assignments, or share. You have to state and demon-strate that you respect each boy's right to say "No, I'm not ready yet" if a topic feels too unsafe or threatening.

Once the boys begin to develop some trust in one another and in the cother-apists, they share on a less superficial level about current problems in their lives. When one group member requests help with a problem, you will probably find that you can tie in that problem area with issues related to abuse and, thus, involve the entire group in discussion and problem solving. For example, if a teen is sus-pended for fighting at school, you could explore the following issues with the en-tire group by asking these questions:

- Is anger allowed and safe at home?
- Does someone encourage you to fight because that is the "masculine" way to respond?
- Does anyone tell you that you should not be angry?
- How do you honestly feel toward the offender? Toward your parents?
- What do you want the end result to be when you get into a fight?
- What are some other ways to get the same end result?
- What do you think are the long-term consequences of fighting?
- How do you think aggressive behavior relates to your experience of being abused?

This minimally structured format makes it possible for you to ensure coverage of the most important issues for molested boys; at the same time, the adolescents receive encouragement and practice in making choices about their group time.

Correcting Problematic Behavior. Behavior modification techniques are not used with this age group. If a boy is not participating, is constantly distracting others, or is using the group time to discuss something totally unrelated to abuse, he is re-moved from the group and asked to spend some individual time confronting his resistance and determining whether he wants to find some solutions for over-coming it.

A common source of resistance is that the boy does not believe that his shar-ing in group will be kept confidential. With some additional planning you can assist a boy in overcoming his reluctance to talk. For example, if he is a dependent of the court, you can give him a copy of any progress summary you write before you send it. In this way you give him a sense of control, and it may be possible to renegotiate what is written if he is uncomfortable with it.

Another situation that may cause difficulty is one in which a boy's parent is calling frequently and asking what he is doing in the group. To handle this situation, you might decide to inform the parent that you prefer to speak with him or her in conjoint sessions with the boy present, so that he can hear directly what you are sharing in response to the parent's intrusiveness.

Group Session for Boys Ages Fifteen Through Eighteen

For boys ages fifteen through eighteen, it is best for you and your cotherapist to impose only minimal structure. In this way the members share responsibility for choosing the therapy issues to be addressed and for using their time effectively. You need to emphasize the boys' ability to share what is going well for them and what issues or concerns they need help with. At the beginning of each session, therefore, you will want to have a sharing period during which you listen carefully for priority areas that will engage the entire group. This approach requires you to have a range of activities and techniques available at a moment's notice.

During some sessions, the members may bring up very little. Consequently, for each session you need to have prepared at least one activity or other idea if the boys do not lead you in any particular direction. To select activities and ideas, consider important themes or symptoms the boys have repeatedly mentioned.

Preparing a Child to Leave Group Therapy

If you have chosen to limit the life span of your groups, the termination of group therapy depends on the group's ending date rather than on the individual progress of each boy. If you have decided on working with ongoing groups, however, you will be dealing with the important task of evaluating a member's readiness to leave. The following discussion will assist you in determining whether a child is ready to leave therapy.

Meeting with the Child

When you are faced with the prospect of a child's leaving a group, you will need to meet with him. During the meeting you need to reinforce the empowerment theme by asking for and considering his impression of his progress and his readiness to leave the group. Encourage him to explain why he feels that discharge is appropriate. Remind him of the problems specified in his treatment plan and ask specifically about the current status of each. You need to determine whether changes have occurred in each problem situation and whether each problem has been resolved, has decreased in frequency or severity, or has become less troublesome.

Often a boy will want to leave group just when he is facing a critical time in his therapy. It is important to explore whether something happened to trigger his decision. Consider the following possibilities:

- Is the boy angry about being confronted by you (or your cotherapist, if you have one)?
- Does he have an unresolved conflict with another group member?
- Did the perpetrator come into contact with him and somehow pressure him not to talk in therapy?
- Have any group topics or disclosures made him so uncomfortable that he does not want to continue?

Assessing Relationships with Significant Adults

After you have met with the boy to discuss his request to leave the group, you will want to get in touch with his parent and other significant adults involved and ask the same questions about his progress on the problems specified in his treatment plan. In addition, you need to assess the child's relationship with the significant adults in his life by obtaining answers to the following questions:

- Is the boy able to talk with parents (or other significant adults, or both) and listen to their viewpoints even if those viewpoints differ from his?
- Does he have an effective way of dealing with conflict that arises with these adults?
- Is he responsive to parental discipline?
- Is an adult (either a parent or a parent surrogate such as a grandparent, an aunt, an uncle, a friend's parent, or a coach of a sports team) available to him and willing to serve in a supportive role?

After you have obtained answers to all necessary questions, compare the boy's responses to those of the adults. If the adults' responses vary significantly from the boy's, again meet with the boy to address this discrepancy openly. For example, you might say to him, "It seems that you and your teacher have different opinions about how well you respond to authority. Can you tell me more about what happens when you argue at school?"

Also, if there is not at least one adult in the boy's life who can provide consistency, support, and nurturing, and he is not able or willing to ask for help when he needs it, he is not ready to be discharged. One very important goal of therapy is that the boy learns to reach out for help when he has a problem and understands this is not a sign of weakness.

Discussing Discharge with the Group

You will also need to address the issue of the child's leaving with the entire group. Discuss how a poorly timed or poorly planned discharge can negatively affect the progress a child has achieved in therapy. Also explain that each boy presents with a different set of problems, a different support system, and a different response to the treatment; consequently, decisions about discharge are made on an individual basis.

Ask the other group members to give feedback on the boy's readiness to stop group therapy. A boy is frequently more ready to accept constructive criticism from peers than he is to hear the same feedback from adults. If the boy hears something he does not like, this situation will give you a sense of how he deals with conflict, whether he can tolerate uncomfortable emotions, and whether he has the ability to listen to others.

Making the Decision to Discharge

Before you plan a member's discharge, you need to consider whether the boy has improved in the following areas since the time of your initial assessment of him:

- Overall functioning
- Behavior at school
- Relationships with peers
- Relationships with parents and other significant adults
- Psychiatric symptomatology

Small positive changes in each of these areas will add up to an overall improvement in functioning. However, if there is either no improvement or deterioration in any particular area, you need to advise against discharge.

You also need to answer the following questions, keeping in mind that you are looking for a positive change since the time the boy entered the group.

1. *How would you assess the boy's ability to tolerate discussion of the molestation?* Can he remember the abuse without being overwhelmed by his feelings? Does he still withdraw, shut down, become angry, bounce off the walls, or get silly? For example, it is an improvement for the angry boy to verbalize his anger instead of

destroying property or verbally abusing someone in his presence. Similarly, the boy who previously withdrew and refused to participate has improved if he sticks with the group's activities or discussion and shows some verbal interaction.

2. *Has he fully disclosed what happened to him?* If it is known or suspected that the boy continues to maintain secrecy about certain aspects of his molestation, consider discharge from the group only if it will be followed by individual treatment. A medical exam, another victim's disclosure, or input from the offender can indicate there is a different story—usually of more extensive sexual acts than the boy is willing to talk about. Denial, shame, or other issues contributing to continued secrecy will need additional therapeutic work.

3. *Has he stopped repressing the impact of the molestation?* Regardless of his age, each sexually abused boy needs to directly confront and acknowledge the pain he has experienced. Without this acknowledgment, he is at higher risk for engaging in offending behavior due to his belief that "it did not affect me, so it will not affect this child either." Additionally, it is important for him to feel the emotions as fully as possible rather than to disconnect or disengage from them.

4. *How well has he worked through the traumatic aspects of his abuse?* James (1989) notes that there are four important aspects to helping children integrate and achieve mastery over a trauma:

- Fully examining what happened
- Symbolically recreating the experience so that he no longer perceives himself as a victim
- Expressing thoughts and emotions related to the abuse
- Looking at the trauma realistically without minimizing or exaggerating

5. *Does he still act in helpless or self-victimizing ways?* When there is a problem, does he demonstrate effective problem-solving efforts, or does he give up? The child may be at risk for additional abuse if he believes he is powerless and unable to make an impact on his world. The child who views himself as a victim usually behaves in a manner congruent with this belief and needs much cognitive work along with practice in assertive, powerful behavior.

6. *Does he take age-appropriate responsibility for himself?* You are looking for a balance here, between taking no responsibility (always blaming others or the situation, or giving excuses) and feeling wholly responsible for things that are beyond his control. Either extreme is harmful to the child. Some of the activities in Part Two address ways to discuss responsibility so that it is perceived positively and as an important aspect of empowerment.

7. *Does the boy blame himself in any way for the sexual abuse?* Does he place responsibility where it belongs, on the offender? If he does blame himself, it is nec-

essary to explore and clarify why. If there is something he feels he could have done differently, acknowledge this and plan with him how he could implement these actions in the future. Assist him to understand that learning new skills following a painful experience is empowering and helps him move on from it.

8. *Have there been any occurrences of sexualized behavior toward other children of any age?* Has the boy exhibited any other abusive behaviors? If not, the boy can be discharged. If so, however, he remains at risk for offending behavior and clearly needs additional group intervention or a different therapeutic modality. If there is a court mandate for treatment, use this leverage to keep him in therapy until the behavior is under control. If there is no court mandate, you cannot make a child stay in treatment. Instead, ensure that both the boy and his parent understand their accountability and the potential consequences of allowing the child to leave treatment, which could involve dealing with the judicial system or incarceration.

Discharging the Child

If your evaluation has shown that the child is ready to leave the group, discharge him. If your evaluation has shown that he needs to stay, apprise him and his parent of that fact. If the boy and his parent remain intent on his leaving therapy, have them sign a written document stating that you are opposed to discharge and listing the reasons you discussed.

Before the child leaves, meet with him and his parent. Clarify that it may be necessary for the boy to return for additional treatment in the future and that this does not mean he has failed in any way or that therapy was not effective. Explain that a person's needs are different at different ages and depend on circumstances that cannot be anticipated or predicted ahead of time.

Give examples of times that may be especially difficult or symptoms that can recur during periods of high stress or vulnerability. If the boy experiences a major loss (such as the death of someone close) or a series of losses, he may become depressed and require additional intervention. When he begins dating relationships or becomes sexually active, he may have new concerns or questions about the impact of the abuse. Finally, situational changes, such as a parent's remarriage, having contact with the offender, or legal proceedings that require the boy to testify, may exacerbate memories of the abuse.

If you are discharging the child with a recommendation that he continue some kind of therapy, be careful that you do not convey the message that he has failed or has not participated in the group adequately. Some issues may need more thorough resolution in an individual or family therapy modality. Family therapy is indicated especially when significant adults have difficulty supporting a child's progress or inadvertently reinforce negative behaviors.

If the boy clearly benefited from the group but made slow progress due to excessive absences or other factors, another time-limited cycle of group therapy specific to sexual abuse may be indicated. If the boy is repeatedly demonstrating sexually abusive behavior toward others, you must refer him to perpetrator treatment.

Finally, repeated academic failure or continued behavioral problems in the school environment suggest that a special education evaluation is in order. Coaching a parent through the process of requesting and receiving an evaluation is well worth the investment of time. Many boys who have been sexually abused progress more rapidly in their recovery when small, appropriate changes are made in their school programs. Some possible changes to consider include the following:

- A switch from a male to a female teacher (if the offender was a man) or from a female to a male teacher (if the offender was a woman)
- Adjusted physical education requirements (if public changing of clothes creates discomfort)
- Smaller class size so that he gets more individual attention and instruction
- Supportive counseling at school if particular situations occur there (such as anger outbursts, crying spells, or flashbacks)
- A transfer to a new school if peers are exacerbating the problems by taunting about abuse

Conclusion

This chapter provided essential information on group therapy with sexually abused boys. When you combine this information with the activities in Part Two, you will have all the tools you need to plan and conduct group therapy sessions.

CHAPTER FIVE

WORKING WITH PARENTS AND SIGNIFICANT ADULTS

When you decide to work with a sexually abused boy, you need to establish a relationship with a significant adult in his life (his parent, his guardian, or another person who has assumed a custodial role—referred to here as "the parent"). The boy's treatment will be greatly enhanced if you and his parent can create a therapeutic alliance and work together toward his recovery. This chapter addresses ways in which you can establish and maintain a relationship with the parent that will allow you to exchange important information that will assist you in your therapeutic efforts.

Developing a Therapeutic Alliance with the Parent

The ideal situation for creating a relationship with a parent would be to conduct an ongoing support group for parents of molested boys or even individual therapy for each parent. However, depending on the scope of services you provide and each child's circumstances, you may have only one or two face-to-face meetings with a parent (during the initial assessment and when you release the child from therapy); you may have regular meetings; or you may see the parent only sporadically, when crises arise. However, you need to try to establish some kind of regular contact, whether it is face-to-face, over the phone, or in writing.

Sending a Letter to the Parent

After the initial assessment session, you might want to send a letter to the parent outlining basic information about the child's therapy:

- The day and time of the child's sessions
- Expectations for consistent attendance
- Confirmation of transportation arrangements
- Confidentiality guidelines
- Treatment goals
- An invitation to meet with you at any time to ask questions or discuss concerns

A sample letter to a parent is shown in Exhibit 5.1. Note that this letter encourages future interaction with the parent and states that the therapist will contact the parent regularly.

Educating the Parent

Early in the relationship, you need to educate the parent about sexual abuse and its ramifications. You can do this in meetings, over the phone, or through written materials. Here is some of the information you will want to provide (see Chapters One and Two):

- Inform the parent that many boys are sexually abused, and large numbers of men report having been molested as children.
- Explain that the term *sexual abuse* addresses the types of sexual contact the boy experienced; the age, size, and power differential between the boy and the abuser; and the use of force, bribery, and threats on the part of the abuser.
- Counter common myths ("Sexual abuse is not harmful to boys," "Molestation is usually committed by strangers," and so on) with accurate information.
- Describe the behavioral symptoms of molested boys.
- Inform the parent about what to do if he or she suspects additional or continuing sexual abuse.
- Describe the immediate action steps to take within the first week following a boy's disclosure of sexual abuse (if disclosure has not already occurred).
- Describe long-term action steps to take to improve coping and facilitate healing.

Dealing with a Parent's Resistance and Fears

Unfortunately, not all parents are able and willing to cooperate with you in their children's therapy. Each parent has his or her own beliefs and feelings about sexual abuse,

EXHIBIT 5.1. SAMPLE LETTER TO PARENT.

Dear Mrs. Jones:

Thank you for your participation in Jimmy's evaluation last week at our clinic. The purpose of this letter is to confirm the details we discussed about Jimmy's participation in the boys' group.

His group will be meeting here at the clinic every Wednesday from 3:00 to 4:30 P.M., starting January 6.

Regular attendance is expected and is necessary for Jimmy to get the most benefit from his therapy. If he is ill, please keep him home. If for any reason he cannot attend, please contact the clinic by 12:00 on Wednesday at the latest, so transportation can be canceled. Absences without notifying me in advance will jeopardize Jimmy's continued participation.

Our van driver will be picking Jimmy up at Benson School by 2:30 and taking him to your home after the group session is over. It is your responsibility to sign the paperwork necessary at the school to authorize this arrangement.

We respectfully request that you honor the confidentiality of Jimmy's group sessions by not pressuring him to talk about his experiences in the group. If he chooses to share with you what he does or learns in the group, that is fine. Of course you will be notified immediately if there is any concern about Jimmy's safety or well-being. As we agreed, the priorities for Jimmy's treatment will be the following:

1. Expressing and managing his anger without aggressive or verbally abusive behavior
2. Understanding how he has been affected by the abuse by his grandfather
3. Improving his social skills and relationships with his peers

In closing, please remember that I am available by phone or in person to talk with you about any concerns or questions you might have about Jimmy. I will be checking in with you regularly to see how things are going at home and school, and I look forward to working with you and your son.

Sincerely,

therapy, and parenting. These beliefs and feelings often lead to resistance to therapy, and this resistance must be at least partially overcome before you can develop an effective alliance with the parent.

For example, the parent may not believe treatment is useful or may be skeptical because previous therapeutic encounters seemed threatening. Or the parent may not believe the boy was molested, may be uninformed about the damage caused by sexual abuse, or may think the best course of action is to forget what happened. The parent who is court ordered to obtain therapy for the child often feels angry about this authority and resents being told what to do.

Sometimes a parent feels terrified of therapy without understanding why. (They may be survivors of childhood sexual abuse, for example, whose own memories often surface only when their child also is molested.) Sometimes you may encounter a parent from a severely dysfunctional family who views the abuse of a child and the child's needs as low priorities compared to the demands of everyday living.

Often you will find that you can help a parent view the therapy in a more positive light by explaining the process carefully and taking that parent's wishes for the child into consideration in guiding the therapy. This approach involves helping the parent identify some goals for the boy. Ask the parent what he or she wants most to see change or improve for the child. A parent may be focused, for example, on behavior at home (staying out of trouble, acting less defiantly), school performance (working up to his ability, paying attention, and getting the work completed), or getting along better with peers (no fighting, playing cooperatively, developing friendships).

A more sophisticated parent may be able to identify more subtle problem areas dealing with emotions, such as the boy's ability to handle his anger better or to feel better about himself. If a parent can be helped to put into words what she or he would like to see happen for the child, you will then be able to discuss therapy goals and processes so that the parent understands how these issues will be addressed. (You will also need to convey these goals to the child.)

For example, if a parent is most concerned about the child's anger and how he expresses it, you can help by explaining the following:

- The therapeutic goal of encouraging expression and acknowledgment of all emotions, including anger
- The reasons why a boy who has been sexually abused may feel angry, including anger at a parent for not protecting him (see Chapter Three)
- Session rules, which set limits on verbally abusive language, threats, and any hands-on behavior, and consequences for such behavior (see Chapter Four)

- Some examples of how you will work with anger during the sessions, such as providing safe alternatives for physical release of anger, helping the boy identify precipitants for outbursts, exploring what other feelings are underlying the anger, and reinforcing personal responsibility for behavior at all times

Once you have pinpointed the source of the parent's resistance—generally denial or fear of some kind—you can work with him or her on removing that resistance.

Confronting a Parent's Denial

You will see many forms of parental denial about the reality of the child's molestation, at all stages of contact. This defense may be used in reaction to strong feelings of responsibility, shame, or anger. In a case involving incest, for example, the parent may find it overwhelming to face the changes necessary in order to reunite the family. Other parents typically respond to all stressful or painful situations with denial; in fact, they may never have had the opportunity to learn how to move past denial and how to cope more effectively.

You may encounter any of a variety of parental behaviors that stem from denial: no-shows for counseling appointments, refusal to follow through with recommendations from the police or child protective services, taking a boy out of counseling prematurely, stating that the boy has not been hurt by the abuse, and discouraging the boy from any attempts to talk about the abuse.

There are several ways to address denial. One is to point out the parent's own losses arising from the child's abuse. The parent may not have recognized this crisis as a loss issue for himself or herself, and may need to grieve. Once you have explored this idea, introduce the typical stages of coping with loss as outlined by Kübler-Ross (1969). Learning about these stages will help the parent understand his or her own reactions and that denial is not abnormal; doing so will also set the expectation that denial is temporary and can be worked through.

Another way to approach denial is to reframe therapy as one possible way to prevent future difficulties for the boy and his family. Still another approach is to reinforce the parent's power to make choices in response to the abuse and then to give some feedback about the potential consequences of those choices.

In addition, sometimes an analogy about the use of medical services is helpful. What does the parent do if a child hurts himself or develops symptoms of an illness? What usually happens if the parent seeks immediate attention? You can reinforce the notion that usually the problem does not progress, costs are lower, and the child feels better sooner. Contrast this situation to the negative results that may arise from doing nothing: the problem may become significantly worse, the child will feel miserable for a longer period, and the costs of treatment (which may include additional visits to doctors or even hospitalization) will probably be much higher. Similarly, denial about the need for boys to talk about and resolve problems resulting from their molestation may appear to be effective as a short-term solution; in the long run, however, denial results in much higher emotional and financial costs.

If you discover that the parent has a long-standing pattern of denial, you may have to delve into the situation more deeply to determine what the parent ultimately fears, what payoffs the parent receives from denial, and who in the parent's life encouraged denial or avoidance as a response to painful events. Keep in mind that exploration of this kind is often the first step for parents to recover memories of their own childhood abuse.

Exploring a Parent's Sex-Role Expectations

Although accepting the reality of child sexual abuse is never easy for a parent, it is generally easier to seek help and provide support for a daughter. Sex-role expectations play a major part here. Victimization conjures up descriptions of a boy as helpless, weak, or fearful—just the opposite of the words most often used to describe a boy: *strong, in control, assertive.*

When parental expectations reflect societal expectations, these "shoulds" ("My son should be strong") interfere with the parent's ability to accept the reality of the abuse and to appropriately support and assist a male child who has been molested. The following are some of the damaging assumptions that result from this kind of thinking:

- Something is wrong with him, or he would not have been molested.
- He should have known what to do to stop it.
- He was chosen because he is feminine.
- Being molested will make him less than a man.
- My son must be crazy if he needs counseling.

When you encounter this kind of response, include both mother and father in your efforts to educate and intervene, if at all possible. Some authorities on sexual abuse have suggested that the father is more likely to encourage a boy to resist and avoid the reality of molestation and the need for treatment (Porter, 1986). Discussion with parents about their feelings and reactions to molestation of a male child can bring into the open their sex-related expectations and erroneous assumptions.

Your essential therapeutic goal in this situation is to change the parents' perception of their boy as "damaged" due to the abuse. Instead, you want to instill in them the perception that their son is a normal child reacting to an abnormal event that happened to him.

Addressing a Parent's Fear of Homosexuality

An underlying worry for many parents of boys molested by a male is whether or not the abuse will "cause" their sons to become homosexual (Gilgun & Reiser, 1990). This fear may be communicated unconsciously or consciously to the boy. Fears of homosexuality can underlie much of the resistance to therapy and the denial about the impact of sexual abuse.

When a boy has been molested and picks up on subtle or not-so-subtle messages from the parent that he may be homosexual, he may have extreme reactions when his sexual orientation is questioned: sexual acting out, promiscuity in an attempt to "prove" masculinity, or both; homophobic statements and actions; avoidance of any discussion about sexuality; an exaggerated "macho" stance; or even assault. In addition, you need to be aware that feelings and questions about sexuality choices tend to be more prevalent in the teen and young adult years. You may be the only person with whom a young man feels he can talk about these feelings and concerns.

If you find that the parent fears homosexuality, you need to provide information on the subject that is accurate and free from bias and judgment. You also need to create a safe environment in which to discuss the impact of abuse on sexuality. Correcting misinformation about homosexuality can be effective in lessening the parent's concern that abuse in childhood will inevitably lead to a homosexual lifestyle. The following is some general information that you might want to share with the parent:

- It is estimated that approximately 10 percent of the population is homosexual.
- Homosexual preference is believed to be determined not by a single causative factor but by an interplay between early learning, biology, cultural values, social influences, and personality.
- Homosexuality is not defined solely by sexual experiences with persons of the same gender.
- Homosexuality is not considered a psychiatric disorder.
- For many people, homosexuality is unnatural and therefore unacceptable. For others, however, sexual orientation is seen as just one aspect of a person's being, and a same-sex orientation is just as acceptable as a heterosexual orientation.

If the family has a religious affiliation, find out what the particular church teaches about homosexuality and then explore whether the parent agrees with the church's doctrine in this area. Some parents find that they do not agree with the church philosophy about homosexuality. Another important area to investigate is whether the molested child has been counseled by anyone from the church, so that you can take this into consideration in the boy's therapy.

Also let the parent know that the issue of homosexuality will be addressed in therapy sessions with the boy and that the following points will be emphasized:

- Sexual abuse by a male does not cause a boy to be gay.
- Every boy, regardless of his sexual orientation, is a worthy human being.

Addressing a Parent's Fear That the Child Will Abuse Others

Another sensitive issue for the parent may be the relationship between childhood abuse and later offending behavior. Although research in this area is certainly not complete, it is true that most adult and juvenile perpetrators of sexual abuse have experienced childhood abuse of some kind. Unfortunately, parents often leap to an incorrect assumption that their molested children will grow up to act out sexually against other children. In other words, they may assume a causal link and also communicate it to the boy either subtly or overtly, resulting in significant fear, hopelessness, and sometimes a damaging self-fulfilling prophecy.

If you encounter this erroneous assumption, you need to confront it directly, preferably with both parents as well as the child. State that current knowledge indicates that although a minority of sexually abused children do grow up to repeat the cycle with offending behavior, the majority do not. Then you need to emphasize that the following mediating factors, which are under parental control, are what make the difference:

- The absence of other types of physical and emotional abuse
- The presence of appropriate adult male role models
- The absence of substance abuse
- Effective and prompt therapy to address the problems created by sexual abuse
- Parental understanding of power and control dynamics, along with willingness to follow through with necessary changes
- Accurate, age-appropriate, and ongoing sex education

Inform the parents that although certainly the boy will need ongoing reinforcement and support from them in order to prevent abusive behavior, abuse is not inevitable. Also explain that in therapy with the boy you will be addressing the fear of becoming an offender.

If the boy has already sexually victimized another child, you will need to encourage the parents to do the following:

- Fully acknowledge the offense, without minimizing it or blaming the child.
- Sort out their feelings about themselves and the boy.
- Understand and change family behavior patterns that may have contributed to the sexual abuse.
- Examine issues for the other children in the family (especially protection from sexual abuse).
- Modify destructive ways of maintaining family balance, such as protecting the offender or keeping family secrets.
- Learn general parenting skills (by attending courses or reading informative materials; see the Resources section at the end of the book) as well as specific skills needed to manage a child who has been abusive.

Recommending Help for a Parent Who Has Been Victimized

Depending on various circumstances and the way in which the family was referred for therapy, you may know before you meet the boy whether one or both of his parents have been abused as children (physically, sexually, or emotionally). However, it is more often the case that you do not know this for a fact. In some cases you will suspect that a parent was abused, on the basis of the information you have gathered.

When you do suspect abuse, you need to create an atmosphere for the parent in which he or she feels safe enough to remember and disclose that abuse. You also need to assist the parent in recognizing how his or her own unresolved abuse issues will affect the effectiveness and speed of the boy's recovery from molestation.

Keep in mind that your recommending ongoing therapy for a parent can be perceived as threatening, just as it can for a child. The parent may insist that sexual abuse had no impact or may deny the abuse because of some negative stigma that is still attached to therapy. It is very likely, however, that the parent has never received effective treatment. Sometimes a parent becomes willing to seek treatment, though, when you emphasize that such treatment would be beneficial for the child as well.

How a Parent Can Help

You need to learn what each boy needs and wants from his parent in order for him to cope effectively with the sexual abuse he has experienced. To gain a clearer

understanding of children's situations, my colleagues and I often ask boys to identify their "wishes" with regard to their parents. Following are sample replies:

> "I wish that my mom hadn't been gone so much and that my dad had
> enough control to stop himself." (Age eight)

> "I wish my mom would stop taking drugs and come back and live with us."
> (Age eight)

> "I wish my mom hadn't worked nights and then slept during the day. I had
> to have a baby-sitter, and he was the one who molested me." (Age ten)

> "I needed love. I needed protection. I wanted my mom to come out and
> stop it." (Age twelve)

> "During my molesting I needed a person to talk to about my molesting."
> (Age thirteen)

> "I needed my mom and dad's love and backup." (Age twelve)

> "I needed love and I also needed counseling and I also needed protection."
> (Age fourteen)

> "I think I needed support from my parents most of all (when I told)
> because I had held it in for so many years (five at least) and I wasn't sure
> what kind of reaction I was going to get. And fortunately I received that
> support from my mother, and she did what she could to get me help and
> let me know that I was OK." (Age eighteen)

The theme of support comes through clearly in these comments. When a parent asks you what he or she can do to help the child cope better with sexual abuse,
you can discuss a number of ways to provide the necessary support:

- By helping restore the child's personal power
- By protecting the child from further harm
- By validating the child's feelings
- By enhancing the child's self-esteem
- By encouraging the child to safely manage his anger
- By enforcing privacy and boundaries in the home
- By providing sex education for the child

Restoring the Child's Personal Power

You need to emphasize to the parent that the most critical issue addressed in therapy is the restoration of the child's personal power. Explain that by regaining a
sense of power, the child can overcome feelings of helplessness and victimiza-

tion and can begin learning and using effective problem-solving skills. There are several therapeutic goals related to restoring power, and you need to share these with the parent:

- To assist the boy in identifying when he feels helpless, powerless, or out of control
- To develop the boy's awareness of situations that generate such feelings and the people most likely to precipitate such feelings
- To help the boy understand the connection between sexual abuse and power (that many offenders are motivated by power and control rather than sexual gratification)
- To reinforce positive methods of regaining a sense of mastery and self-control (identifying personal choices and the resulting consequences, learning problem-solving skills, and so on)

The parent's understanding and acceptance of these goals is critical, as the parent must, whenever possible, avoid situations in which the boy feels helpless, powerless, or out of control. The parent also must avoid reinforcing a child's perception of himself as a victim. You need to help the parent see that although the child is not responsible for any aspect of his sexual abuse, he is responsible now for his actions and their impact on others.

Encourage the parent to allow the boy freedom of choice whenever possible by helping him identify potential solutions to problems and then choose one of those alternatives. You may need to work especially hard with an authoritarian parent who does not want to give up any decision-making power to the child.

Ask parents to praise examples of the positive use of power and to implement immediate consequences for actions that are abusive or hurtful to others. For example, an aggressive child who typically punches his younger sister needs to receive praise when he chooses to leave the room rather than have another physical fight. When he does punch her, consequences need to be specific and implemented immediately so that the boy sees a negative outcome associated with that behavior.

Finally, you need to assist in identifying what areas or issues cause conflict between the boy and the parent. If disagreements are constant and about many aspects of the child's life, the parent needs to choose a maximum of three areas on which to focus. This approach reduces the number of confrontations; constant battles only exacerbate the boy's attempts to stay in control.

Protecting the Child from Further Harm

Immediate safety and protection issues must be addressed first, both with believing and denying parents. Longer-term protection issues cannot be addressed when a parent still denies the abuse. Clearly, the issues are more complicated when the offender is a family member and living in the same home with the child. When this is the case, child protective services or the legal system (or both) frequently place external controls on the parent.

If these systems are not involved, however, it generally falls to the parent to figure out how to prevent further abuse from occurring. If the parent is unwilling to consider this important need and fails to implement reasonable protective actions, the child remains at risk, and the family requires urgent intervention to prevent reoccurrence of abuse.

In most circumstances, the boy's wishes can be taken into consideration in planning safety precautions. If the molestation was by a member of the extended family and the child wants to continue going to family get-togethers, the parent can have the child supervised at all family functions by a responsible adult who does not deny that abuse occurred. The parent can also limit the amount of time spent with the family to ensure that continual, close supervision is possible. If the boy was molested by an older sibling of his best friend and wants to continue his friendship, the parent can make the friend's home off-limits yet allow the friend to have visits and overnight stays. If the boy was molested by a neighbor who has been verbally harassing the family since charges were filed, the parent can obtain a restraining order and also send the boy to a relative's home until all legal action is completed. If a child's soccer coach was the offender and the boy wants to continue to play on the same team, the parent can request suspension of the coach based on the allegations or transfer the boy to another team or another league to play.

There is one circumstance in which a boy's request cannot be granted: when he is minimizing the seriousness of the sexual abuse and wants unsupervised contact with the offender. Regardless of the relationship between the offender and the child, safety controls must be set into place to prevent further victimization.

Additional protective actions to recommend to parents depend on the individual needs of each boy. The following are some suggestions:

- Limiting or eliminating contact with individuals who do not believe the child was molested or who do not support treatment goals
- Learning what things or places trigger flashbacks for the boy (for example, men with beards, the bathtub or shower)
- Initiating immediate contact with school staff when there are school-related problems, so that effective interventions can be coordinated between school, mental health staff, and parents
- Seeking the aid of an advocate if the child will be going through the court process, to ensure he has necessary support and preparation

- Practicing assertiveness and saying "no" when the parent intuitively feels a person or situation is not safe for the boy

Validating the Child's Feelings

The parent must learn how to validate and encourage the child's expression of feelings besides anger, such as sadness, loneliness, and confusion. As mentioned before, boys are frequently socialized to believe that these feelings are unacceptable for them. The parent must be aware of not only his or her own messages to the child about feelings but also the messages provided by other significant adults in the child's life.

Enhancing the Child's Self-Esteem

A person's self-esteem is a significant determinant of his or her behavior and ability to cope with life events (Oaklander, 1978). The child who is sexually abused clearly suffers a loss in self-esteem. The parent needs to know that rebuilding self-esteem requires a sustained effort on the part of all adults involved with the boy. This means that the parent needs to inform significant adults about what happened to the boy and recruit them in the effort to help him.

For example, teachers who are unaware of the molestation history or uninformed about the impact of sexual abuse may unintentionally reinforce low self-esteem with actions or words. Father figures who have not been involved with any treatment with the child may be completely unaware of ways in which they are contributing to the child's negative self-image.

Before you work with the parent to teach him or her ways to bolster the child's self-esteem, it is helpful for the parent to identify ways in which his or her own self-esteem was bolstered or impaired as a child. Ask questions such as these:

- What did your parents say or do to help you feel good about yourself?
- What words or actions made you feel you were less important or not as worthy as others?

When you have this information, it is usually easier to come up with ideas for fostering the child's self-esteem that the parent views as useful. Although they appear very simple, the ideas listed here can have powerful influence on a boy when used consistently and honestly by the adults in his life. Practice these ideas with the parent until he or she feels comfortable using them:

- Give descriptive, specific praise.

- Give descriptive, specific criticism focused on behavior, not on the boy himself (for example, "I don't like it when you yell at me from downstairs. Come upstairs when you need to talk to me").
- Listen to and accept all feelings.
- Be honest and sincere with compliments to the child. Phoniness and insincerity only reinforce mistrust.
- Use "I" messages to give feedback (for example, "I feel angry when you ignore my directions to clean up your room").
- Provide choices and give opportunities to solve problems and make decisions whenever possible.
- Model self-esteem by not putting yourself down. Demonstrate doing things that show you think highly of yourself.
- Avoid teaching the boy to base his self-esteem on accomplishments or attributes. Every child is valuable and worthy, regardless of skills, appearance, or accomplishments.

A parent may also need support in identifying how children show they have low self-esteem. Some behavioral clues include cheating in games ("I'm no good if I don't win"), bragging, self-critical statements, frequent "I can't" statements, giving up easily or not even trying, or unwillingness to try anything new or different.

Encouraging the Child to Manage His Anger

For many parents of molested boys, concerns about anger management are the reason for seeking treatment. It is a common message in our society that expressions of anger are acceptable for boys and men, whereas other feelings are less acceptable. Conversely, for females, expressions of anger are frowned on and usually chastised.

When a boy has been sexually abused, anger may be his only safe outlet for expressing the overwhelming emotions that result. In this situation the child may be presenting with one or more of the following symptoms: oppositional or defiant behavior, fighting, running away, self-abusive actions, destruction of property, and temper tantrums.

When you can help the parent understand the losses that the child has experienced as a result of being sexually abused—along with the parent's own losses— the parent may be able to understand the child's anger better. Also, you might let the parent know that expressing anger is a necessary part of the recovery process. You may want to bring up the stages of grief again and explain that anger is just one stage in the process of recovering from loss.

You and the parent also need to examine the boy's role models for handling anger. Let the parent know that the child learns what has been modeled for him; if significant adults in the boy's life engage in abusive language and fighting, he has not learned different, more appropriate means of releasing anger. If the parent is sensitive about having physically abused the child, at this point he or she will probably manifest significant denial or resistance. Obviously, family norms are not changed overnight and may require significant time in therapy to modify.

Ask the parent what he or she believes are acceptable ways for the boy to express angry feelings. By this time it is hoped that the parent recognizes the importance of expressing anger and comes up with some appropriate suggestions. If not, provide some suggestions from the anger-release activities in Part Two: pounding a pillow, ripping up newspaper, using a racquet to hit a racquetball against a wall or fence, kicking a punching bag, and going to a safe place where the child can yell or swear as much as he likes. Once you have reviewed these responses with the parent, you can schedule a session with both parent and child for the purpose of creating plans for working with the child's anger.

Emphasize that the boy needs to hear what behavior is unacceptable at home and at school, while also hearing that his angry feelings are understood. He needs to hear what methods of dealing with anger are acceptable to his parent, and he needs to be allowed to choose which of the acceptable ones he wants to implement. Perhaps the parent and child together can be responsible for getting whatever is necessary for the redirection of behavior (buying a punching bag or selecting a safe place to yell). Finally the child needs to hear—and the parent must practice—how he will be redirected if he begins to act out anger inappropriately.

Throughout this process, the parent's own anger about what has happened to the child and the resulting consequences must be explored. Is the anger under control? How does the parent express it? Also, if there is a court order to attend therapy, the parent may feel angry toward any individual who is involved with court recommendations. Some parents have great difficulty acknowledging the rage they experience; some even focus their anger on the child and blame him for the abuse. Others turn their anger inward and become immobilized by self-blame.

Like the child, the parent too needs validation and an effective, safe way to express anger. You need to help the parent explore several issues:

- What feelings is the parent repressing or refusing to acknowledge?
- What does the parent believe will happen if he or she does not feel angry anymore?
- What purposes does the parent accomplish by acting in anger?
- Is the parent's current method of expressing anger effective and not harmful to others?

When a parent accepts that a behavior or attitude is not helping him or her achieve what is desired, that parent may be motivated to try something different.

Enforcing Privacy and Boundaries in the Home

All children who have been molested have had their physical boundaries violated. Although this is only a part of the violation a boy feels, it is an important one. Whether the child is three or eighteen, he needs to feel in control of who is touching his body and when. You can assist parents to recognize and meet this need by introducing the following guidelines:

- Do not touch the boy (for example, for a hug or to rub his back) without first asking his permission.
- Use discipline methods that do not involve physical punishment.
- Insist that any adult in close contact with him (teachers, coaches, and extended relatives) also follow these guidelines.
- Respect his need for privacy. Knock before entering his room and make the bathroom off-limits to other people when someone is using it.
- Set a clear limit on any physical contact with which the boy feels uncomfortable.
- Give the boy permission and encouragement to tell someone that he does not want to be touched.

Providing Sex Education for the Child

When a boy has been sexually abused, the parent must examine the effectiveness of his or her sex education efforts with the child. Although parental feelings of guilt and responsibility often accompany exploration of this topic, past and future communication about sexuality needs to be addressed. It is common for parents to have such thoughts as, "If only I had talked to my son about sex before, maybe the abuse could have been prevented."

To help you recommend to the parent how to approach the situation, ask the parent to think about and then discuss the following areas:

- What were the patterns of communication in your family of origin? Were there any taboo subjects?
- What are your beliefs and values about sex education for children?
- How do you model good communication in the home?
- How do you usually respond when your child talks to you about friends, school, wishes, or problems? How do you invite or discourage him from talking to you?

- Are you giving congruent, consistent messages? Do your words match your actions?
- What feelings of your own may prevent you from listening fully to your son?

Accurate sex education includes both factual information and discussion of values, choices, peer pressure, birth control, and pregnancy. Molested boys desperately need this information in order to clarify the confusion they commonly experience.

Another common reaction that has an impact on sexuality is a boy's feelings of guilt and of being damaged. Your explaining how these areas will be covered during therapy will help parents. You also need to educate them about normal developmental stages in children and what is appropriate information for children at different ages (see the Appendix).

Although sex education may be covered in therapy and at school, emphasize that the child's needs for information will change over time and that the parent needs to provide ongoing clarification. Books are available to read with children of all ages and are an excellent means of beginning dialogue about sexuality. Other possibilities include attending a community presentation together or watching a movie that addresses some related area, such as adolescent pregnancy. These activities can stimulate further discussion.

Discussion of HIV and AIDS is an important aspect of sex education. Even very young boys have some awareness about the possibility of illness or injury after molestation. Frequently a boy believes that if a male molested him, he is now infected. You can anticipate a range of possible reactions from both the child and the parent, ranging from occasional uneasiness when the topic is raised, to intense and paralyzing anxiety. Discussion around obtaining an HIV blood test, and all its implications, is more effective when it is done with the individual boy, rather than in a group setting. As you gather the details of a boy's sexual abuse, these details will indicate whether testing needs to be considered (for example, if drugs were injected during the molestation, if there were multiple offenders, if any offender was male, if sodomy or oral copulation were involved, or if the child was involved in prostitution).

Working with Other Significant Adults

In addition to custodial parents and stepparents, there may be other adults who are influential in the molested boy's life. These possible contacts can include the following people:

- A parent who is estranged or who has sporadic contact with the boy
- A child protective services worker who is responsible for supervision of the family
- A teacher or school counselor
- A probation officer responsible for supervision or monitoring if there has been involvement with law enforcement
- A grandparent who shares caretaking duties

Because children's circumstances can vary dramatically, you will have to assess your need for collateral contacts in the case of each individual child. The following steps are recommended in determining the need for your involvement with other significant adults. First, decide whether making contact with the person is mandatory, desirable, or necessary only on an as-needed basis. For example, it would be mandatory for you to have contact with an overly authoritarian teacher who is aggravating power and control issues with an abused boy. Also mandatory would be your contact with a court social worker who is insisting on group therapy "no matter what" and who does not recognize assessment or screening criteria. If a boy is functioning without major difficulty in school, then your contact with his teacher would be a low priority and would be indicated only if a specific need arises.

Second, obtain necessary releases from the parent and inform the boy and that parent about what you plan to discuss with the collateral individual involved. Be certain that you have their agreement about the contact and that you are very clear in explaining the purpose of your contact. For example, there are many parents and boys who will oppose anyone in the school system having knowledge of the sexual abuse, or who fear documentation of the molestation in school records. This is understandable, and you must maintain their wish for privacy.

In such a situation, it is possible to problem-solve with the boy and his parent to arrive at a form and content of communication with school staff with which they feel comfortable. A letter with clinical recommendations for dealing with problematic school behaviors, based on your knowledge and experience with this particular boy and eliminating his background history, may be agreeable for one family. Another child may be comfortable only if he is present with his parent to hear all that is being said to his teacher. Some adolescents prefer written information from the therapist, if they are able to see the letter before it is sent.

In some situations, especially where there is court or legal involvement, a boy may have only minimal control over what is shared. You will need to talk about this from the beginning of his therapy, so that there are no surprises. It is important to inform clients that attendance, compliance with recommendations, any new information about the sexual abuse, and general progress are typically included in a summary to the court.

Third, plan your collateral contacts with a realistic assessment of how much available time you have. Although a highly involved teacher may want to update you weekly about school behavior, or a court social worker may request written monthly progress reports, time limitations may affect your ability to comply.

Finally, be aware that you may be in contact with a particular individual only once. It is critical to prioritize what is necessary to cover, from your perspective as well as from that of the collateral individual. You can prepare an agenda prior to the appointment by asking specifically what the person wants or needs. If you initiate the contact, be sure your agenda has clear priorities.

Be aware that ignoring the impact of other significant people can directly or indirectly sabotage the child's treatment progress. The boy whose parents, teacher, extended relatives, and social worker have all received information about how to support his recovery will clearly do much better than a child whose support system lacks this knowledge.

Keep in mind that even a very brief collateral contact can create significant results. One young adolescent shared in a group I led that his health teacher said that abused children grow up to be abusers themselves, which led to much anxiety and confusion for him. Although he did not want to identify himself as sexually abused to his entire class, he did want to take advantage of the opportunity to educate both his teacher and his peers. We agreed together that I could contact the teacher, let him know how his comments had been interpreted, and request that he clarify this issue with his class. The teacher was receptive to this feedback and provided corrected information to his students. Overall, speaking up was an empowering experience for the boy.

Conclusion

Establishing a relationship with a boy's parent or with other significant adults in his life can be difficult, but it is essential to the success of therapy. With proper education and understanding, parents and others can become your allies in therapy.

CHAPTER SIX

HANDLING CHALLENGES

This chapter offers suggestions for handling challenges that you may encounter in therapy with sexually abused boys. It covers problematic behaviors and challenging situations in both individual therapy and group therapy as well as challenges related to external factors and to administration.

Individual Therapy

The following are some common problematic behaviors that you may face in individual therapy:

- Continually seeking physical contact
- Experiencing drastic mood shifts
- Failing to attend sessions consistently
- Forgetting session content
- Departing from treatment prematurely
- Recanting the abuse
- Refusing to acknowledge documented molestation
- Remaining silent during individual sessions

These behaviors are discussed in detail in the following sections.

Continually Seeking Physical Contact

Frequent requests for physical contact are to be expected, especially with very young boys. It is difficult for many boys to make direct requests for what they want; it is more likely that they will show you.

You need to set limits on physical contact. At the same time, though, you need to validate the importance of physical contact and nurturance and to give comfort to a child when he needs it. (Keep in mind that most perpetrators ignore a child's needs, so you need to provide a different experience.)

When a child asks for physical contact, first remind him about the rule of "no physical contact" without first receiving permission. Explain that you are not rejecting him but respecting his rights. Then request and receive his permission before giving him a hug or a pat on the back or placing an arm around his shoulder.

You can assist a child in gradually decreasing the amount of physical contact he needs by helping him set a goal to be reached during his sessions. For example, you and he may decide that you will hug at the beginning and again at the end of the session only. Then be consistent in enforcing the limits.

Also discuss nonphysical ways to feel nurtured, such as by receiving consistent, positive, honest, and specific feedback. Always validate the boy's feelings and help him understand them and recognize his self-worth.

Finally, you may want to check with the parent to see if the boy is equally needy at home. Ask how the parent manages the situation and what the family's norms are concerning physical contact. You may want to do the same with his teacher. What you learn will be helpful in your intervention with the boy.

Experiencing Drastic Mood Shifts

The inability to regulate emotion is common among traumatized children. Keep in mind that children attempt to cope with intense feelings, such as those that accompany a traumatizing event, with whatever means are available to them. Sometimes the child may exhibit very restricted, tightly controlled play, use of words, and affect. He may have numbed himself to the pain by shutting himself down or by concentrating intensely on something else.

Eventually, the feelings build to a level at which the child's coping mechanisms no longer work. This is when you will observe an explosion of emotions and activity that seems to come from nowhere. You may also see this kind of mood shift when a boy experiences a flashback.

When the shift occurs, you need to explain, in age-appropriate terms, the impact of trauma on feelings and behavior. Clarify that the boy "explodes" because it is the best coping method available to him at the time. Let him know that you want to help him learn some alternatives that may work better.

Your objective is to desensitize the boy to overwhelming emotions gradually, helping him tolerate a little more intensity over time so that outbursts decrease in frequency. As you and he go through these shifts together, you need to work on developing the child's trust in you so that eventually he will allow you to care for him. As trust and caring develop, you can begin to explore how the boy feels when he is cared for.

Over time the boy will realize that caring soothes his feelings of anxiety, fear, and anger. Once he understands this, you can teach him a few simple techniques as alternatives for soothing himself. Your specific choices will depend on the child, but here are some examples:

- Holding a soft material or item (such as a blanket or stuffed animal)
- Engaging in a favorite creative activity, such as artwork
- Exercising or engaging in other physical activity
- Repeating or reading calming statements
- Drawing a picture (or being given such a picture) of a safe and secure place and then visualizing going there
- Deep breathing

Failing to Attend Sessions Consistently

When you begin to see a pattern of frequent absences, confront the boy immediately and ask for an explanation from him and from his parent. See if the reasons given by the child are the same as those given by the parent.

Depending on the reasons you are given, you may need to check out their validity by talking to the boy's doctor, teachers, social worker, or the person responsible for his transportation. For example, if the reason given is frequent illness, find out whether the child is being seen by a doctor and whether the parent is following through with medical advice.

If legitimate school problems are the reason, determine whether the school staff can negotiate or compromise to ensure that therapy is a priority. If transportation is the problem, try to arrange alternative transportation that is reliable and consistent.

If you find that the reasons are not legitimate, you need to determine (1) whether the parent truly supports the child's participation in therapy and (2) whether the boy is coming to sessions because he chooses to or because someone is forcing him to come. You also need to find out if something is happening in connection with therapy that the boy wants to avoid. For example, are peers teasing him because he leaves school early to attend a session?

If you find opposition or defiance on the part of the parent or child, be very clear about their responsibility for any consequences if you decide ultimately to terminate the therapy because of failure to attend. Make your requirements simple in a written behavioral contract, and request that both the child and parent sign it. Finally, if the family is under any type of court supervision, you need to notify the social worker that continued participation is in jeopardy due to poor attendance. Usually the leverage that a social worker has is enough to improve the family's compliance.

Forgetting Session Content

It can be disconcerting to begin winding down an individual session with a routine question such as "What was your favorite part of today's session?" only to have the child respond with "I don't remember." There is evidence that memory for traumatic events is processed differently, and levels of awareness can fluctuate (James, 1994), resulting, for example, in unremembered flashbacks. If you observe a child repeatedly acting out the trauma he experienced, and he does not recall this or respond to you while it is occurring, this may be a flashback episode.

Another alternative is that the child is dissociating. James (1989) suggests that any child who demonstrates memory impairment needs to be evaluated for dissociative behavior and describes some tools to assist in this evaluation. The indicators of dissociation that you are likely to observe include the following. If you do observe any of them, make sure you consult with someone with expertise in this area.

- Appearing unaware of surroundings
- Staring off, as if in a trance
- Extreme withdrawal
- Denial of behavior that you have witnessed
- Appearing disoriented or confused

During a dissociative episode, talk to the child as if he were present and can hear you. When his awareness of surroundings returns, explain to him that "going somewhere safe" is his way of coping with the abuse.

In cases involving either flashbacks or dissociation, ask the boy's parent or teacher or another involved adult to keep a log of what is happening each time the boy has such an experience. Also ask the child to notice and remember or keep track of the circumstances. Your objective is to identify what triggers the episodes: an emotion, some kind of sensory experience, a particular behavior, or even a particular object that reminds the child of the trauma.

Once you detect a pattern, you can develop some management strategies to help the boy feel more in control. For example, you may suggest reducing contact with a triggering object, practicing assertiveness during uncomfortable sensory experiences, or asking for help when certain feelings arise. Convey to the child that his knowledge of triggers is empowering and that it will help him manage these experiences.

Departing from Treatment Prematurely

A boy's departure from treatment before you think he is ready to leave can trigger feelings of loss and abandonment for him. These feelings are most acute when you and the boy have been working together for some time.

If you are given any notice of the child's leaving, discuss these feelings with him. Review the dynamics of loss: describe the stages of grief and what happens when a person experiences concurrent or multiple losses, and explain why anger and sadness are normal reactions. Let him know that feelings of loss tend to accumulate, which helps him understand times when emotions seem out of proportion.

If possible, have a final session with the boy to address leaving therapy. Although the parent may minimize the value of a final session, it is important. Elicit the boy's feelings about the change, say good-bye, and provide closure for his treatment. If you can, give him something tangible that will be a positive reminder of the work he has done in therapy, such as a stuffed animal, a book you have read with him, or a picture frame for his favorite artwork.

If the reasons for departure have to do with hostility on the part of the boy or parent, you may not be able to hold a good-bye session. Sending a card or letter instead is another option for providing some closure.

Recanting the Abuse

If a boy begins to deny that the molestation occurred, be very gentle with him. Reflect his wish that the abuse had never occurred. Acknowledge that it is often very difficult to talk about situations that cause painful memories.

Assess for any recent changes in his circumstances that may be triggering the denial, such as recent contact with the perpetrator, an upcoming court appearance, pressure from his family, or a parent's overt antagonism toward therapy. Keep in mind, too, that memories—especially traumatic ones—can change over time. You can continue to address the residual effects of the abuse even if a boy has recanted.

Refusing to Acknowledge Documented Molestation

A boy often refuses to acknowledge molestation after another child discloses sexual abuse and states that your client is also a victim. In this situation, you commonly find that he is being brought to therapy for the sole purpose of disclosure. Effective therapy will not occur unless you clarify for the boy, his caretakers, and any social service or legal professionals that you will not force him to talk before he feels ready. If you do not make your purpose clear, sessions will feel like an interrogation, an investigative interview, or a means to trick him. You will establish an ongoing power struggle rather than create a safe and supportive atmosphere.

The reality is that boys sometimes do not feel safe enough to talk about their abuse until they are much older, physically bigger and stronger, and living away from home. If this is the case with one of your clients, you can still address the residual effects of the abuse without emphasizing the etiology: clarifying and expressing feelings, providing age-appropriate education concerning sex and safety, and reducing problematic behaviors. Every few sessions, ask the boy whether he feels ready to talk about what happened to him, but always respect his decision.

Remaining Silent During Individual Sessions

Find out how verbal the boy is at home and school. Does his silence appear limited to therapy sessions, or is he silent in other areas of his life also? A persistent unwillingness or failure to speak in social situations could indicate selective mutism. When this is the case, consider that the extent of trauma is likely to be severe. Therapy with this child is usually much more gradual and less direct, so that the boy is spared further fear.

Failure to speak can also be related to severe depression, highly oppositional behavior, any of a number of communication disorders, a pervasive developmental disorder, a psychotic disorder, severe mental retardation, or inability to use language. (Also see "Silence in Group Sessions" in this chapter.) A consistently nonverbal child can test your patience; if you are able, share your reactions with someone who might be able to help, such as another staff member or a supervisor.

Another circumstance that can cause a boy to be silent is that of his being forced into therapy. If this is the case, try to negotiate or compromise with the party who insisted on therapy. If therapy has been mandated by a court, let the child know that you and he can probably reach some agreement about his participation that accommodates his needs and also makes good use of his sessions.

Mandated Therapy with a Young Boy. In mandated therapy with a young boy, you will need an enticing array of supplies to maintain his interest. Offer him a choice of artwork, games, toys, puppets, and outdoor recreation activities if possible. Make the sessions as nonthreatening as possible and avoid any direct interpretations of his play until he begins to trust you. Instead, as he plays make comments and ask gentle questions. Keep your initial discussions about the purpose of therapy very brief. Let the boy know that although the choice about talking is up to him, choosing to talk will help you help him faster. Remind him at the start and end of each session that you would like to hear his voice, his opinions, and his feelings.

Mandated Therapy with a Teenager. In mandated therapy with a teenager, you may find that the boy uses silence to establish control. You will have to be inventive in offering "hooks" to gain his interest and help him see the value in coming to sessions. Find out what he likes to do, and then see if you can use any of those things in therapeutic activities. If he likes music, for example, listen to his favorite artists with him; ask him to explore the meanings of certain songs; ask how the songs make him feel; discuss the use of music as a coping skill when he is stressed, angry, or unable to sleep; invite him to write his own songs or create his own music.

Group Therapy

In group therapy, members may engage in problematic behaviors either rarely or consistently, depending on the composition of the group. In addition, certain situations may arise that require careful management.

Problematic Behaviors

The following are some of the problematic behaviors you may face in groups:

- Acting aggressively
- Developing cliques or subgroups
- Dividing cotherapists
- Using power and control in dysfunctional ways
- Prematurely disclosing the details of abuse
- Engaging in sexualized behavior

- Remaining silent in group sessions
- Violating confidentiality
- Violating group rules or norms
- Being unwilling to give feedback

These behaviors are discussed in detail in the following sections.

Acting Aggressively. Aggressive behavior (sometimes called "acting out") refers to a child's demonstrating his feelings in an inappropriate way. When a child acts out, he usually is doing so because he is unable to express his feelings in words or is unable to tolerate his emotional response. In responding to a boy who is acting out, you need to accomplish two goals: (1) enforce previously set rules concerning unacceptable behavior and (2) help the boy learn how to control his behavior (thereby teaching the other group members as well).

Assault—on you, your cotherapist, or one or more group members—is the most serious form of acting out that you might experience. It is more likely to occur in highly restrictive settings (such as a hospital or residential treatment center) and during procedures involving physical restraint. Regardless of the setting in which your group operates, however, you need to plan in advance how you will intervene in the event of an assault. You must decide what to do both when you are alone with the group and when you are working with a cotherapist.

Here is one plan you might consider: first give immediate feedback that the behavior is unacceptable. Be sure your tone of voice is loud enough and commanding enough to get the group's attention. Focus on the unacceptable behavior and tell the boy specifically what he needs to do instead. Do not criticize the responsible boy or allow peers to criticize him. Give him as many options as possible to regain control of his behavior. For example, you can offer time to talk, a change in seating arrangements, a time-out from the group, a physical outlet to release energy, art materials for drawing, or paper for writing. Use physical restraint only as a last resort; if you use this approach, you need a minimum of three to four adults who are trained in managing assault. Then you must ensure the group's safety by removing the responsible child from the group or moving the rest of the group to another location.

A successful intervention with aggressive behavior involves helping the child understand that he can control his anger without harming himself or anyone else. Consequently, later, when the child is able to calm down, you need to review with him what happened. Help him identify what triggered the behavior and identify more appropriate options for the next time the trigger occurs. If he is enough under control at this point to rejoin the group, reinforce with all members present that everyone gets angry, everyone has different triggers for their anger, and everyone is personally responsible for controlling his behavior.

If you feel that the responsible boy can tolerate it, ask him if he wants some feedback from his peers. If possible, allow the other members some time to vent their feelings about what has occurred. They may express anger with you or with the child who acted out; they may express fear or anxiety; they may even experience flashbacks about similar incidents in their own lives. After the group session, you need to discuss the incident thoroughly with your cotherapist, sharing observations and personal reactions.

An incident severe enough to cause injury or property damage warrants a boy's immediate suspension from the group, so that all members can see that you are willing to ensure the safety of the group. When you suspend a boy, it is a good idea to use a written behavioral contract stipulating clear conditions for his return to the group as well as consequences for further aggressive behavior. Work with the boy in writing this contract, in order to reinforce his responsibility for his behavior and his ownership of the agreement.

If at some point the child returns to the group but continues to have outbursts that jeopardize group safety, you must discontinue his attendance of group therapy. You may want to treat him in individual therapy, in which case you can consider group therapy again when he has established better control. It is important to consider all available options before you permanently terminate the boy's participation. If the boy or his parent is seeing another therapist and if you have a signed release of information from the parent, you may want to contact that therapist to obtain feedback before you make final plans for the boy.

This plan works well with worst-case scenarios, but you may also adapt it for less serious incidents. In addition to aggression, you need to watch for and immediately deal with other behaviors, both verbal and nonverbal, that are abusive or can lead to abusive acts in the group. Some of these behaviors are relatively subtle, such as denying responsibility, blaming others, and making excuses; others are not so subtle, such as making threats, intimidating members, and provoking members to act out. All these behaviors must be confronted immediately and dealt with in a consistent manner each time. For more information on behavior management and violence prevention, contact the Crisis Prevention Institute, Inc. (telephone: 800-558-8976) or the Professional Assault Response Team (PART) (telephone: 916-723-3802).

Developing Cliques or Subgroups. The majority of abused children experience some degree of social isolation or have minimal skills in developing positive relationships. Therefore, if some of the boys in your group are developing friendships with one another, those friendships can facilitate recovery. Sometimes, though, a clique or subgroup interferes with the group process and impedes therapy.

When a clique forms, determine the extent of its interference with the group before you decide to use it as a topic for discussion. Examples of the kind of disruption that warrants intervention are scapegoating of a group member, refusal to work with anyone in the group outside the clique, or threats between two cliques. You can intervene in any of the following ways, starting with the first option and progressing to the next options only if the first does not work:

1. Directly address the development of the clique with your group members and the problems you have seen caused by it, and state your expectation that the boys can resolve this issue. Encourage them to take responsibility for resolving the problem. State that if they do not resolve it, you will step in to impose some changes.
2. Change seating arrangements in the group.
3. During activities, assign each boy a partner outside his clique.
4. Encourage empathy by implementing role plays in which one child is scapegoated or left out of peers' activities; then lead a discussion about the results.
5. Work with the individual boys in the clique to encourage friendships with group members outside the clique; in this case you can establish a behavioral goal for each clique member. Emphasize the choices available for developing new friendships outside the group setting as well.

If none of these interventions is effective and the disruption continues to be severe, you may need to disband the group and start over with a new combination of boys.

Dividing Cotherapists. Behaviors that may indicate a boy's desire to pit one cotherapist against the other include the following:

- A child asks to meet with only one therapist after group.
- A child responds verbally to only one therapist and ignores the other.
- A parent reports to one therapist that his or her boy has spoken negatively or critically about the other therapist.
- A child appears to be attempting to persuade his peers to make one of you the "bad guy."

When any of these behaviors occur, you need to deal with them immediately. The child who initiates such behaviors has much less control when the subject is discussed openly in the group.

First point out the behavior and then explore the feelings behind it. State that although it is normal and natural to feel more comfortable with one person than with another, behavior that purposely excludes one therapist tends to switch the group's focus away from its purpose—to help the group members. You might want to compare the behavior with playing one parent against the other. Request that the boy who exhibited the behavior share his concerns with both therapists present, and let him know that this is an assertive way to take responsibility for resolving the problem. Also explore whether the boy's feelings of helplessness are contributing to the behavior. Finally, both you and your cotherapist need to emphasize that you are working together as a team to provide the best therapy for the group.

Using Power and Control in Dysfunctional Ways. Some dysfunctional uses of power and control that you may see in a group include the following:

- Passive-aggressive behavior
- Manipulation
- Provocation
- Ridicule
- Scapegoating
- Sabotaging your efforts or those of your cotherapist or the other group members
- Silence (when used as a power ploy; see the section "Remaining Silent in Group Sessions" in this chapter)

Point out these behaviors immediately after they occur, identify them as dysfunctional power and control behaviors, and then discuss them as a group issue. Explain why regaining a sense of power and control through positive means is so important for abused boys (see Chapter One). Discuss how self-empowerment and self-control are positive, whereas exerting control over others is not. Invite the group to discuss the feelings that may trigger a desire to control others. Then encourage the boys to offer more positive alternatives for managing their feelings and obtaining what they need. Reinforce the principle that each boy always has a choice about his own behavior. During the entire discussion, set a positive example by refusing to engage in any form of power struggle in which one person is "right" and the other "wrong."

Prematurely Disclosing the Details of the Abuse. Upon starting the group, some boys may begin talking immediately about every detail of the molestation. Premature disclosure is problematic for a number of reasons. It can be too threatening for some boys to tolerate. When a boy discloses prematurely, you can anticipate overwhelming anxiety on the part of the other members; this anxiety may in turn lead to disruptive behavior. Premature disclosure can also result in feelings of extreme vulnerability on the part of the boy who shares, which may cause him to drop out of the group.

To prevent this occurrence, you need to use activities in the early stages of group development that emphasize building rapport, creating a safe atmosphere, and clarifying the goals and purpose of the group. If you are unsuccessful in preventing the behavior, be sure to validate and praise the boy's willingness to share about what happened. Also explain that it is common to feel anxiety about sharing the abuse details and that some boys just want to get it over with early. Then use redirection and explain that the group will share details together at a later date; state that waiting a while to share the information will give the members time to grow closer and feel safer with one another.

After the group session, check with the boy who shared to see if anyone is pressuring him to talk about the abuse. He may also believe that he can be finished with therapy once he tells about what happened. Explain that group therapy involves much more than disclosing the details of the abuse.

Engaging in Sexualized Behavior. Sexualized behavior needs to be confronted immediately and labeled as inappropriate. Try to uncover the motivation for the behavior so that the boy can understand it better himself; for example, is he trying to get his peers' attention? Is he attempting to provoke someone in the group? Are current group topics making him uncomfortable enough to try to avoid them? Is this his way of bringing up questions or concerns about sex?

It is very common for younger children to be confused about the differences between physical affection and sexual behavior, so you need to explain the difference. Point out that using words and discussion are more likely to have a positive result. Also remind the entire group of the group rule about not touching you, your cotherapist, or the other members without permission. Reinforce the idea that each boy is accountable for his own behavior, which includes following this rule.

If the incident is severe, work with the child to develop a contract with clear consequences for recurrence of the behavior, including the possibility of suspension or termination of group membership. For example, any sexual touching or sexual act with another person warrants such a contract. In the event of consensual sexual behavior, both boys need to be held equally accountable, and you need to develop a contract with each.

Sexualized talk is common and can be very disruptive. If it is not addressed promptly, it can escalate quickly and waste the group's time. Explain your guideline for discussion of sexuality: questions or concerns about any aspect of sexuality can be openly discussed in the group, whereas sexual talk for the purpose of disrupting or provoking others is not acceptable. It is also useful to help the boys explore what feeling states precipitate this type of conversation, as it is usually triggered by anxiety.

Remaining Silent in Group Sessions. A boy may be silent in a group for any of a number of reasons. For example, he may be highly fearful, or he may have experienced physical punishment for speaking up in the past. You also need to consider whether his silence is an effort to exert control over you and your cotherapist.

Ask the group to share with this peer their thoughts or opinions about the meaning behind his silence, or what he might be feeling. Point out that, in general, the more actively involved group members are, the more benefit they receive from therapy. Some children respond well if you gently invite them to participate by asking nonthreatening questions.

It is not a good idea to allow a persistently silent child to remain in the group. You can set a time limit with him to help increase his verbal participation. If he chooses not to do this, you can recommend individual therapy with the possibility of returning to the group when he feels ready to join in. (Also see "Remaining Silent During Individual Sessions" earlier in this chapter.)

Violating Confidentiality. Violation of confidentiality can occur for a variety of reasons. You may find out about it by hearing boys talking in the waiting room about something that happened to a peer, for example. You may also hear confidential things about the group from parents whose sons have shared with them.

When a child has violated confidentiality, you need to meet with him to restate and clarify the rule about confidentiality. Then examine the circumstances. Some violations happen by accident. This is common with young boys, for instance, and may be motivated only by a desire to share something significant that happened in the group.

Deliberate violations, in contrast, are cause for concern. For example, it may be that the child wants to get a peer in trouble or to convince a parent that he is not as "bad" as the parent thinks he is. Another serious problem that you might uncover is pressure from someone else to tell what happens in the group, in which case you need to contact the person who is exerting pressure and discuss the importance of confidentiality.

After a violation has occurred, you need to discuss what happened with the group. You may either describe the situation specifically, or you may choose to state simply that the violation occurred, without identifying the offender. Explain that the violation must not happen again. Restate the rule of confidentiality and its importance for the group in terms of developing trust, cohesiveness, and safety. If, after this group discussion, the same child commits a second violation, it may be that he is not yet ready for group membership.

Violating Group Rules. Anticipate periods of oppositional or limit-testing behavior in any group. The boys test in order to evaluate the limits of their power with you and with their peers. Testing in different relationships is one way in which they learn whether it is safe to trust again.

It is important for boys to experience limits without rejection or punitive measures. One of your goals in dealing with violations is to encourage a healthy balance of assertiveness and compliance with authority. You need to avoid an authoritarian stance, because it will not only essentially guarantee more oppositional behavior but also further disempower the group members. Instead, discuss each violation with the group and use it as an opportunity to remind each boy that he is responsible for making the choice to cooperate.

Gil and Johnson (1993) advise that when therapists are tested, they may need to increase containment of both behavior and emotions of the group members, reduce elements that may be distracting the group, modify the reinforcement system, or use a more proactive style. Dealing with violations gives you a chance to evaluate your structure and management of the group to determine whether you need to alter anything. Consider, for example, whether you are recognizing and adequately acknowledging group members for complying with your wishes.

For some infractions, you may choose to ask the group members to determine what corrective action is to be taken. If the members cannot reach agreement within a set time period, with guidance from you and your cotherapist, then you can implement a behavioral contract with the boy involved.

Sometimes you will find that one group member has ongoing difficulty in following the rules. In this case the best approach is to address your concerns with him individually.

Being Unwilling to Give Feedback. One of the most important benefits of group therapy is peer feedback. In some groups, however, the boys are unwilling or unable to confront each other. If you find that one or more members are not giving feedback, point out your observation to the group; encourage the reticent boys to identify what is holding them back. (For example, a child may be feeling unsafe, may be afraid of a peer's anger, or may be worried about not being liked by his peers.)

Explain the benefits of hearing the ideas and experiences of other molested boys. Encourage the members to establish a group goal of assertive communication. Be sure to define *assertive communication* and give some examples. If a majority of the group members continue to resist giving feedback, conduct one or more of the activities in Part Two that address assertiveness skills, self-esteem, and anger management. Remember also that you and your cotherapist must model giving constructive feedback to the boys.

Problematic Situations in Groups

Any number of events can affect a group in such a way that you and your cotherapist must intervene. These are some situations that call for action:

- When a planned activity is ineffective
- When a group member experiences a personal crisis unrelated to his abuse
- When one group member's abuse history is markedly different from everyone else's
- When a cotherapist's style clashes with yours
- When a cotherapist leaves the group
- When a group member is molested again
- When a group member discloses that he molested someone

The following sections describe these situations and suggest ways to handle them.

When an Activity Is Ineffective. Planned treatment activities are not always effective. This happens more commonly with a group of young boys than with an older group. Several things can go wrong: most or all of the boys may complain, refuse to participate, or become agitated and act out.

Consequently, prior to each group session, you need to prepare at least two activities so that you have an alternative if necessary. If you frequently find that your first planned activity does not work, you need to reexamine the needs of the group and adjust your planning accordingly. You may find that you need to change the group's structure, place more or less emphasis on certain topics, or change the pace.

Also keep in mind that a high anxiety level, inattention, disinterest, and disruptive behavior might be related to the topic being addressed rather than to the activity. In this situation, reflect what the boys may be feeling so that they can continue to practice clarifying and expressing their feelings. If the topic is difficult but necessary, set a time limit on dealing with it and then switch to something relaxing or fun. If possible, gradually increase the time limit in such situations so that the boys can increase their tolerance for uncomfortable feelings. If only one member exhibits the previously mentioned behaviors, meet with him outside the session to explore what is causing him anxiety.

When a Group Member Experiences a Personal Crisis Unrelated to His Abuse.
In this situation, one approach is to make arrangements to conduct short-term concurrent individual or family sessions for crisis intervention. Often, however, this approach is not possible; also, some crises have applicability to the other members' situations and are better dealt with in the group. Another advantage to using

group time in this way is that the child in crisis can benefit from feedback from his peers; he may not only feel less alone but also receive some useful ideas to implement or adapt.

When you take the group approach, allow the boy in crisis as much sharing time as you can. This may mean abandoning any activities you had planned. Many times you will find that a crisis issue is at least tangentially related to molestation and, therefore, constitutes a useful group topic. An example is when a child experiences a death in his family. You can make comments such as these: "When you have been molested, you also are faced with many losses. It's important to have help in grieving and saying good-bye. It takes time to heal from your losses. When you're grieving as a result of a loss, you will experience many different feelings: numbness, sadness, and anger, for example."

When One Group Member's Abuse History Is Markedly Different from Everyone Else's. When one group member's experience is significantly different from that of his peers, he requires additional sensitivity from you and your cotherapist. He has the potential for increased shame and embarrassment as well as a sense of being different. Certain events—such as assault by a group, ritualistic sexual abuse, or abuse in adolescence—can make a boy's participation in the group more complicated.

You need to address this situation in your approach to group sharing of abuse experiences: emphasize that although the individual circumstances of the boys' abuse may differ, many of the common aftereffects are similar. Focus on the shared feelings and behaviors and deemphasize the specific details. Explain that because each traumatic experience is different, each group member has faced different challenges and learned some things along the way. Encourage the members to share what they have learned, as a means of helping one another.

When a Cotherapist's Style Clashes with Yours. It is important to assess your cotherapist's theoretical orientation, expertise, and style before you begin doing group therapy together. Even when you have made a careful assessment, however, you may find later that your style and that of your cotherapist are so different that they confuse the group members. For example, one of you may have an active and directive style, whereas the other prefers to allow the group process to develop on its own. In such a situation it may be difficult for the group members to develop a uniform understanding of the group's rules and norms.

Such differences need not mean that the two of you cannot work well together. They do mean, however, that you and your cotherapist must thoroughly discuss your differences ahead of time so that you can establish a way to work comfortably together and without contradicting each other. Try to take advantage of each person's strengths so that they blend harmoniously. Realize, though, that some tasks or roles cannot be assigned to just one therapist. If only one of you intervenes when members' problematic behaviors must be corrected, for example, you are setting up a "good guy–bad guy" dynamic.

Make it a priority to work with your cotherapist to model behavior for boys. Consider the following issues:

- Are you taking responsibility for your feelings and expressing them when appropriate?
- Are you demonstrating responsible behavior?
- How are you handling things that make you angry before, during, and after group sessions?
- Are you setting limits in a consistent manner?
- Are you clearly communicating your expectations?
- Are you demonstrating to the boys that taking care of yourself is a top priority?

When a Cotherapist Leaves the Group.   Even with careful pregroup planning, sometimes a cotherapist must discontinue working with a group. Unless it is an extreme emergency, you should have some notice so that you can prepare the group members. Give them as much notice as you can, up to a limit of three or four weeks.

During that time, anticipate behavioral reactions to loss, abandonment, or betrayal. It is common to see increased acting out, withdrawal, and anger. This presents another opportunity to further explore how the boys have experienced issues of abandonment and betrayal in the past.

Offer a formalized process to say good-bye, preferably an experience that encourages everyone to participate and to share positive memories and feelings. If possible, have a good-bye session during which you and your cotherapist share your own feelings about the change. Let the boys know that even though saying good-bye can be difficult because they feel sad, it is better than having unresolved feelings and things left unsaid.

Unless your cotherapist leaves unexpectedly in the first two months of a time-limited group, it is recommended that you not try to introduce a replacement. It is less disruptive to continue with only one therapist until the group ends. However, be aware that certain groups may require another therapist in order to ensure safety and effectiveness.

When a Group Member Is Molested Again.   If a group member discloses additional abuse, praise his willingness to speak up. You may need to shift the group emphasis for a while to provide support for him, but continue to allow all the members an opportunity to talk and raise concerns.

A new disclosure often triggers difficult reminders for the members. Encourage all of them to offer as well as receive support, even if they feel uncomfortable. Also be aware that other members may be considering sharing new information about their abuse; remind the boys that secrets begin to lose their power once they are shared and that the group is a safe place for sharing.

Make sure that you comply with all necessary reporting of new abuse incidents. Generally you will need to contact child protective services, the police, or both. Remind the boys of this legal requirement and discuss it as a necessary exception to the rule of confidentiality. Also let them know that after an incident has been reported, the boy involved may be interviewed by police or representatives of the legal system.

State clearly that you do not know specifically what will happen after you have made your report. Be especially careful not to promise the child that he can continue coming to the group regardless of what happens. (Once the incident becomes known, the child's situation may change drastically. For example, he may be removed from his home as well as from therapy.)

When a Group Member Discloses That He Molested Someone. One of the most difficult challenges encountered in doing therapy with sexually abused boys is when a group member offends. You need to discuss the episode with the group, educating about offending behavior and conducting activities that teach the risks of offending and the skills that can prevent it.

Point out that the abusing child has made a positive choice in disclosing the incident instead of keeping it a secret. Let him know, however, that you will *not* minimize or excuse his actions. Explain that your goal for him is to be accountable for his behavior, which includes admitting it completely, accepting the consequences that follow, and taking whatever steps are necessary to prevent recurrence.

The other group members need to see that even though your emphasis is not punishment or anger, you consider the incident to be serious. Review what factors make sexual activity abusive, so that all the boys understand why this particular situation is considered offending behavior. Anticipate significant levels of anxiety, anger, scapegoating, and disruptive behavior as the group reacts to this stressor. Make sure all members understand that you are obligated by law to report the incident to the police, child protective services, or both.

In addition to the required reporting, you will need to help the abusing boy tell his parents. You and he can work on this issue in private, outside the group.

Give him as many options as possible for approaching and notifying the parent, and then let him choose the option he wants.

If he is unable or unwilling to follow through for any reason, notify the parent while the boy is present; he needs to hear the conversation. During this conversation, you will need to assess how appropriate the parent's response is and also evaluate whether the home is safe for the boy to return to. The following conditions may be considered unsafe for the child:

- The parent is enraged.
- There is a history of physical abuse or substance use in the family.
- The boy's victim is a sibling or someone else living in the home.

It is also important to consider if there is anything happening in the family that overtly or covertly supports offending behavior. For example, it is a red flag if a parent expresses little concern about the behavior ("Boys will be boys") or anger at you for discussing the incident seriously.

You need to determine whether it is clinically appropriate for the child to continue in the group. If the following conditions are met, you may be able to continue his treatment in the group:

- He admits to the offense and demonstrates motivation to change.
- This is a first offense (antisocial or violent behavior has not been repeated).
- There is no substance addiction or psychotic process.
- The behavior was not violent and did not involve physical force.
- There were no bizarre or ritualistic acts.
- There is a capable adult who is willing and able to provide supervision in the home.

If any of these conditions are not met, the boy needs to be removed from the group and placed in a different form of treatment. When you and the boy ultimately discuss your decision, explain that you are taking this action not to punish him but to help him with specialized care so he can change his behavior.

The specific treatment you recommend will depend on what you believe he needs and the availability of various options. Some alternatives to consider are individual therapy (with you or with another therapist), an offenders' group, substance abuse treatment, or immediate family intervention. Also, you may be in a position to advocate juvenile court involvement, so that a court order can be used to ensure compliance with treatment.

You must monitor your countertransference reactions closely, so that you do not impede therapeutic progress by expressing anger or reacting in a punitive manner. You need to serve as a caring helper, confronter, teacher, facilitator, and reality tester.

Challenges Related to External Factors

Not all challenges arise from the boys themselves, from the situations that develop during a group session, or even from your efforts to coordinate and work harmoniously with a cotherapist. Some arise from external factors, such as the following:

- The child's insurance will not authorize coverage.
- The child's living situation changes.
- The child's parents do not support treatment, or they sabotage it.

The following sections explain how to intervene when you are faced with problems arising from these factors.

The Child's Insurance Will Not Authorize Coverage

When a child's insurance carrier has refused to cover therapy, you need to contact the case manager. Your objective is to convince the case manager that abuse-specific therapy is necessary and to explain why either individual therapy or group therapy (depending on your choice) is the most appropriate intervention for this boy. First make it clear that you provide specific treatment for molested boys or that your individual therapy plan is to address sexual abuse issues. Depending on the case manager's clinical experience, you may need to give detailed information about what you do in sessions and why you do it.

Be prepared to explain to the case manager how your therapy can alleviate particular symptoms. In addition, when you are recommending time-limited group therapy, emphasize that the time limitation makes therapy less expensive than the option of an ongoing group. Also point out that group therapy is typically more cost effective than individual, residential, or in-patient treatment.

Be sure that you have also addressed any additional treatment needs by making the necessary referrals. Let the case manager know if you are recommending a psychiatric consultation for medication, encouraging the parents to attend a community support group, or attending school meetings yourself to ensure that the boy's school placement is adequate.

It is much more likely that you will receive approval if you maintain certain guidelines in your treatment setting. Be sure that you use a psychiatric diagnosis and develop a treatment plan that is consistent with this diagnosis. On your treatment plan, specify clear and measurable treatment goals in behavioral terms.

If you have difficulty obtaining authorization, you may have to give even more clinical information to justify the treatment. In this event, issues of confidentiality and trust are involved, and you must let the boy know that you are obligated to talk to the case manager about his case and why it is necessary.

The Child's Living Situation Changes

Families move, parents separate, and courts make decisions. These events and others can result in a change in a child's living situation. If he can continue attending sessions, they can be a stabilizing factor for him. If there is a new adult legally responsible for the child, contact that person as soon as possible to determine if he or she is willing to have the child continue. If this person presents obstacles, consider some creative alternatives, such as carpooling, a short-term attendance contract, or waiving the fee for therapy if possible. If the child is a dependent or ward of the court, you might ask for support from his social worker or his probation or parole officer.

If the change (such as an immediate move out of the state) results in an unavoidable termination of treatment, make every effort to carry out a good-bye session with the child. The opportunity for closure is important for both of you.

The Child's Parents Do Not Support Treatment, or They Sabotage It

You will encounter all degrees of parental involvement and influence, ranging from active support to sabotage. Many parents who do not support therapy perceive therapists to be threatening or critical, no matter how you interact with them. Lack of support or involvement is usually manageable; sabotage of treatment is not. Examples of sabotage include pressuring the boy to recant, not allowing the boy to attend sessions regularly, or refusing to follow through with your treatment recommendations (such as obtaining a medication evaluation).

You and the parent need to discuss the sabotage or lack of support without violating the child's confidentiality. Identify the problem as you see it; then ask the parent to do the same from his or her point of view. Ask directly if the parent is willing to resolve the problem in order to help the boy. If so, identify some solutions together and ask for the parent to choose one to implement. Afterward you need to put your requests in writing, along with the parent's decision and a time frame for evaluating whether the solution is working.

If the parent is involved in some kind of therapy and has signed a release of information, you may want to call a case conference for all involved professionals—you, your cotherapist (if you have one), the parent's therapist, and the child's social worker or probation or parole officer. You can share necessary information as a team and coordinate interventions. For example, you might be ready to send a termination letter to a child who has not attended therapy for four weeks and whose home phone has been disconnected. You might plan differently, however, if the mother's therapist were to tell you that the mother recently lost her job, has symptoms of depression, and is struggling to pay the bills.

If a parent refuses to consider possible solutions, remains hostile, or is unwilling to talk with you, you may need to turn to child protective services or the child's probation or parole officer as a last resort. You need to weigh this option carefully, as it may have the unfortunate consequence of triggering even more resistance from the parent or precipitating a family crisis.

Talk to the child directly if therapy must be terminated because of a parent's sabotaging behavior. He needs to understand he is not being punished and that this is something beyond his control to change. Ask what he would like to see happen, as he may bring up ways to intervene that you have not considered. Discuss alternatives to lessen his feelings of powerlessness.

Administrative Challenges

Two administrative challenges will require your attention in every child's case:

- Documentation of treatment
- Evaluation of therapy

Documentation of Treatment

Documentation requirements vary, depending on the treatment setting, but here are some general guidelines:

- Be sure that the child, regardless of his age, knows his individual treatment emphasis.
- Be as specific as possible in describing a child's behaviors. (Compare "Appears less depressed" to "No tearful episodes this week, ate entire snack, reported sleeping well with no nightmares.")
- Limit your treatment plan to a maximum of three problematic behaviors that are observable and measurable. These are the areas that you will target for improvement.
- During any contact with a parent, ask specifically about the child's progress in the identified problem areas: Has the parent noticed any changes? If so, what are they? Is the child using any new skills at home? Has he shared new knowledge with anyone in his family? Document the responses so that over time your records will reveal whether the child's treatment has been effective.

• If the boy has any school-related problems, make monthly calls to his primary teacher to ask the same kinds of questions and record the answers.

Do not make the assumption that positive changes you observe in the therapy setting will automatically be carried over to home and school. Also do not assume that everyone involved with a child will view changes in the same way you do. For example, a previously oppositional boy who has become very depressed usually becomes easier to manage at school; therefore, his teacher is not likely to be pleased at the results of your efforts with the child to encourage him to express his anger openly.

Include in your case document any homework assignments that you give the boy and the outcome of those assignments. If you use a behavior modification system, document his progress week by week.

Evaluation of Therapy

As of this writing, there are no published research studies that evaluate treatment effectiveness for sexually abused boys (Watkins & Bentovim, 1992). So far, evaluation is limited to feedback from the boys, from parents and other adults involved, and from therapists' informal assessments of changes seen in the course of treatment. However, you can still use assessment measures at the start of treatment, obtain feedback from the aforementioned sources just prior to the end of therapy, and then evaluate progress. It is also advisable to carry out a six-month and twelve-month follow-up to assess how the boy is doing, from both his and the parent's point of view.

Friedrich, Luecke, Beilke, and Place (1992) suggest using the following outcome measures:

Achenbach Child Behavior Checklist

Child Sexual Behavior Inventory

Child Depression Inventory

Piers Harris Self-Esteem Inventory

Martinek-Zaichkowsky Self-Concept Scale

Roberts Apperception Test for Children

Achenbach Teacher Rating Scale

Companies that sell testing and assessment measures are good sources. Four such companies are as follows:

Psychological Assessment Resources, Inc. (800-331-8378)

Western Psychological Services (800-648-8857)

The Psychological Corporation (800-211-8378)

University Medical Education Associates (802-656-8313)

Additional measures are the Children's Manifest Anxiety Scale, suggested by Hack, Osachuk, and DeLuca (1994), and the Nowicki Test of Locus of Control, recommended by Johnson and Berry (1989).

Conclusion

Providing individual and group therapy for sexually abused boys presents many challenges, but it also offers many rewards. I keep the following anonymous saying in several places at home and where I work so that it is always in my awareness:

A hundred years from now it will not matter what my bank account was, what type of house I lived in, or what kinds of clothes I wore, but the world may be much different because I was important in the life of a child.

You will make an important difference if you choose to meet the challenges of helping molested boys resolve their victimization. Effective therapy can empower boys to move on to a future that is physically, emotionally, spiritually, and mentally healthy.

PART TWO

STRUCTURED ACTIVITIES TO USE IN THERAPY

ABOUT THE ACTIVITIES

This chapter introduces the structured activities in Part Two. Each activity is addressed to a group facilitator, as it is most commonly used by a therapist in group settings. However, you can easily modify most of the activities for use in individual therapy.

Why Structured Activities Are Important in Therapy

My colleagues and I run primarily time-limited groups rather than ongoing or open-ended groups (see "Group's Life Span" in Chapter Four). Limiting groups to six or nine months is both a selling point to our clients and a challenge to us. The time limit means that we are continually faced with start-up of a new group.

Our beginning goal is an ambitious one: encouraging boys to address the difficult issue of sexual abuse while we work to build group cohesiveness, establish trust and safety, and keep the boys coming to therapy. Even if you prepare extensively and provide an extremely effective orientation to group therapy, you will probably find achieving this goal difficult, too.

Using structured activities like those in Part Two will help you meet the challenge. All the activities presented in this book have been created to accomplish specific goals in a limited time frame; all of them address the issues associated with sexual abuse, and many of them accomplish secondary goals associated with group process. The activity design is flexible enough to serve the members of a group, who represent a wide range of needs, or to give effective individual treatment for one boy.

In addition, all the activities are based on the primary goal of therapy with sexually abused boys, regardless of their ages or personal circumstances: *restoring a sense of empowerment after sexual abuse.* Consequently, the therapeutic tasks involved in the activities are those that develop boys' awareness of personal power as well as the necessary knowledge and skills to use that power effectively and in positive ways. The boys learn that

- They are in control of many aspects of their lives.
- They have choices about their own behavior, regardless of the behavior of others.
- They can make choices.
- They are responsible for their personal choices and the consequences of those choices.

As you use the activities over time, you will find that the boys begin to think differently about their sexual abuse. Slowly their behavior will change as a result of their new beliefs. As they regain their personal power and practice using it in the safe environment of therapy, they will shed the image of themselves as victims.

Through participation in therapy in general and in structured activities in particular, boys learn to let go of something else as well: any problematic behaviors they may have adopted as a means of coping with what happened to them. Such behaviors, rather than the abuse itself, are often the catalysts for therapy. Most of the activities in this book address dysfunctional behaviors in four areas that often cause difficulties for molested boys (see "Sexual Abuse of Boys" in Chapter One):

- Isolation
- Impaired relationships
- Sexually abusive behavior
- Homophobia

The activities that pertain to sexually abusive behavior represent a proactive attempt to prevent molested boys from becoming molesters. (It is important to note, as stated elsewhere in this book, that having been molested does not necessarily mean that a boy will molest others. In fact, this is a rare occurrence, but molested boys and their parents often fear future molestation on the child's part.)

Activity Format and Presentation

All the activities in Part Two are presented in the general order recommended for time-limited therapy, either with a group or with an individual boy. They are not intended to be used rigidly, one after the other, though, nor will all of them be useful to you in all situations or with all clients. However, you will probably find that they spur your own creativity in developing treatment ideas.

The components of each activity are as follows:

- Activity number (1 through 50) and title.
- Target ages (Some activities are designed for a specific age range. When the target age is designated "all," the activity can be used with boys of all ages.)
- Abuse issue(s) addressed
- Objective(s)
- Rationale
- Procedure
- Common responses
- Handouts, if any

You will notice that the time required to run the activity is not one of the components. This is because the time varies greatly, depending on a number of factors, such as the participants' ages, how many boys are in attendance, their individual needs, and whether you are using the activity in a group setting or with an individual.

In addition, you will note that most activities describe responsibilities to be assumed by a cotherapist. This represents my belief that therapists who work in pairs are particularly effective in a group setting. However, if you do not plan to work with a partner, you can easily assume all the facilitation responsibilities yourself.

ACTIVITIES

◆ ACTIVITY 1: Definitions

Target Ages
- All

Abuse Issues Addressed
- Confusion about sexuality
- Denial

Objective
- To help boys recognize the characteristics that define sexually abusive behavior

Rationale

Misinformation about what sexual abuse is and is not needs to be addressed early in the group's existence. Many boys enter treatment with the perception that they experienced sexual encounters rather than sexually abusive incidents. Consequently, the group needs to establish a common definition of abuse.

Procedure: Part 1

To encourage participation, use an informal and unstructured approach similar to brainstorming. Using this activity as the first or one of the first gives the boys a chance to begin talking about sexual abuse immediately. It sets the expectation that every participant may challenge the denial of sexual abuse and may discuss how molestation has affected his life.

Begin the activity by acknowledging that most boys do not receive adequate information about sexual abuse because of a common and incorrect assumption: that sexual abuse does not happen to boys. Also state that the participants may find it difficult to ask questions or clarify areas of concern because of another incorrect assumption: that boys are supposed to be knowledgeable about everything concerning sex.

It is recommended that one cotherapist be in charge of recording participants' responses and that the other initiate a discussion by asking "What do you think sexual abuse or molestation means?" The cotherapist responsible for recording writes down all of the boys' contributions, thereby demonstrating how varied the understanding of the term is. Be sure that no answers are labeled as "wrong," as you want to encourage the boys to talk. Emphasize that everyone learns about sexual abuse differently, and as a result it can be difficult to agree on an exact definition. Be sure to include the various characteristics of abuse:

- Use of force or coercion
- Disparity in power or status
- Lack of mutual consent
- Age and size differences between the child and the abuser, which make it possible for the child to be overpowered
- Secrecy

Encourage the boys to consider same-sex versus opposite-sex involvement as well as any covert actions that may be involved (such as pornography, voyeurism, or exposure of genitals). You and your cotherapist must be able to talk easily about sexual acts, as this modeling makes it easier for boys to acknowledge what has happened to them.

Procedure: Part 2

Part 2 involves discussing and deciding on a group definition of sexual abuse that can be referred to throughout the life of the group. Establishing a clear definition and leaving it posted is helpful in orienting new members, educating parents, and assisting boys in recognizing previously unidentified abuse.

During this discussion you also need to highlight the socialization issues involved in abuse. Ask the boys whether either of the following incidents constitutes sexual abuse or molestation:

- A fourteen-year-old girl has intercourse with a thirty-year-old man.
- A fourteen-year-old boy has intercourse with a thirty-year-old woman.

Most boys will not identify the second situation as abusive; instead, they generally perceive the fourteen-year-old boy as "lucky."

Common Responses

During this activity, younger boys frequently exhibit silly and attention-seeking behavior due to their anxiety about the topic. Let the boys know that it is common to feel nervous or anxious when discussing difficult topics with new people, but set clear parameters so that they know what is expected of them. For example, you might say, "This activity is for talking and sharing. After we finish we can do some playing or go outdoors."

Older boys often deny that the reported behavior was abusive. Encourage them to talk, but at this point do not challenge or confront them about their denial. (When confrontation occurs early in the group process, before the group has achieved mutual trust and rapport, those confronted may drop out. Also, making a boy feel "wrong" only creates an unwanted power struggle.) Instead, point out similarities between the boys' stories. Then point out the differences and emphasize that people have different opinions, just as they often have different feelings about the same event.

◆ ACTIVITY 2: TV Interview

Target Ages
- All

Abuse Issues Addressed
- Isolation
- Feeling different or damaged

Objective
- To encourage interaction and sharing

Rationale

A group therapy session makes it more difficult for boys to isolate themselves. Through group interaction they realize that although they may feel isolated, different, or damaged, there are other boys who have also been molested and who share the same feelings.

Procedure

Ask the boys to assemble into pairs, or assign pairs. If there is an uneven number of boys, you or your cotherapist can form a pair with one boy.

State that in each pair the two will take turns playing the role of a TV reporter: the first boy to play the reporter will interview the other (using questions provided) to find out information about him that will be used later in introducing him to the group; then the boys will reverse roles and repeat the interview process. Explain that if all interview questions are answered and there is still time left, the interviewer may ask additional questions if he wants to. After the interviews have been completed, the boys in each pair will introduce each other to the group.

Most boys want to write down answers to the interview questions, so you will need to provide paper, pencils, and portable writing surfaces. Allow at least twenty to thirty minutes for the interviews and another thirty minutes for the introductions. *Note:* Younger boys may require some help and possibly more time with the interviewing process than older boys. Also, although sample interview questions are included at the end of this activity, feel free to change questions or add others depending on the composition and needs of the group.

After the introductions have been completed, ask the boys to compare how they felt about the activity before they participated in it to how they feel afterward. Following are some sample questions:

- Do you feel differently about talking now than you did before the activity? If so, in what way?
- Are you better acquainted with your peers because of the mutual sharing? How?
- What did you find that you have in common with other people in this group?

Common Responses

Some boys withdraw because they feel too "different" or ashamed to share information about themselves. Periodically remind the boys during this activity and others conducted early in the life of the group that all the members are present because they have experienced sexual abuse. Point out commonalities and acknowledge that each boy will also be different in some ways from each of his peers.

You may also find that one or more boys complete this activity with exaggeration, boasting, or bragging. At this point it is too early in the life of the group to confront such behavior unless you already have established a strong therapeutic relationship with those particular boys. Describe your expectation for honesty in sharing. Also acknowledge the boys' efforts when they support one another, are empathic, or attempt to connect with one another; these behaviors help enhance sharing and build group cohesiveness.

TV Interview for Boys Ages Seven Through Twelve

1. What is your first name?
2. If you have a nickname, what is it?
3. How old are you?
4. What school do you go to?
5. With whom do you live?
6. What is your favorite hobby?
7. How did you find out about this group?
8. When is your birthday?
9. If you could change one thing at home, what would it be?
10. Have you been in counseling before? If so, what did you think about it?
11. Do you have any pets?
12. What would you like to do for a living when you grow up?
13. Complete this sentence: One thing I would like to see happen in this group is . . .
14. If you could say anything at all to the person or people who molested you and it would be safe to do so, what would you say?
15. How are you feeling (honestly!) about being here today?

TV Interview for Boys Ages Thirteen Through Eighteen

1. What is your name?
2. What do you like to be called?
3. How old are you?
4. When is your birthday?
5. What school do you attend, and what grade are you in?
6. What is the one thing you like best and the one thing you like least about school?
7. With whom do you live?
8. What is your favorite hobby, sport, or extracurricular activity?
9. Who suggested that you come to the group?
10. Have you had any experience in therapy? If so, what was it like for you?
11. What would you like to change most by coming to this group?
12. How do you feel about being here?
13. How did you tell about the abuse?
14. What was your family's response?

◆ ACTIVITY 3: Completing a Self-Evaluation

Target Ages
- Thirteen through eighteen

Abuse Issues Addressed
- Denial or minimization
- Responsibility for one's own behavior

Objective
- To encourage each boy to complete a self-evaluation and share at least one answer with peers

Rationale

Many boys have little awareness of how they have been affected by sexual abuse. Addressing the impact early in treatment helps them recognize what they need help with, thereby maximizing the benefit of treatment.

Procedure

It is recommended that you do this activity in two parts over two sessions. Because of its length, completing the self-evaluation stimulates thinking and discussion, which you do not want to cut short because of limited time.

Give the boys pencils and copies of the Self-Evaluation Form. Explain that the list of statements includes problems that are common with boys who have been molested. Ask each boy to read the list of statements first and place a check mark next to all statements that are true for him. Once he has completed this, he can complete Part I of the self-evaluation. State that responses will be kept confidential and that there are no right or wrong answers. Explain why honesty is necessary: when you and your cotherapist know what each boy wants or needs, you can direct group discussions and activities to meet those goals.

Allow plenty of time for the self-evaluation. Then ask for volunteers to read at least one response each to the group. If the members choose to and enough time remains, you can begin discussion at this point; if there are many questions and insufficient time, you may ask the boys to hold their questions until the next session.

Common Responses

Mistrust is to be expected among sexually abused adolescents, so you may be challenged on your statement about confidentiality. State the exceptions to confidentiality (see "Establishing and Maintaining Trust" in Chapter One) so that it is clear that you cannot guarantee total confidentiality. Suggest that the boys proceed slowly and cautiously in rebuilding trust with new people.

Affirm a boy's choice if he decides not to complete the activity. At the same time, however, point out there are consequences, such as slower progress in treatment, if you and your cotherapist have to figure out each boy's needs on your own.

Self-Evaluation Form

List of Statements (Place a check mark next to any statement that is true for you.)

I feel different from other people because of the abuse.

My body is damaged.

I feel guilty about what happened.

I'm filled with anger.

I'm afraid a lot of the time.

I don't enjoy things the way I used to.

My future looks awful.

I don't think things are ever going to get better.

I'm not eating or sleeping the way I did before the abuse.

I don't like to be around other people, and I stay by myself a lot.

I don't know what I feel about the person who abused me.

I'm tense or worried most of the time.

I feel lousy about myself.

I feel confused about how sex should be for me now.

I blame myself for what happened.

My moods change all the time.

I can't control much of anything now.

I can't trust very many people now.

The molestation doesn't affect me much.

I have to be on the alert all the time now.

I don't see friends much anymore.

I feel terrified of certain things.

My eating is all messed up.

I think I would be better off dead.

I think about dying.

I've tried to hurt myself since the abuse.

I can't seem to get along with other kids anymore.

I want to do sexual things with other kids.

I get into fights or blow up a lot at other people.

I don't want to do what grown-ups tell me to do.

I'm having a lot of trouble sleeping well at night.

I feel like running away from home.

I feel "spacey" or in another world a lot of the time.

I feel sick often.

Things have gone downhill for me at school.

I use drugs or alcohol to avoid thinking and feeling.

Self-Evaluation Questions, Part I

1. How do you think the abuse affects your life now?
2. What do you think your life will be like in ten years?
3. If the molestation had not been reported, what would your life be like now?
4. List three of your best qualities or strengths.
5. List three things about yourself that you sincerely want to change.
6. Do you think there is any way to tell if a person is a molester? If so, please explain.
7. If you had three wishes, what would they be?
8. How has being molested affected your feelings toward your mother?

Self-Evaluation Questions, Part II

1. How has being molested affected your feelings toward your father?
2. List three goals for yourself (other than in therapy) for the next six months.
3. List three goals for yourself in this group.
4. If you could say anything to the person or people who molested you (and be completely safe, without any possible consequences), what would you say?
5. Have you had recurrent, intrusive memories of what happened? When? How often?
6. Why do you think that the abuse happened?
7. Rate your overall trust level right now from 1 (no trust at all in family and friends) to 10 (complete trust in family and friends).
8. Is there anything about the molestation that you have not discussed with anyone? If so, how can we help you feel safe enough to talk about it now?

◆ ACTIVITY 4: Creating Group Rules

Target Ages
- All

Abuse Issues Addressed
- Powerlessness
- Oppositional or defiant behavior

Objectives
- To have each boy verbally demonstrate an understanding of group rules and the reasons for their use
- To encourage each boy to express his feelings about rules, limits, and authority figures

Rationale
Every boy needs to know your expectations regarding his behavior in the group. Involving the boys in developing rules is empowering to them, and it enhances their ownership of both the rules and the group process.

Procedure
Ask the members to brainstorm, discuss, and then decide on their group rules. Give a general explanation of why rules are needed and why it is important that the boys be actively involved in establishing the rules. Although you and your cotherapist need to give input, encourage reality testing, and give final approval to the rules, the boys need to decide together what rules they believe are important to have.

Encourage the boys to be in charge of this process as much as possible, limiting feedback to clarification and pointing out safety issues and possible ramifications ("What will happen if the rule is 'Talk whenever you want to' instead of 'One person talks at a time'?") Given this opportunity, the boys can select age-appropriate guidelines and also learn about what makes groups run smoothly. Also ask the members to determine any consequences for not following the rules.

Explain that you must impose a few rules that are nonnegotiable (Chapter Four), such as the following:

- No betraying confidences about what is said in the group
- No substance abuse
- No hands-on behavior toward another person

You might encourage the boys to establish rules for you and your cotherapist, too. For example, the members might decide that each of you will show any progress summary to the boy concerned before sending it to court or school.

Be sure to bring up the issues of power and control. (*Note:* Activity 6 includes an extended discussion of these issues.) Ask the boys how they feel about rules, limits, and authority in general. Explain that molested boys often resist rules, because regaining control is so critical after they have been victimized. Emphasize that it is common and understandable for boys to react with defiance to anything that triggers feelings of helplessness or powerlessness or reminds them of their abuse.

Provide some examples of negative power behaviors: coercion, manipulation, bribery, inflexibility, unwillingness to compromise, constant limit testing, bossiness, excessive demands, extreme passivity, and giving up after minimal effort.

Common Responses

Many groups develop a wide range of rules; others decide that none are needed (no control); still others create extremely rigid and unrealistic standards (too much control). Explain that a group with no rules results in chaos and no benefits for the members, whereas an overly controlled atmosphere is more characteristic of a jail than a therapy session.

Emphasize that the purpose of rules is to ensure the safety of all members and to provide the best therapy experience possible. Explain that your goal is to help the boys learn to control themselves, not to control their behavior for them.

When the boys suggest extremely different rules that conflict with one another, negotiate a compromise. For example, you might suggest beginning with a minimum of rules and then reevaluating after one month to see if more or less structure is needed.

◆ ACTIVITY 5: Establishing a Ritual for Starting or Ending Sessions

Target Ages
- All

Abuse Issue Addressed
- Anxiety

Objective

- To foster recognition of the positive benefits associated with a consistent group routine

Rationale

Rituals add structure add stability to both time-limited and ongoing, open-ended groups. Establishing and following a ritual for starting or ending group sessions (or for both) help orient new members, reduce anxiety for current members, and help the new boy join in. A ritual also allows established members to model sharing and self-disclosure, thereby reinforcing a sense of trust and safety in the group setting. A closing ritual also serves to end the sessions on a positive note.

Procedure

Let the boys know this will be a group decision-making process, which involves communication and compromise. Tell them that they will be selecting a ritual for starting and ending every group session, with final approval resting with you and your cotherapist.

Give some examples to get them started, and encourage all the members to share their opinions so that they will feel a part of the decision-making process and responsible for the final outcome.

Following are some examples of introductory rituals:

- Sharing name, age, length of time in the therapy group, and identity of perpetrator
- Sharing the best part of the previous week and the worst part of the previous week
- Sharing an honest feeling about coming to group therapy, with an explanation
- Sharing a goal for today's session

Here are some examples of closing rituals:

- Each boy tells what he thinks the purpose of today's activity was.
- Each boy tells one thing he learned today in the group.
- Each boy describes what or who helped him today in the group, and how.
- The boys share an empowering affirmation.
- The boys and therapists participate in a group hug (no sooner than six weeks into the life of the group).

Emphasize that each boy has the right to decide whether he will participate in any ritual. He is also responsible for communicating his feelings assertively about his participation. If the boys choose to have a group hug, it is done in a circle, with arms across shoulders or around one another's waists. Watch the process closely and intervene if any of the following situations arises:

- Someone is hugging too hard.
- Someone appears uncomfortable and is not speaking up.
- Someone looks pressured to go along with the group.
- Someone makes sexual comments or gestures.
- Several boys seem unwilling to participate.

After the hug, spend some time exploring with the boys what kinds of messages are sent (at school, from parents, by TV commercials and magazines) about boys and men hugging one another. Ask these questions:

- When was the last time you were hugged by your father, your grandfather, or a friend?
- How do boys learn that it is OK for girls and women to hug but not acceptable for males?

Make sure the boys clearly understand the purpose of a group hug. The boys need to learn that all physical closeness or affection is not hurtful. Point out that a group hug is not sexual, coercive, or in any way abusive.

Common Responses

If the group adopts the hug as a ritual, be aware that male therapists must be comfortable in modeling nonsexual touch with boys. If you or your cotherapist is at all reluctant, group members will recognize this and may follow your lead. Some boys may not participate at first, but most choose to join once they feel emotionally safe in the group.

Sometimes a group hug triggers sexualized behavior or comments such as "I like this; I must be a queer." Any sexualized behavior and comments need to be labeled and confronted immediately, with an explanation about why they are unacceptable. You can also encourage members to identify what they are feeling so that they can better understand how their feelings affect their behavior.

◆ ACTIVITY 6: Brainstorming Power Behaviors

Target Ages
- All

Abuse Issues Addressed
- Powerlessness
- Sexually abusive behavior

Objectives
- To assist each boy in identifying which of his behaviors increase his sense of being in control
- To assist each boy in describing those behaviors

Rationale

It is important to clarify early in therapy that sexual abuse is a misuse of power and control. You cannot assume that boys understand this concept.

Procedure

Have the boys brainstorm what power means to them. If you are working with young boys, ask them to think about television or movie characters they perceive as powerful and what it is about those characters that makes them this way.

Record all ideas contributed by the boys. Then give a simple definition of power, such as the one that follows, and explain why power is so important in therapy for sexual abuse: *"Power* refers to the ability to influence or control things or people. A person can have *influence* with another because of his role or position (for example, boss and subordinate) or because of his relationship with another. *Control* refers to the ability to govern, regulate, or manage something or someone. It also refers to exercising power over or dominating another person."

Let the boys know that *power* as it is used in their therapy emphasizes control of oneself, rather than negative uses of control over other people. Explain that each boy can regain a sense of personal control and personal power without harming others if he uses rational thinking, develops his strengths, and increases his mastery of skills.

Boys also need to become familiar with what powerlessness is, and their own personal experience with this feeling. *Powerlessness* is the perceived lack of personal power or control over circumstances, experiences, or the environment. Ask the boys to complete this sentence: "I feel powerless when . . ." After you have received their responses, ask them to complete another sentence: "I feel powerful when . . ."

If they need help getting started, offer examples: "my energy level is high," "my health is good," "I get compliments," "I accomplish goals that I've set," "I learn something new," "I'm with supportive people," "I study hard," or "I break a bad habit."

Common Responses

It is very likely some boys will share beliefs that constitute a risk factor for the development of offending behavior: equating sex with power, thinking of sex as a way to control someone else, feeling powerful when angry, and so on. These types of responses give you an important clue regarding which boys will need extra help in developing a sense of empowerment and self-control.

Younger boys may express confusion about this discussion. If so, you need to simplify your explanation of the importance of power and control for molested boys. Some of the books listed in the Appendix contain excellent material to help younger boys understand this concept.

◆ ACTIVITY 7: Coping Through Relaxation

Target Ages
- All

Abuse Issues Addressed
- Anxiety
- Anger

Objective
- To have each boy select and describe a safe, relaxing scene from nature that he can use to help him relax

Rationale

When boys are able to recognize anxious and angry feelings, they are ready to learn effective coping strategies as an alternative to acting out. Physical and mental relaxation can be done independently in most situations and does not require an adult's help or supervision.

Procedure

Instruct each boy to find a comfortable position for himself, sitting or lying down. Ask the boys to close their eyes. If they tell you they do not feel safe with their eyes closed, tell them to leave their eyes open. Explain that this activity will be like a daydream. You might want to talk briefly about stress, common stressful situations, what stress does to the body, and common emotions related to stress. State that everyone experiences stress and must learn to cope with it or eliminate it in healthy ways rather than respond by drinking, using drugs, smoking, overeating, or denying the problem. Explain that stress that is not handled effectively can eat away at people's energy, can make them physically ill, and ends up replacing their positive feelings with unpleasant ones. Tell them that relaxation is a coping skill that reduces stress and has only positive effects.

Describe deep breathing very simply. Explain that you want each boy to breathe in slowly and deeply through his nose and exhale (blow the air out) through his mouth. By placing one hand on your stomach and one on your chest, demonstrate how deep breathing involves the abdomen as well as the chest. Have the boys practice this to work toward physical relaxation.

To have the boys practice emotional relaxation, encourage each of them to daydream about the most peaceful place he knows. Have them pay attention to as many details as possible, using all of their senses: touch, smell, sight, hearing, and taste. If you choose, you may use a guided-imagery exercise. When all senses are incorporated into the imagery, the experience is more vivid and detailed. An example follows:

I want you to sit back in a comfortable position and close your eyes if you can. Take a deep breath and let it out slowly. Take another deep breath and let it out even more slowly. Pay attention to your arms. Shake them a little bit and then let them rest at your side.

Notice your legs. Are they in the most comfortable position? Get as comfortable as you can. See if there is any part of your body that is hurting or feels tight. Rubbing it gently or taking more deep breaths may help that part relax. Feel comfortable and peaceful.

Now I want you to imagine you are walking down a long path, surrounded by trees. It is cool and very quiet. You hear only the wind in the trees and some birds chirping. Smell the fresh air as you walk, taking in deep breaths as you go. Your body feels strong and at peace. The path takes you to a large, green meadow. The sun is shining, the sky is blue, and the meadow is filled with lush green grass.

As you walk across the meadow, you see a clear blue pond ahead of you. Sit down next to the pond and look into the water. Reflected in the water you see a rainbow. As you look at each color, your body feels more and more relaxed. Your mind becomes calmer and more peaceful with each color. First you are seeing red [pause for ten to fifteen seconds after each color]. Now orange, yellow, green, blue, purple, violet.

Take another deep breath and let it out slowly. Bring your imagination back to this room. You're with your friends, and you feel relaxed and calm. When you are ready, go ahead and open your eyes.

If you want, you can use a guided-imagery exercise during each session, perhaps as part of a starting or closing ritual. As a starting ritual, it helps everyone become focused and ready; as a closing ritual, it helps boys ease out of a tense activity or an emotional discussion.

One caution is necessary: *Never use guided imagery to trigger memories of sexual abuse.* All therapists who work with abused clients should be aware of the debate over "false memories," previously mentioned in Chapter Four. All guided imagery and visualization used in our groups are positive in nature and done for the sole purpose of relaxation. The use of guided imagery does not direct or lead the boys to think of any specific person or abusive event in their past. We do not use any form of suggestion or suggestive questions about abuse with visualization or guided imagery. Whitfield (1995) recommends that if these techniques are to be used in a more specialized manner, it is essential that the therapist have adequate training, including, for example, formal study, receipt of certification or a license if needed, and regular consultation and supervision.

As an alternative to guided imagery, you might ask each boy to make a large drawing of his favorite place or the place where he feels most comfortable and safe. The boy can take this drawing home and use it to practice relaxation there when he needs it. A great place to put it is next to the boy's bed. Encourage the members to practice in the morning and before going to sleep at night for best results. Like any skill, relaxation becomes easier with practice and as boys begin to experience its benefits.

Common Responses

When they are first learning, younger boys often exhibit anxiety through restlessness and fidgeting. Help the restless child verbalize what he is feeling and explore the precipitants for feelings of anxiety or fear, internal or environmental. Generally the precipitants involve some type of perceived threat.

Older boys may downplay the importance of relaxation or guided imagery, but they usually welcome guidance in learning a skill that is easy to do, does not cost anything, and has no harmful effects. Help each boy identify one situation or place in which relaxation will benefit him.

To emphasize the point that relaxation and stress reduction do not happen without some action on a person's part, you and the boys can make a poster of ideas for reducing stress and then hang it on the wall for quick reference and a reminder. Have the boys brainstorm ideas and then draw, paint, or use magazine pictures on poster board to represent these ideas. If the boys need help coming up with ideas, here are a few: crying, exercising, intense physical activity that focuses energy, humor, writing, working on a hobby (such as reading, watching television, or playing games), being around other people, listening to music, and taking time out from a stressful situation.

◆ ACTIVITY 8: Affirmations

Target Ages
- All

Abuse Issues Addressed
- Low self-esteem
- Powerlessness

Objective
- To have each boy write at least two personal affirmations that he agrees to use and practice while attending therapy

Rationale
Critical statements, the attitudes of others, or feelings of shame or guilt can reinforce a child's tendency to engage in negative self-talk. Building skills in using positive self-talk helps a child feel better about himself and gives him a better sense of self-control.

Procedure
Give each boy a pencil and a copy of the Guidelines for Creating and Using Affirmations. Review the guidelines with the group, starting with a brief definition of affirmations: positive statements about oneself that usually begin with "I" and are stated in the present, as if they are already true. Then go over the characteristics of affirmations one by one. Ask the boys to picture in their minds how they would like things to be if they could completely create their lives and their circumstances.

Describe affirmations as coping thoughts, in that they remind a boy that he is in charge and can manage. Explain that they can be used to cope with even the most critical problems related to sexual abuse. Then encourage each boy to identify what those problems are for him, to choose the problem that is his biggest challenge (regardless of what other people may have told him), and to write at least two affirmations designed to help him overcome that problem.

Emphasize that thoughts are completely within the individual's control and can be changed when they create problems. Explain the concept of a self-fulfilling prophecy: "If you think something repeatedly, such as 'I'm fat' or 'I'm ugly,' you will believe that it is true. When you internalize or accept this belief, it will become your reality, because you will be viewing everything that happens to you from that perspective."

Some boys may need help with this task. Porter, Blick, and Sgroi (1982) identify ten areas where sexually abused children are likely to develop problems. Examples of affirmations related to those issues follow and are offered to assist the therapist in developing powerful, individualized statements with the boys.

"Damaged Goods" Syndrome

- I feel great about my body.
- My body is healthy and perfect.

Guilt

- I believe the molestation was _____'s fault.
- I deserve to be safe and protected at all times.
- I did the right thing in telling.
- I made the best choices I could at the time.

Fear

- I take action to help myself feel safe.
- I ask for help whenever I'm feeling afraid.

Depression

- I deserve to be happy.
- I begin and end each day with positive thoughts.

Low Self-Esteem

- I love myself exactly the way I am.

Poor Social Skills

- I choose friends who are kind and who like me.
- I am a good friend to others.

Repressed Anger and Hostility

- I talk about my angry feelings without showing angry behaviors toward others or myself.
- My anger is under control.

Impaired Ability to Trust

- I get to know people gradually and carefully.
- I practice trusting a little bit more each day.
- I feel good and safe with trustworthy people.
- I trust myself to do the right thing.

Role Confusion

- I deserve to act like a ___ -year-old and do ___ -year-old things.
- I am a child in my family.
- I have fun being just ___ years old.

Self-Mastery and Control

- I am in charge of my feelings and my behavior.
- I work out problems in a way that is good for me and for others.
- I am responsible for making good choices for myself.
- I know how to deal with this problem.
- I am responsible for taking care of my needs.
- I can create a plan to work this out.

If a boy seems stuck, encourage him to think of abuse-related problems in terms of the negative messages he has received about the molestation. Then ask him to choose the one message that troubles him the most.

Once all boys have created their affirmations, explain the next step: posting their affirmations in several prominent places and then reading them and saying them often to internalize them. Also discuss other ways in which the boys can remind themselves of their affirmations, for example, by making a tape recording that repeats affirmations for ten to fifteen minutes and then listening to the tape every night before falling asleep. James (1989) suggests a variety of creative options.

Common Responses

Adolescents may criticize this activity with such comments as "Positive thinking is a bunch of bull." Using your knowledge of their hobbies and interests, provide some examples of the importance of doing something consistently over time in order to experience positive results: "At the start of football season, are you back in shape after only a few days, or does it take longer? When you learn a new language, are you able to converse fluently right away? Learning any new skill takes time, commitment, and patience to practice."

Recommend to the boys that they try using affirmations at least twice each day for a month before making any judgments about their effectiveness or usefulness.

Guidelines for Creating and Using Affirmations

1. Start with "I" and use short, simple phrases that are easy to remember.
2. Write each affirmation in the present tense, as if it were already so.
3. Use positive words and statements ("I'm beautiful" instead of "I'm not ugly.")
4. Keep the affirmations in different locations so that you can review them regularly (in a school notebook, in your wallet, on the bathroom mirror, on your bedside table).
5. Repeat affirmations at least twice daily, preferably aloud.

◆ ACTIVITY 9: Letting Go of Blame

Target Ages
- Seven through eleven

Abuse Issues Addressed
- Guilt
- Blaming oneself
- Powerlessness

Objectives
- To help each boy begin the process of letting go of blame, both verbally and cognitively, for his molestation
- To help each boy understand that he is not responsible for his molestation

Rationale
Many boys believe they are responsible for causing their own sexual abuse and for family disruption following disclosure. The guilt and self-blame they feel can be immobilizing. They need to learn skills associated with protecting themselves so that they will feel safer and less vulnerable.

Procedure
Distribute pencils and copies of the Responsibility Worksheet. If the boys are older, tell them to follow the instructions and complete the worksheet by marking X's in the appropriate places.

If the boys are younger, read the statements aloud, pausing after each statement and asking each boy to mark an X in the appropriate place.

Invite the boys to share their responses, and lead a discussion based on the results. State that any boy who marked four or more X's in the I Agree column or the

I Do Not Know/I Am Unsure column needs to work on letting go of the notion that he is responsible for his abuse and regaining his sense of empowerment and control. (Note that you will need to know each boy's results so that you can give extra attention to the boys who need it.)

Common Responses

Many boys will state that they do not know how they feel. If this happens, reassure them that it is normal to have conflicting feelings. This concept can be difficult for younger boys to understand, and it warrants frequent discussion. The use of a poster depicting feelings helps in explaining the concept. Most children's posters include expressive faces and words to describe the feelings depicted by each face. You might also write down some words that denote feelings and keep the list posted.

An abused boy may be self-destructive if he feels he deserves to be punished for the abuse, so explore this carefully with any child who responds affirmatively to the last statement on the checklist. He will need to be assessed for the need for hospitalization, and an immediate safety plan must be implemented. Although a detailed assessment for suicide risk is beyond the scope of this book, the following are some important areas to address. You need to determine the following:

- Whether he has a plan to harm himself
- Whether he has the means to carry out such a plan
- Whether he has made any previous attempts
- What level of support and supervision is available for him at home

Because of their past experience, some group members may be able to offer ideas about ways to alleviate suicidal thoughts. Encouraging them to share their ideas is a good idea.

Responsibility Worksheet

	I Agree (✔)	I Do Not Agree (✔)	I Do Not Know/ I Am Unsure (✔)
1. I do not deserve to be safe and protected.	( )	( )	( )
2. It is my fault if someone abuses or molests me.	( )	( )	( )
3. There is nothing I can do if someone tells me to keep a tricky secret.	( )	( )	( )

	I Agree (✔)	I Do Not Agree (✔)	I Do Not Know/ I Am Unsure (✔)
4. I have no adults whom I can talk to if something is bothering me.	( )	( )	( )
5. Even if I feel scared, I cannot tell an adult if someone touches me in a confusing way.	( )	( )	( )
6. I should get into trouble if I do not tell right away about something bad that happened.	( )	( )	( )
7. I am old enough and strong enough to have stopped the abuse if I had wanted to.	( )	( )	( )
8. If something bad happens, I cannot do anything about it.	( )	( )	( )
9. I often feel that things are out of my control.	( )	( )	( )
10. If I were different in some way, the molester would not have chosen me.	( )	( )	( )
11. I should be punished for what happened.	( )	( )	( )

◆ ACTIVITY 10: Taking Responsibility for Yourself

Target Ages
- Ten through eighteen

Abuse Issues Addressed
- Blaming oneself
- Taking responsibility for oneself

Objective
- To have each boy select one environment (for example, at home, at school, with friends, or in the group) in which he will work on assuming responsibility for himself

Rationale

Eliminating self-blame and assuming responsibility for oneself are critical to recovery. Each boy needs to learn to focus on what he can do about any given situation, thereby changing his perception of himself as a victim to one of being a survivor.

Procedure

Prominently post the following statements:

- Responsibility is a gift because it gives me the power to make changes.
- I always have a choice, and choice is freedom.

Ask the boys to share what they think about these statements. Boys usually view responsibility as something difficult and negative, so you must reframe it positively. Explain that by taking responsibility a boy can become aware of the control he has in any situation and that this awareness gives him new options for problem solving.

Work individually with each boy to discuss any decisions or choices he made about the sexual abuse, such as keeping it secret or telling. Encourage him to consider how and why he made these decisions. Point out that he may have made those choices because of a limited perspective, a lack of awareness of options, or misinformation. Emphasize that people do the best they can to cope, regardless of what happens, and that in the future each boy will have new choices to make about his own behavior and recovery from abuse.

Characterize blaming as the opposite of assuming responsibility for one's own actions. Reinforce the fact that blaming others keeps a person in the role of victim; as a victim he expects others to make things better for him. If those other people do not come through (which is generally the case), the victim becomes angry and resentful and still does not have what he wants.

By this time the boys will have a good understanding of the importance of empowerment, so emphasize this point: *when you blame others, you give them control over you and your life.*

Common Responses

If some of the boys mistakenly assume that you are saying they are responsible for being molested, correct that misperception. State that responsibility for the abuse *always* falls on the offender. It may take more than one session to ensure this is understood.

◆ ACTIVITY 11: Forgiving Yourself

Target Ages
- Ten through eighteen

Abuse Issues Addressed
- Blaming oneself
- Self-esteem

Objective
- To give each group member the opportunity to write a letter of forgiveness to himself

Rationale
Boys need to hear repeatedly that they are not responsible for the abuse they experienced; their offenders are. Acknowledge that at the time of the abuse, under those circumstances, the boys were victims. Point out that each boy is no longer a victim because he is no longer powerless; each boy must come to perceive himself as a survivor, not as a victim. Helping boys give up inappropriately blaming themselves for the abuse can help them accept appropriate and realistic responsibility for their actions in the present and future.

Procedure: Part 1
Distribute pencils and copies of the Forgiving Myself handout. Ask each boy to complete each statement as thoroughly as possible.

After everyone has finished, ask members to share their answers. Then ask them the following questions:

- In what ways are you blaming yourself?
- Did the perpetrator say that the abuse was your fault?
- Are you ashamed because your body responded to the molestation or some aspect of it?
- Did someone tell you that getting molested means you are a failure?
- Do you feel you should have been able to prevent or stop the abuse?
- Do you think you brought the abuse on yourself for some reason?

State that blaming themselves for the abuse can create anger, resentment, and hate. Instead, the boys need to forgive themselves.

Procedure: Part 2
Distribute pencils and paper and instruct each boy to write a private letter of forgiveness to himself, even if he does not yet feel that forgiveness. Then encourage

those boys who have significant difficulty with self-blame to read their letters daily until they are able to forgive themselves.

Common Responses

Just as many boys feel strongly that they will never forgive those who molested them, many also feel the same way about forgiving themselves. You may need to reframe blame by explaining an aspect that is not often discussed: the boy who accepts blame for being abused may feel less helpless than he would otherwise, because the blaming gives him a sense of control over the abusive situation.

Explain that there are healthier ways to regain control. The decision to forgive oneself is a means of letting go and moving on in a positive way.

Forgiving Myself

1. Reporting the abuse was wrong because . . .
2. How I feel when I talk about being molested:
3. What I think other people will feel when they know I was molested:
4. Something that I am afraid of when I talk about being molested is . . .
5. When I forgive someone, I feel . . .
6. How I felt after I told about being molested:
7. What I think other kids would say if they knew what happened to me:
8. Whom do people usually blame when a boy is molested? When a girl is molested?
9. I am ashamed of . . .
10. True or false: Something must be wrong with a boy if the abuse felt good or was enjoyable.
11. I must have brought the abuse on myself, because . . .
12. A boy is a failure when . . .
13. I believe I should have been able to stop the abuse because . . .
14. I feel most hateful toward . . .
15. I do not deserve to be protected, because . . .

◆ ACTIVITY 12: Feelings Wheel

Target Ages
- Seven through thirteen

Abuse Issues Addressed

- Feeling different or damaged
- Isolation
- Depression

Objectives

- To enable each boy to recognize impulsive behavior
- To foster less frequent use of impulsive behavior while in the group

Rationale

Identifying, labeling, and clarifying feelings helps boys realize that others share similar emotions. Isolation lessens as they become aware of shared reactions and experiences.

Procedure

Give each boy a pencil or a felt-tipped marker as well as a sheet of paper at least 8½ by 11 inches (larger is better). Instruct each boy to draw one circle to cover most of the sheet; another, smaller circle inside the first; and a third circle inside the second one. Ask each boy to label one circle (it does not matter which) with the words *Parents or People who take care of me,* another with *Perpetrator,* and the third with *Me.*

Instruct each boy to think about what feelings he has right now toward each of these three people or groups of people and write down as many feelings as possible in the respective circles. Emphasize there are no right or wrong feelings and that talking about feelings honestly helps build trust.

When everyone has completed the task, announce that the boys have created "feelings wheels" and ask for volunteers to share whatever they choose about their drawings. Then lead the group in a discussion in which you make these points:

- People's feelings affect how they behave.
- Feelings can change over time.
- Ambivalent feelings are normal.
- All boys who have been molested share common feelings.
- The feelings that are the most difficult to talk about also are the ones that are most important to discuss.

Then take the discussion about feelings and behaviors in a slightly different direction by asking the following questions:

- What behaviors get you into the most trouble?
- What feelings tend to go along with these behaviors?

State that molested boys of all ages need to learn and practice how to connect their feelings to their behaviors. Define impulsive behaviors as those that are done quickly, without thinking prior to acting. Then ask whether the problematic behaviors they just cited are also impulsive.

Explore the societal norm that feelings are not masculine. With younger boys, use a poster that has a variety of "feeling" faces on it and includes the name for each feeling. With older boys, ask for contributions of "feeling" words, record these on a poster, and keep it on the wall so that the boys can explore and further define emotions.

Common Responses

The majority of boys will lack awareness of the connection between their feelings and behavior. Emphasize that this is an important concept that they will be returning to often in therapy.

Either before or after the session you might want to contact the boys' parents to see if they are willing to reinforce this topic at home by watching for patterns and then pointing out these patterns to their sons. You might offer examples of phrasing such an observation: "When you go to bed late, you cry a lot more the next day," or "I know doing well is important to you; you look so sad when you don't get an A."

Consider working with the boys to establish a simple cue to use in the group as a reminder to slow down and think before acting. I use the sign language sign for *slow*, which is to place the fingers of your right hand on your left wrist and move them slowly upward toward your elbow.

◆ ACTIVITY 13: Feelings and Behavior

Target Ages
- Seven through twelve

Abuse Issue Addressed
- How feelings influence behavior

Objective
- To have each boy recognize his personal precipitants for feelings of sadness and anger

Rationale

Molestation causes a wide range of feelings. Many of these are uncomfortable for boys to acknowledge and express. It is important for boys of all ages to understand their feelings, however, as well as how those feelings affect their behavior. When they understand why certain behaviors occur, they feel less powerless.

Procedure

Distribute pencils and copies of the Feelings and Behavior Worksheet. If you have completed Activity 12 with the group, display the group's poster of "feeling" faces or words associated with feelings; if you have not completed Activity 12, you can make the poster yourself and display it. (The poster is not used in this activity except as an additional reference for the boys.)

Instruct the boys to complete the statements on the worksheet by filling each blank with a "feelings" word. Clarify that they can refer to the list of words on the worksheet to get ideas (and the ones on the poster, if applicable) but that they must not use the same word more than twice. (This direction encourages the boys to examine more thoroughly the range of emotions that people experience.)

After they have finished, have members share their responses. As they announce their responses, be sure to validate all feelings. Then emphasize the following points:

- There are no right or wrong feelings. They just are, and judgments about them are not helpful to anyone.
- Every boy is unique.
- To respond to any single feeling, each boy has literally hundreds of behavioral options.
- The decision to react with a certain behavior in response to a feeling rests with the individual.

Common Responses

Some boys may refuse to participate because "feelings are for girls, not for guys." Acknowledge that this belief is shared by many boys and is often reinforced by family members and societal norms in general. Reassure the boys, though, that the group is a safe place to express and discuss feelings, if they choose.

You may also be challenged about the importance of feelings. If so, explore what the boy has been told about feelings, and explain again that therapy is to help the boys feel back in control. State that when they can recognize situations, patterns, or feelings that precede problematic behaviors, they have taken an important step toward regaining personal control.

"Feelings" Words

Afraid	Excited	Peaceful
Angry	Fed up	Pleased
Annoyed	Frustrated	Proud
Anxious	Glad	Reassured
Bitter	Guilty	Relaxed
Bored	Happy	Resigned
Cheerful	Helpless	Sad
Confident	Hopeless	Satisfied
Confused	Hurt	Scared
Cranky	Hysterical	Shocked
Creative	Immobilized	Silly
Curious	Interested	Surprised
Determined	Irritable	Suspicious
Discouraged	Lonely	Unsure
Doubtful	Loving	Upset
Eager	Nervous	Uptight
Enraged	Paralyzed	Worried

Feelings and Behavior Worksheet

Instructions: Using the words listed above—and others that denote feelings—fill in the blanks in the following sentences.

1. When I am teased, I feel _____, and then what I do is

   _____.

2. When I am late for school, I feel _____, and then what I do is _____.

3. When my mom or dad hugs me, I feel _____, and then what I do is _____.

4. When my brother or sister blames me for something that is not my fault, I feel _____, and then what I do is _____.

5. When my teacher calls on me, I feel _____, and then what I do is _____.

6. When my parents fight, I feel _____, and then what I do is _____.

7. When I go to school, I feel _____, and then what I do is _____.

8. When I go to bed at night, I feel _____, and then what I do is _____.

9. If I have to talk in front of my class, I feel_____, and then what I do is _____.

10. When I am coming home from school, I feel _____, and then what I do is _____.

11. When I wake up from a bad dream, I feel _____, and then what I do is _____.

12. When I have to do chores, I feel _____, and then what I do is _____.

13. When I have done something wrong, I feel _____, and then what I do is _____.

14. When my mom is not home, I feel _____, and then what I do is _____.

15. At dinnertime, I feel _____, and then what I do is _____.

16. When I am around my friends, I feel _____, and then what I do is _____.

17. When my dad is not home, I feel _____, and then what I do is _____.

18. When I get a gift, I feel _____, and then what I do is _____.

19. When I give a gift, I feel _____, and then what I do is _____.

20. When I get up in the morning, I feel _____, and then what I do is _____.

21. When I visit relatives, I feel _____, and then what I do is _____.

◆ ACTIVITY 14: Creating a Slang Chart

Target Ages
- Seven through twelve

Abuse Issues Addressed
- Anxiety
- Confusion about sexuality

Objective
- To encourage the boys to learn various terms for private body parts

Rationale

All molested boys need to receive accurate sex education and to explore their concerns about sex. (If the boys do not become accustomed to one another's terminology in particular, they will experience high levels of anxiety in the group and will not be able to tolerate discussion and assimilate information.)

Procedure

This activity is most useful as an introduction to sex education. It can also be scheduled immediately after some basic information has already been presented to the boys. Ask the boys to brainstorm all of the slang terms or nicknames they can think of for each of the following body parts, one at a time: *vagina, breasts, anus, penis, testicles.* As the boys come up with ideas, write each on a chalkboard or a poster under the appropriate heading (the "real" name for the body part).

Be prepared to hear some creative terms. You and your cotherapist need to be at ease with this terminology; be willing to get a little silly if the group initially has trouble getting started. If you are anxious or judgmental, the boys will see your discomfort, and the activity will not be as successful.

Eventually the list becomes a "slang chart." With younger boys, you might want to keep it for their further reference; consider transferring it to a more permanent surface and keeping it in the group room.

State very clearly that the boys have permission to use any slang words for body parts during their therapy sessions; at home, however, they must follow their parents' or guardians' rules. Provide a wind-down period or outside activity before the boys leave for home.

You can also use this activity design with different terms for homosexuality, gays, and lesbians, depending on the needs of the group.

Common Responses

You will encounter much silliness with this activity, which can get out of control very quickly if you allow it. Keep the discussion centered on the boys' terms and move quickly through the brainstorming. Acknowledge that most people feel anxious when talking about sex and that the group is a safe place to talk about this difficult topic.

Although most therapists see the value in this activity, other adults often do not appreciate the use of these words, especially at home. Consequently, even though you have asked the boys to follow their parents' rules at home, you may receive complaints from parents afterward. Consider notifying them in advance and explaining the rationale for the activity and for the use of the boys' own slang words during group sessions. Clarify that you will urge the boys to adhere to their parents' wishes at home.

◆ ACTIVITY 15: Making a Floor Plan

Target Ages

- Seven through twelve

Abuse Issue Addressed

- Denial or minimization

Objectives

- To offer the boys an opportunity to share the details of their abuse
- To encourage the boys to practice giving and receiving peer support

Rationale

The boys need to know that their memories of abuse will surface from time to time, along with new recollections; they also need to learn that they can cope with their memories. It is therapeutic for them to remember details and to process the feelings completely, instead of avoiding the memories in order to lessen their pain at the moment.

Procedure

Give a large piece of drawing paper to each member, along with an assortment of pens, pencils, crayons, markers, and various stickers. Ask the boys to close their eyes. Instruct each boy to choose one particular molestation memory and to think about it. Choices are important here, so offer options: the most upsetting memory, the first occasion, the place where it happened most often, or the most vivid recollection. (Keep in mind that for some members it might have been a one-time occurrence and for others the abuse might have gone on for years; for others, there were multiple perpetrators. Try to provide ideas about memories that would apply to different situations.) With a group of younger boys, you might want to be more specific, such as "the first occasion" or "the memory that is most clear."

Direct each boy to see the place in his mind, with as much detail as possible. Then ask him to draw where it occurred (for example, a living room, an apartment, at school, a neighbor's bedroom). State that in order to draw the picture, each boy will pretend to be floating above the location and looking down, with the roof removed so that everything is in plain view.

Encourage each boy to include the layout of the room, doors, closets, windows, furniture, and people. Tell the boys that after they have completed their floor plans, each of them is to choose stickers to place on the drawing to represent himself, the offender(s), and every other person around the location (such as family members). Allow plenty of time to create the drawings, even though some boys will feel so uncomfortable with the memories that they want to get the activity over with in a hurry.

After all floor plans have been completed, offer each boy the opportunity to show his floor plan to the others and, if possible, to talk about it. Explain why sharing the details of abuse is necessary:

- Through sharing, secrets lose their power.
- This represents a chance to have a positive experience in disclosure, since many children are frightened or angered by an investigative or police interview.

Encourage the boys to share as fully as they can about the molestation, but emphasize that no one needs to share anything that he does not want to. This sharing offers each boy a chance to disclose the "who, when, and where" details before he is invited to disclose the more difficult details concerning "what."

You may find it helpful to start with the most verbal child in the group, so that the boys see modeling of open disclosure. If the boys are still reluctant to talk about the abuse at this point, proceed to Activity 16. Remind the boys that sharing details with their peers in the group is therapeutically important and that they have many choices in how to carry it out. Discuss how each boy feels about visualizing an abuse memory and ask whether he feels differently about the experience now than he did then.

You might be able to increase the pace of the process by providing a completed example at the beginning of the activity, so that the members can see what a floor plan looks like.

Common Responses

A boy may share only part of his abuse story and leave out other details. Be careful not to push for full disclosure from each child before he is ready. Acknowledge how difficult it is to share, and validate each individual's disclosure afterward. Let the group members know they may decide to share more during a later session. If any boy refuses to participate, stress that it is his choice and that you will not force disclosure.

A high level of anxiety and restlessness is common when the boys share details of abuse. Consequently, you need to allow time for deescalation at the end of this group activity. You do not want to send boys home with pent-up feelings. Also, the boys deserve positive reinforcement after completing a difficult task; if possible, schedule an outing or other fun activity for them after all the disclosures have been completed.

You and your cotherapist must be prepared with appropriate interventions in case a member is unable to tolerate hearing about his peers' abuse. In this case one of you can work with the child who is sharing while the other manages the group.

Possible reactions include escalating disruptiveness, questioning the truth, put-down comments, unwillingness to be serious throughout the sharing, and name calling. Help the boys recognize when their feelings are building, and offer something they can use to divert their tension (drawing materials, play dough to squeeze, or a stuffed animal to hold). Rather than trying to have everyone disclose during the same group session, you may want to limit the amount of time spent sharing by having perhaps one or two boys share per session.

◆ ACTIVITY 16: Sharing the Details

Target Ages
- All

Abuse Issues Addressed
- Powerlessness
- Anxiety
- Isolation

Objectives
- To encourage the boys to share the details of their abuse
- To offer the boys practice in giving and receiving peer support

Rationale

Previous interviews with child protective services, the police, or other therapists may have felt like interrogations to the boys; the ones who have gone through such interviews may have felt that they were being threatened or that their truthfulness was being questioned. This activity offers a welcome, empowering alternative in that it allows the boys to tell their stories in their own way and to have their methods of sharing respected.

Procedure

Note: This activity may extend through several sessions, depending on how long it takes the boys to prepare and make their presentations on the details of their abuse.

The activity deals with the manner in which each boy was abused—a much more difficult topic than other questions about the abuse that the group may have previously addressed. Provide the boys various media (dolls, puppets, drawing materials, and so on) along with a copy of the Details Questionnaire. Each boy chooses the item he prefers and uses that item to prepare a presentation in which he shares the details of his abuse; the presentations may cover only the areas that appear in the Details Questionnaire, or they may convey more information. Using items in his presentation allows each boy to achieve some emotional distance from the details, which makes the details safer to share.

You need to help the boys understand the purpose of having them share details that are so painful. You can cite the following reasons:

- We have a group goal not to keep secrets.
- It is important for you to hear what happened to others so that you know you are not alone.
- Telling everything can help other boys disclose abuse that previously they were too embarrassed or afraid to tell.
- Most boys say they feel better after sharing these things, even though it is uncomfortable at first.
- Knowing the details of the abuse will help me (or "us" if you are working with a cotherapist) help you in the best ways possible.

Provide as many items as possible for the boys to choose from in conveying their experiences:

Puppets: The boy can have a puppet answer questions about what happened or use puppets to show what happened during the molestation.

Anatomically correct dolls: The boy can use the dolls to show what happened.

Supplies for drawing: The boy can illustrate who was there, where the molestation happened, and other details (see also Activity 15).

Role play: The boy can act out a court situation, for example, in which the judge (a person of the boy's choosing) asks him a set of prescribed questions covering the details.

Paper and pencils for writing: The boy can write the details in narrative form.

A tape recorder and tapes: The boy can record his story away from the group and then play the tape for the other members.

Rehearse with you or a cotherapist, then tell the story: The boy can work with one of you about how to tell his story before disclosing details in front of his peers.

Directed interview: You can work with the boy to devise interview questions about the details that call for simple yes or no responses from him; then you can interview him while the other members observe (especially useful when a boy needs to describe details about specific sex acts but is reluctant to).

Play it safe with SASA: The boys can play this game, which has specific interview questions to answer (see the Appendix).

Details Questionnaire: Give the boy a copy of the Details Questionnaire and ask him to fill it out; he can then read it to the group, or you can do the reading if he feels he cannot talk about the abuse.

Emphasize that each boy may choose from the materials you have provided or use another method with which he is more comfortable; no one is limited to the alternatives you have offered. State that each boy's choice is to be respected by everyone in the group.

Allow plenty of time for the boys to prepare during the session, but also be aware that some methods may require work outside group sessions. You may or may not have some boys ready to make their presentations during this first session.

Common Responses

Some boys may rush through the process of preparing and making their presentations in five minutes. Another boy may take an entire group session to share what happened. Consequently, the sharing may extend into the next couple of sessions.

If a boy appears unemotional and detached during a presentation, ask him what he is feeling; state that shutting down his feelings will not alleviate them or help him feel better. Others may cry throughout the presentations, so it is important for you to set a firm rule ahead of time that no one is to criticize or make fun of anyone else during the sharing.

Some children will probably become enraged. Be sure to intervene as soon as you notice any signs of anger; encourage the child in question to discharge his feelings in some physical but acceptable way before he feels out of control.

Be sure to allow time for deescalation at the end of every group session that includes sharing about specific abuse details.

Details Questionnaire

Instructions: Answer these questions to the best of your ability:

1. How many people have molested/sexually abused/raped you?
2. What are these people's names?
3. For *each person* you listed in item 2 above, answer the following:
   - How old were you when it started?
   - How old were you when it stopped?
   - Did it happen one time? A few times? Many times?
   - Where did it take place?
   - What things did he or she do to you? Ask you to do?
   - Who else knew about it?
   - What happened to make the abuse finally stop?
   - How do you feel when you think about the molester?

◆ ACTIVITY 17: Understanding Everything You Always Wanted to Know

Target Ages
- All

Abuse Issues Addressed
- Confusion about sexuality
- Confusion about sexual identity
- Dysfunctional sexual behavior

Objective
- To assist the boys in writing down and obtaining answers for their questions about sexuality

Rationale

A boy's abuse experience colors how he perceives his sexuality and often distorts his beliefs about sex. Thus, an important part of therapy is exploring and correcting negative or harmful perceptions and beliefs.

Procedure: Part 1

Prior to this activity, it is necessary to provide a foundation of sex education that is appropriate for the boys' age level. Reading a book with the boys or viewing an educational video are two options (see the Appendix for recommendations). Another approach is to invite a specifically trained health educator to come talk to your group.

For latency-aged boys, the foundation would include terms for private body parts, reproduction, and changes experienced during puberty by both boys and girls. For adolescents, you need to cover all of these topics plus discussions of values, peer pressure to be sexually active, personal responsibility, birth control, and sexually transmitted diseases. (To use this activity with very young boys, be sure you know the words they use to describe sex and sexually related topics so that you can communicate at their level when you educate them.)

This activity consumes a minimum of two to three group sessions. First you review the foundation of sex education that you have already provided for the group. Then distribute paper and pencils and ask each boy to write down all the questions about sex or sexuality that he can think of, leaving plenty of space between questions. Emphasize that the questions ought to be ones for which the boys actually do want answers, especially those questions that the boys would not consider asking their parents. Explain that the boys will submit their questions without identifying themselves, so that no one will know who asked what.

After the boys have finished writing, ask them to tear their papers so that only one question appears on each slip of paper, to fold each slip in half, and to place all their slips into a bowl or basket that you have brought for that purpose.

Procedure: Part 2

The boys take turns drawing one slip of paper at a time and reading the question aloud for the group to discuss. Allow plenty of time for this to be certain questions are adequately explored and answered.

Older boys often want to minimize their lack of knowledge and thus hurry over those areas where they need information the most. To deal with this dynamic, you and your cotherapist may ease the boys' anxiety and ensure that critical topics are addressed by adding your own questions on slips of paper. (You can include the ones on the Understanding Everything Worksheet; add others if you want.)

During this discussion, some information is especially critical to emphasize. For example, be sure to point out that there is a wide range of "normal" variation in the age at which boys enter puberty. Listen for examples of unusual or deviant sexual arousal, as this is one risk factor for the development of offending behavior.

Finally, let the boys know that if they need some questions to be answered in greater depth or if they want to ask additional questions, you or your cotherapist will be available for consultation outside the group session. In this way you encourage the boys to come to you with questions that were too uncomfortable to bring up in the group.

Common Responses

If you and your cotherapist are not comfortable talking about these topics, the group dynamics will reflect your discomfort: you will see resistance, disruptiveness, and other problematic behaviors. Disruptive behavior can also occur as a result of anxiety and embarrassment. You need to acknowledge the feelings and set limits on behavior that interferes with the group process. Explain the consequences, such as a time-out, ahead of time if a child is unwilling to follow directions.

Sexualized comments frequently escalate with this activity. If only one child is making them, continue the group while ignoring his comments. If other boys follow his example, you will have to use more directive interventions. Label and confront the behavior as attention seeking and tell the boys how they can get your attention in a positive way.

Often an older boy will make fun of his peers' questions, with an "I know everything" attitude. It is important to validate all questions and to stress there is something for everyone to learn from the discussion. Point out that you and your cotherapist do not know everything either and are always learning.

You might consider informing parents about this topic beforehand. This will ensure that parents will not be completely surprised if their sons ask additional questions at home.

Understanding Everything Worksheet

1. Is masturbation bad for you or weird or wrong?
2. How old does a girl have to be before she can become pregnant?
3. Is it normal to think about sex all the time?
4. Is there anything a boy can do to increase the size of his penis?
5. Can a girl swim during her period?
6. What is a girl's period?
7. How do you know if someone is ready to have a sexual experience?
8. True or false: Having a homosexual experience means that a person is gay.
9. What is a virgin?
10. Do girls enjoy sex as much as guys do?
11. What is an abortion?
12. When is it OK to force someone to have sex?
13. What is the first thing a guy should do if he starts thinking about molesting someone?

14. Is there anything wrong with having sex without using birth control?
15. True or false: Only gay people get AIDS.
16. What are the causes of homosexuality?
17. True or false: Something is wrong with me if I feel "horny" most of the time.
18. Is it OK to look at pornography? Why or why not?

◆ ACTIVITY 18: Discussing the Big "M" Word

Target Ages
- All

Abuse Issue Addressed
- Confusion about sexuality

Objectives
- To encourage the boys to verbalize their anxious feelings
- To build each boy's tolerance of anxious feelings so that he can participate in group discussion more effectively

Rationale
Shame and embarrassment about sexuality in general and masturbation in particular can be acute for the sexually abused boy. Often misinformation and family values can exacerbate instead of alleviate his feelings. Obtaining accurate information about sexuality and masturbation and having permission to discuss self-stimulation can lessen his shame and guilt.

Procedure
You will need to have completed basic sexuality education prior to addressing the subject of masturbation with the group. Keep in mind it may be the first time any of the boys have heard masturbation discussed openly, so you can anticipate giggles, disbelief, embarrassment, and other reactions.

With younger boys, ask if anyone remembers what the word means. If possible, refer to the resources that you used earlier to educate the boys on sexuality. Ask the following questions:

- What are some slang words for masturbation?
- Do you think masturbation is normal?
- To whom have you talked about masturbation? What were you told?
- Have you ever heard masturbation discussed in your church?
- What do you think would happen if your parents found out that you masturbated?
- Do you think most boys and girls masturbate?
- Is it OK to touch yourself when other people are around? What about in private?

For adolescents, you can conduct a more in-depth discussion if you use the questions on the Masturbation Quiz. You can either distribute copies of this handout or simply read the questions to the boys. Whether their answers are right or wrong is not the emphasis of this activity (all the statements are false). Instead, you want to present masturbation in as neutral a light as possible, with the purpose of providing alternative points of view than those the boys may have already heard. (Getting the boys to understand that masturbation is normal is important in terms of later group discussions that will center around prevention of offending behavior.) Make sure that you clarify and expand on the information in the quiz so that the boys are left with no misconceptions.

Common Responses

Laughter, silliness, and extreme embarrassment are common. Some boys may express anger or disgust with you and your cotherapist, because this topic is taboo. If this happens, encourage the boys to keep talking, especially with their peers. You want to present alternative points of view and to emphasize again their ability to make the right choices for themselves.

Some boys may attempt to embarrass you or your cotherapist by asking personal questions about whether and how you masturbate. Be very clear about your personal boundaries by stating that such questions will not be answered because sexuality is a personal and private issue. Refocus the group on the reason for discussion about masturbation, which is to inform and educate.

Masturbation Quiz

Instructions: Decide whether each of the following statements is true or false, and then mark it either *T* or *F.*

1. No married people masturbate.
2. Masturbation is an abnormal activity and very rare.
3. Playing with yourself can cause mental problems, and it physically harms your body.
4. Something is wrong with a five-year-old who touches his or her genitals.
5. Masturbation will stop your sex drive as an adult.
6. Masturbation serves no useful purpose.
7. You should believe what your friends tell you about masturbation.
8. Boys masturbate much more often than girls of the same age.
9. Masturbating with a partner is never part of a healthy sexual relationship.
10. It is OK to masturbate in a public place.

◆ ACTIVITY 19: Sexuality Quiz

Target Ages
- Eleven through eighteen

Abuse Issues Addressed
- Confusion about sexuality and sexual identity
- Homophobia
- Isolation
- Sense of being different or damaged

Objectives
- To develop the boys' knowledge and understanding of sexual issues
- To encourage each boy to share one new thing he learned from this activity

Rationale
Myths, stereotypes, and homophobia are common among sexually abused boys. Parents do not often discuss sex openly with their sons, so the boys need a safe place to get accurate information, express concerns about the impact of sexual abuse, and develop an understanding of the fact that they are not different or damaged because of molestation.

Procedure
Distribute pencils and copies of the Myths and Truths Quiz. Ask each boy to complete the quiz, and explain that the quiz will be used for discussion.

After everyone has finished, announce that the only true statement is the last one. Allow plenty of time for discussion. Ask members if they recall from whom or where they obtained their knowledge in these areas. Remind the group that many people continue to believe the myths described in the quiz. Explore whether there is any adult in each boy's life with whom he feels comfortable enough to further discuss questions or concerns.

Common Responses
You are very likely to encounter statements that condemn homosexuality. Explain that homophobia refers to hatred, fear, and intolerance of a homosexual orientation or homosexual behavior. Clarify that uncomfortable feelings and fears often stem from misinformation. Ask where these erroneous messages come from and acknowledge that there are cultural as well as religious positions on this issue.

Boys frequently express their anxiety through silliness, inattentiveness, disruptive behavior, and withdrawal. Help them recognize the signs that indicate they are feeling anxious, and suggest ways to overcome anxiety (for example, engaging in a familiar activity, such as drawing).

Explain that it is normal to feel a certain level of anxiety when sexuality is discussed, and validate the boys' willingness to talk about difficult topics. It may be necessary to change gears to a less threatening activity so that the anxiety does not become overwhelming.

When a female therapist is involved with the group, the information she provides may be challenged or disputed by members. Underlying this is a concern about whether a woman can understand male sexual abuse. Clarify that one aspect of therapy is to educate the boys about the ways in which sexual abuse, misinformation, painful feelings, and current problems are related. Point out also that it is empowering for boys to be able to clarify misinformation for others, if they choose to.

Myths and Truths Quiz

Instructions: Decide whether each of the following statements is true or false, and then mark it either *T* or *F.*

1. All gay people would change if they were able to.
2. It will hurt a child to discuss being molested.
3. Lesbian and gay male teachers and parents will try to make children gay.
4. In cases of incest, only one child in the family is usually molested.
5. Homosexuality does not begin until adulthood.
6. When sexual abuse of children occurs, a stranger most often does it.
7. Most lesbians and gay men try to seduce straight people.
8. There are always physical signs if a boy has been sodomized.
9. Homosexuality is very rare and unnatural.
10. Only submissive, dependent, weak, or emotional boys are victimized.
11. Homosexuality is classified as a psychiatric disorder.
12. If a boy does not like sexual contact with a girl, he must be homosexual.
13. You can always tell if someone is gay or lesbian by the way the person looks or acts.
14. Females cannot be sexually abusive or child molesters.
15. In a homosexual relationship, one person usually takes the "male" role and the other the "female" role.
16. Sexual contact between older females and boys is a positive experience and/or a "conquest," not abuse.

17. Most gay men want to be women, and most lesbians want to be men.

18. If a boy has sexual contact with another male, it means he is gay.

19. We know the causes of homosexuality.

20. When boys are molested, it is usually by adult male homosexuals.

21. All males who are sexually abused as children grow up to be offenders.

22. "Coming out" or telling others about being homosexual is an easy, comfortable process.

23. Sexual abuse of boys is less serious and has fewer consequences than abuse of girls. (Boys experience little impact, either physically or psychologically.)

24. According to a well-known researcher, about half of the male population and one-fourth of the female population report having had a homosexual experience.

◆ ACTIVITY 20: Learning to Trust

Target Ages
- Eleven through eighteen

Abuse Issues Addressed
- Mistrust
- Impaired relationships

Objective
- To encourage each child to feel more trusting with peers and therapists

Rationale
Boys need help in understanding how pervasively betrayal of trust can affect their lives. To overcome mistrust, they have to learn ways to identify who is trustworthy and to build trust slowly with new people.

Procedure
Distribute pencils and copies of the Trust Checklist and ask the boys to complete the checklist. Encourage them to go slowly and to try to imagine themselves actually in each situation before they respond. Explain that if another person not listed comes to mind, that person's name can be added.

In order for the boys to understand why this activity is important, it is necessary to talk about how sexual abuse usually causes a betrayal of a child's trust. Encourage discussion of the following questions:

- What do you think trust means? (Encourage the boys to consider such factors as continuity, consistency, reliability, acceptance, reassurance, and honesty.)
- How has your trust level been affected since you were molested?
- What would life be like if you decided never to trust anyone again?
- Do you trust everyone the same?
- How does someone earn your trust?

Explain that the group can help boys gradually rebuild trusting relationships. Be sure the boys understand you do not want them to trust everyone automatically; instead, you want them to learn the difference between people who are trustworthy and those who are not.

Common Responses

Often a boy will make all-or-none statements, such as "I'll never trust anyone again for the rest of my life." Emphasize that it is his choice, under his control, to make this decision. Ask the group members to give him feedback about the quality of relationships when there is no trust.

During a discussion on trust, the issue of secrets and disclosure of secrets may come up. Occasionally you will find that a boy spontaneously tells a previously kept secret, which shows some development of trust on his part. Ask him if he needs anything now in connection with the secret (for example, extra support from you, the other members, or someone else; a chance to discuss the secret in depth). If the secret relates to the boy's molestation, remind him and the rest of the group members that you are required by law to report any instances of abuse.

Trust Checklist

Instructions: For each of the numbered situations that follow, place a check mark in as many columns as are appropriate to designate the person or persons you would choose to tell.

Which of the people indicated would you tell if . . .

Mother *(M)* Father *(F)* Grandparent *(G)* Brother *(B)*
Sister *(S)* Therapist *(T)* Friend *(F)*

	M	F	G	B	S	T	F

1. You made an embarrassing mistake.

2. You had a medical problem that worried you.

3. You felt angry enough to hurt someone.

4. You got an "F."

5. You thought you had a problem with drugs.

6. You wanted to have a girlfriend.

7. You wanted to kill yourself.

8. You thought you made someone pregnant.

9. A friend hurt you.

10. You felt lonely.

11. You decided to run away.

12. You thought about killing yourself.

13. You knew your mom was upset and
    needed some help.

14. You were still being molested.

15. Someone threatened you.

16. You were pressured by friends to use drugs.

17. You saw a good friend shoplift.

18. You were being physically abused at home.

◆ ACTIVITY 21: Taking a Trust Walk

Target Ages
- All

Abuse Issues Addressed
- Mistrust
- Impaired relationships

Objective
- To encourage each child to interact with at least one group member with whom
  he has not previously established a relationship

Rationale
Molested children experience a profound betrayal of trust, which has a significant
impact on their relationships with others. They need to practice taking the risk involved in reestablishing trust, and they need to take the process gradually and carefully, in small steps.

Procedure

This activity is not recommended until group members have become well acquainted with one another and are responsive to limits you have set. If there is
any antagonism between members or if cliques are developing, do not use this
activity. Be sure there are at least two adults available to supervise this activity.

Select a large outside area where it is possible to set some definable boundaries, such as a park or a school playground. Divide group members into pairs,
and give each pair one blindfold. Ask each pair to decide who will be the first boy
to wear the blindfold while the other boy leads him somewhere. *Caution:* If you observe any signs of discomfort about the blindfolds, do not use them; have the boys
close their eyes instead.

Give instructions as follows: "Your first priority is safety. You will be stopped
immediately if we observe any unsafe behavior. Decide together if you and your
partner want to be physically touching during the activity, such as holding hands
or holding on to the leader's shoulder. It is fine if you choose not to be physically
touching in any way."

Then interrupt your instructions to talk about the importance of respecting
personal space and boundaries. Interact with your cotherapist to demonstrate.
The two of you stand facing each other, with several feet of distance between you;
then you both move progressively closer and closer to each other until one of
you is uncomfortable and speaks up. Emphasize that trust is enhanced when you
respect another person's personal space and boundaries.

Proceed with the instructions: "The leader's task is to take his partner on a
tour of the area and to describe it using as many senses as possible. ('Smell the
flowers,' 'Feel the wind on your face,' 'Listen to the cars in the distance.') The
leader needs to talk continually, paying special attention to and warning his partner about any possible pitfalls."

Ask the pairs to spend ten minutes walking. The adults will notify each pair
when the ten minutes is up, and then ask the partners to switch roles and repeat
the walk.

After the pairs have completed their walk and reassembled together as a
group, encourage discussion of how the activity felt. Ask the following questions:

- How did it feel to be led without being able to see? Did your feelings change
  the longer the tour went on?
- Was it harder to be the leader or the partner being led?
- What did you observe about yourself that can help you with current trust
  problems?

Common Responses

A boy may withdraw during this activity if he feels pressure to participate. Encourage his participation by offering as many choices as possible to help him feel more relaxed; for example, he might start by being the leader, pair with you or your cotherapist, or only observe the walk initially.

Occasionally you may encounter overt hostility when the trust walk is introduced. Do not have a child participate if this is his reaction. Instead, address the hostility directly and explore it with him to gain better understanding of why it is coming up now. (He may be pushing people away to avoid any further hurt; he may be reminded of an experience with someone important who betrayed him; or he may feel threatened by any physical contact with his peers.) Offer any interpretations carefully, as you want him to continue talking about the issue as fully as possible.

◆ ACTIVITY 22: Deciding Who Will Know

Target Ages
- All

Abuse Issues Addressed
- Fears
- Powerlessness
- Loss of control

Objective
- To decrease secrecy by sharing about his abuse with one person of his choice

Rationale

Every boy needs to decide for himself whether people are told about his molestation and which specific individuals are told. The process of decision making can seem difficult, yet it is empowering for him to experience having choices.

Procedure

On a chalkboard or a large poster, draw a number of circles and label each with a role. Include *teacher, neighbor, best friend, coach, friend's mom, aunt, uncle,* several labeled *friend,* and so on. Leave some of the circles untitled, as the boys may add more roles.

Distribute paper and pencils and ask each boy to write down all of the people who know that he was molested. One way to get a thorough list is to ask each boy to recall the circumstances surrounding his disclosure: who was involved, with whom did he speak, and what events have occurred since that time. If he cannot remember a particular name, help him identify the person somehow, by role or description. Examples are "the cop who came out after I told my mom" or "the lady who talked to my class about abuse."

Ask each boy to put a check mark next to each individual whom he told or whom he agreed could be informed. There is likely to be extreme variation in responses. For some boys the victimization remains essentially a secret; for others, parents may have told anyone who would listen.

Next, ask if any of the boys who have not previously informed their teachers now want to do so. Write those boys' names inside the circle labeled *teacher.* Go through each circle in this manner. Ask for volunteers to share their reasons for each response and list those reasons.

Finally, discuss the positive and negative consequences that might occur if a boy discloses as well as those that might occur if he continues to keep the secret. (A primary fear to talk about is the fear of what others will think, say, or do in response to the knowledge.)

As deciding whether to tell friends is a common dilemma for boys, ask if anyone has already told a friend and would like to share the friend's reactions. Emphasize that no one is able to predict accurately or control the reaction of another person.

Common Responses

Anger may be precipitated during this activity if a boy has had no control over who was told about his abuse. Point out that such an experience contributes to a boy's feelings that he is helpless and not in control. Then make comments such as "You could not control what happened then, but what positive choice can you make right now?" and "It is OK to feel angry, but not OK to be abusive or destructive."

This activity also frequently identifies parents who have told about the abuse indiscriminately and, consequently, need guidance in respecting personal boundaries and maintaining some sense of privacy for their son. You can then emphasize these areas in your contacts with the parents. It might be helpful to educate the boys that sometimes parents tell others only because they need support as well.

◆ ACTIVITY 23: You and the People Around You

Target Ages
- All

Abuse Issues Addressed
- Developing empathy
- Preventing sexually abusive behavior

Objective
- To allow each boy to participate in at least one role play involving the development of skills and his verbalizing wants and needs in a direct, clear way

Rationale

Boys are often not encouraged to consider the impact of their behavior on others, or the feelings of others. Without this encouragement, they tend to act impulsively and only later may become aware of the effects of their behavior. A boy's acceptance of responsibility for himself includes his consciously recognizing and evaluating potential effects before he makes a decision to act.

Procedure

Announce that the boys are going to be involved in role plays during this session. Explain that role plays are often used when people want to learn or practice new skills or learn to empathize with others. Provide a simple definition of empathy: seeing things from another person's point of view.

Depending on the age and sophistication of your group members, you may need to help each boy individually prepare for his role ahead of time. Another group may do fine with just the instructions "Play this part" or "Pretend you are this person."

Select role plays that are applicable to the boys' own lives. After each role play, be sure to talk about it so that the observers can give feedback and you can emphasize recognizing and considering another person's feelings.

Some sample role plays follow; each involves only two roles.

- Two boys give feedback to each other, both positive and negative, about their appearance.
- Your mom or dad is talking for the first time with the person who molested you.
- You try out for soccer and make the team. Talk to your best friend, who was not selected.
- Your neighbor is mad at your parent for putting up a new fence.

- Your brother has just ruined an important project you were doing for school.
- A teacher has lost control of a boy who clowns around in the classroom.
- A therapist has to talk with a child who prefers to remain silent.
- A new boy in town is trying to make a friend on his first day of school.
- A busy, stressed-out dad is asked by his son for a ride to football practice.

Common Responses

Some members will see this as a fun or silly activity and will not take it seriously. They will exaggerate or behave so that peers will laugh and maybe join in. If only one boy is reacting this way, try to withdraw all attention from his disruptive behavior so that he is not the focus of the group. Ignoring him will either lessen the behavior or cause him to be even more disruptive. Tell him that you expect him to participate without being silly or exaggerating, and give him options if he chooses not to do so (for example, sitting quietly and watching, or leaving the room).

Boys will also express varying levels of understanding about empathy. Provide examples that demonstrate this concept, such as caring, support, listening, understanding and acknowledging feelings.

◆ ACTIVITY 24: Making and Keeping Friends

Target Ages

- Seven through twelve

Abuse Issues Addressed

- Isolation
- Impaired relationships

Objective

- To assist the boys in identifying and sharing negative beliefs that add to their sense of isolation

Rationale

A peer support system is vitally important for boys who are healing from sexual abuse. They need to learn how to interact socially with peers, to engage in age-appropriate childhood activities, and to use peer support as they gradually become more independent from their families.

Procedure

This activity requires some advance preparation and three adults (preferably three therapists). Sketch out a role play for two boys (played by the other two adults) who are meeting for the first time on a playground. In the role play, you want to show the boys several examples of poor social skills (problematic behaviors) that will interfere with making and keeping friends.

Start the session with the role play. Immediately after the first problematic behavior, stop the role players and ask the group members to identify that behavior. Use a question such as "What is he doing that will make others not want to be around him?" When someone correctly identifies the problem behavior, write it on a chalkboard or a poster. Then have the players resume their roles. Follow this same procedure for each example of problematic behavior. Behaviors that can be demonstrated through the role play include the following:

- Not asking for or using someone's name
- Bossiness
- Selfishness or unwillingness to share
- Threatening
- Boasting
- Teasing
- Kicking
- Hitting someone
- Withdrawing and refusing to speak
- Manipulating someone
- Responding in a hurtful way to the other person's request for feedback

After the role play, work with the group members to establish a list of positive social skills. (Start with the recorded list of problematic social skills and ask the boys to identify opposites; then ask the boys to contribute their own ideas of positive social skills.)

Before the boys leave, make and distribute copies of the positive list.

Common Responses

Watching someone being hurt by a peer's comment can trigger boys' memories of similar hurtful experiences. Spend some time on the value of giving simple, nonthreatening feedback with the purpose of helping someone rather than hurting him. Point out that comments on someone's behavior that are painfully blunt or attacking serve no useful purpose; instead, they hurt the other person and usually provoke angry retaliation. Remind the boys of the principles of giving legitimate feedback.

If you have time, have the boys practice giving feedback, and correct any errors they make. Explain that for the group members to be effective in helping each other, they need to give and receive feedback that is honest, significant, and respectful.

Additional intervention can include helping the boys identify outside interests or activities they enjoy that are not solitary. Although some ideas may need parental involvement and financial support (for example, joining an organized sport), others are free and can be carried out by the boy on his own.

◆ ACTIVITY 25: Creating "Self" and "Offender" Drawings

Target Ages
- Seven through twelve

Abuse Issues Addressed
- Feelings about the perpetrator
- Powerlessness

Objectives
- To offer each boy an opportunity to experience the calming and relaxing effects of drawing
- To encourage each boy to identify and illustrate at least one personal strength

Rationale
Art therapy is a useful technique for helping children express emotions and regain mastery. Art-related activities can be calming and relaxing, which gives a child some control over upsetting emotions.

Procedure: Part 1
Supply a large piece of paper for each boy, and a variety of felt-tipped markers and other drawing instruments. If you have plenty of time for cleaning up and have a group of boys with good impulse control, you can use paints.

Instruct each boy to pretend that he owns a magic wand; ask him to imagine that he can use the magic wand to turn the person who molested him into an animal. Ask him to think for a moment about what kind of animal he would choose.

If this is difficult for a boy, ask him to imagine the offender as a make-believe creature. Once he is able to visualize the creature or animal, ask him to draw it, leaving plenty of room on the paper to draw something else later. Allow plenty of time and encourage the boys to include as many details as possible.

Procedure: Part 2

Do not begin part 2 until all boys have finished part 1. Instruct each boy to imagine that with the same magic wand he can turn himself into any kind of animal or creature he wants. Ask each boy to think for a moment about the kind of animal or creature he would choose and then to draw that figure on the same page with the offender figure. Again, encourage the boys to include as many details as possible.

After the boys have completed their drawings, ask each to describe his offender and self figures by answering the following questions:

- What are the characteristics of your "offender" creature?
- What is it about this creature that reminds you of the offender?
- What are the characteristics of your "self" creature?
- What is it about this creature that reminds you of yourself?
- If your "self" creature could say anything to your "offender" creature and be perfectly safe, what would he say?

Share any observations or interpretations that encourage a sense of empowerment. You might ask such questions as the following:

- How is your "self" creature strong, powerful, smart, or creative?
- Which of your abilities could you use to outsmart the "offender" creature?

Reflect all feelings that the boys convey. Then encourage group members to be in control of what they want to do with their drawings. Some may want to take their drawings home, destroy them, or display them in the group's meeting room.

With time-limited groups, it is very useful to do this activity early in the treatment process. Write down the boys' comments and your observations, and save the drawings. Then, toward the end of treatment, conduct this activity again; ask the boys to compare the two sets of drawings, and discuss how the boys have changed since the beginning of therapy.

Common Responses

Sometimes a boy has difficulty attributing anything positive or powerful to his "self" creature. If this is the case, keep his drawing and encourage him to think some more about his positive qualities until the next group session. If he still has trouble, ask the group members to provide some feedback.

◆ ACTIVITY 26: Differentiating Anger That Helps from Anger That Hurts

Target Ages
- Seven through twelve

Abuse Issue Addressed
- Anger

Objective
- To encourage each boy to recognize his responsibility for the consequences of his own angry behavior and to demonstrate his awareness of that responsibility

Rationale

In attempting to manage out-of-control behaviors, many parents mistakenly convey the message that anger itself is bad or wrong. One of the tasks of therapy is to clarify that anger is a normal and justified response to being abused. How a boy chooses to express that anger, however, determines whether it is helpful or harmful.

Procedure

This topic is addressed through discussion and teaching initially. Role playing is also a good way to demonstrate and practice "healthy" anger. Begin the activity by describing a few examples of "healthy" anger. It is important to make the descriptions simple and concrete. Consider comments such as the following: "*When you are physically threatened,* it's OK to use anger or aggression to protect yourself. *When someone violates your boundaries,* it's OK to use anger to set limits with that person and say no. *When you are afraid of someone or something,* it's OK to use anger to overcome your fears or mobilize yourself to take some action."

Normalize anger as a justified response to any kind of abuse: "Most boys who have been abused feel anger, and need to express it in order to feel better." Let the boys know that any time you see this expression of anger in the group, you will support it.

Then explain that although the emotion itself is neither good nor bad, how someone chooses to let it out can be either healthy behavior or destructive behavior. Define a hurtful response to anger in this way: "Anger is hurtful when you use it to control, intimidate, threaten, manipulate, or harm someone else. It never feels good to another person to be controlled, intimidated, threatened, manipulated, or harmed."

Explain that when each boy becomes angry, he needs to stop for a moment and think about a behavioral response designed for self-protection, not for hurting another person or damaging property.

Common Responses

Boys often have no experience with the positive expression of anger, because no one has modeled it for them. You may have to make a special effort to point out in the group any examples that demonstrate such positive expression, so that members can learn to differentiate. Depressed boys in particular will need much encouragement to recognize and verbalize anger.

◆ ACTIVITY 27: Identifying Your Anger Zone

Target Ages
- Seven through thirteen

Abuse Issues Addressed
- Anger
- Aggression

Objectives
- To help each boy identify both negative and positive (ineffective and effective) responses to anger
- To encourage the boys to start substituting positive, effective responses for "acting out" when they become angry

Rationale

"Acting out," or behaving as if one were out of control, is a common residual for young molested boys and generally occurs when they are angry. They need to learn to release their feelings physically in an alternative way that is safe and effective.

Procedure: Part 1

To begin this activity discuss how anger is experienced differently by different people. As a result, effective ways to release or discharge anger will also vary from individual to individual. Jewett (1982) suggests helping children identify which part of their body energy goes to when they are angry (mouth, hands, or legs and feet) then finding safe outlets to release anger using that same area.

Ask each boy to remember the last time he felt extremely angry. Ask the following questions:

- Who was there?
- What happened to make you so angry?
- Did anyone tell you not to be mad?
- What was your first reaction—yelling, running away, hitting, slamming doors, breaking something?

Next ask the boys to give examples of the ways in which they have responded so far when feelings of anger have arisen in the group. Record and post their answers.

Then ask, "What kinds of angry behaviors help you feel better afterward?" Circle or highlight at least one behavior for each boy that reduces his anger and label with each boy's name. This list will give you an idea of the anger zone for each of your members. You, your cotherapist, and the boys will find the list helpful in redirecting angry behaviors so feelings can be released. Activity 28 is needed to complete this discussion area.

Procedure: Part 2

Distribute paper and pencils and ask each boy to make a list of all the people, situations, and circumstances that have caused him to feel anger or resentment. After all boys have completed the task, ask them for examples and help each boy recognize any patterns. Before ending the group, encourage the boys to practice positive responses to anger as much as possible, both in and outside the group.

Common Responses

Some boys may never have felt a sense of relief or release from their anger, for a variety of reasons. For example, the modeling provided by a boy's significant others at home may involve a different body zone than the one he prefers. Parents may also have difficulty permitting a child to express anger in certain ways, such as swearing or yelling. Sometimes they shut the child down before he has adequately ventilated what he is feeling.

Be sure to let the boys know that everyone is different and that the purpose of the activity is to find what works best for each of them. Offer to help the boys experiment in the group so that together you can monitor how they feel after using different techniques.

Not all boys act out in response to angry feelings, and you need to address this issue. Explain how keeping angry feelings inside can lead to other types of problems, including depression and physical illness. Emphasize that everyone is different in regard to what he feels and what he chooses to do about it.

◆ ACTIVITY 28: Releasing and Resolving Anger

Target Ages
- All

Abuse Issues Addressed
- Anger
- Aggression

Objective
- To assist each boy in creating a list of nonaggressive alternatives for managing his anger

Rationale

Boys need to learn nondestructive ways to express uncomfortable emotions. This activity gives them the opportunity to try out new behaviors in a nonthreatening environment.

Procedure

Note: Complete Activity 27 prior to conducting this one.

Place the boys into three groups, depending on where in their bodies they feel a surge of energy in response to anger: (1) mouth, (2) hands, or (3) legs and feet. Give each group a variety of supplies and ask the boys to make an item that will assist them in discharging anger with their preferred area of the body. Here are the kinds of supplies you will need, divided according to the three groupings:

"Mouth" group: materials for creating something to be used in "voicing" anger, either literally or figuratively: paper, stapler, and writing utensils to make a journal; a cardboard box, scraps of newspaper or paper towels, and a cardboard tube (from which the boys construct a "yelling box" by filling the box with wadded newspaper or paper towels, and cutting a hole in the box lid into which the tube can be inserted, thus enabling a boy to yell into the tube and not disturb others); chewing gum or a chewy kind of candy; and a tape recorder and tape so that a boy can record his feelings when he is angry

"Hands" group: clay and such instruments as mallets, cookie cutters, and dull knives for cutting; foam cuttings to rip and stuff into something, pillowcases or paper bags, scissors, and fabric markers (for creating items such as punching bags, covered with words and pictures to represent anger triggers); newspaper to rip up; drawing paper for scribbling or drawing the focus of angry feelings; sponges to throw in a room where nothing will be damaged; any other supplies for writing and drawing

"Legs and feet" group: a pillowcase and paper (or old T-shirts or foam) to tear up and stuff into the pillowcase, age-appropriate materials for closing the pillowcase after stuffing (for creating a stuffed ball that can be kicked or stomped on); sturdy cardboard boxes and felt-tipped markers or other materials (for decorating boxes and then kicking them in an outdoor area)

To get the groups started, you may need to suggest some ideas. Usually the children themselves will come up with additional ideas once they have the supplies; then you can use their ideas as examples in subsequent groups.

In addition to practicing methods of physical release, children can also be taught how to resolve anger by analyzing or thinking through a situation differently in order to decrease their feelings of anger. (This concept is addressed more fully in other activities that address prevention of offending behavior. However, beginning to discuss it here will start the boys thinking about alternative ways to release or control anger.)

If you do not have the resources to provide materials for creating objects, you and your cotherapist may act in a role play in which you play two close friends, one of whom ignores or rudely dismisses the other. The one who is dismissed needs to speak out loud some of the thoughts that would lead to angry feelings, then act aggressively in response to the anger. Then carry out the role play again, with the one who is dismissed using a different approach, rethinking the situation aloud, and then acting nonaggressively but effectively. During subsequent discussion, compare the two role plays; encourage the boys to think about what they can do in response to their anger while they are in the situation. Emphasize that they need to begin practicing the skill of reframing the ways in which they think about situations that provoke their anger. You want to help the boys understand that when they are angry it is empowering to recognize the feeling and consciously choose to do something about the anger that releases it and is not harmful to anyone. This is in contrast to getting angry and reacting impulsively. That is when children feel the emotion is controlling them.

Common Responses

Some parents become very upset with concrete methods for discharging anger and do not understand the purpose or value of such methods. Be aware that some parents typically do not encourage any expression of anger (as a result of believing that the child "should not be angry") and therefore will need to explore the dynamics of their own anger in addition to dealing with their children's anger. Consequently, prior to conducting this activity, you will need to inform the parents about what the children will be doing with the items they make and bring home.

It is a good idea to write the instructions for completing this activity and the limits you set on the use of the created items; then you can send the written instructions home with the children so that parents can review them. Explain in the instructions that this activity encourages children to devise creative and appropriate ways to regain their personal control.

◆ ACTIVITY 29: Differentiating Assertive from Aggressive Behavior

Target Ages
- All

Abuse Issues Addressed
- Anger
- Aggressive behavior

Objective
- To foster each boy's understanding of the differences between assertive and aggressive behavior

Rationale
The boys need to recognize there are long-term negative consequences to expressing anger aggressively. A healthier alternative is to learn and practice assertive behavior.

Procedure
Begin by providing simple, clear, age-appropriate definitions of assertiveness and aggressiveness. Following are some examples of ways to define assertiveness:

- Asking for what you want or need
- Standing up for yourself and your rights without being hurtful to others
- Expressing your feelings and thoughts

Explain that assertive communication is direct and clear and does not attack the other person. Then offer examples of ways to define aggressiveness:

- Doing or saying something that hurts or threatens someone else
- Getting what you want at the expense of another person

Younger boys find it easier to distinguish between the two if you ask them to test any given behavior or comment by asking themselves, "Is this a mean thing to say or do?" Explain that if the answer is yes, usually the behavior is aggressive.

Write two or more brief role plays that involve common situations for boys in the age range with which you are working; each role play needs to portray a situation in which one person wants something from a second person. Make one of the role plays illustrate the use of aggressive behavior in getting something; then create one or more that illustrate assertive behavior in getting something. In the entire set of role plays, make sure that there is at least one example from a home situation, one from a school setting, and one that involves interacting with a peer.

If you are working with a cotherapist, the two of you will act out each role play, one at a time, during a group session. If you are working alone, choose a group member to play the role of the second person (who receives your aggressive or assertive behavior); you and he need to step away from the other group members for a few minutes so that you can coach him specifically on what you want him to do. (For the role plays to have the intended effect, you want the boy to respond negatively to your aggressive behavior and positively to your assertive behavior; although you need to explain this, the boy will probably have an inclination to react the way you want him to.)

After each role play, ask the boys to share whether they thought the boy who wanted something used aggressive or assertive behavior. Ask such questions as the following:

- On what did you base your decision?
- In which role plays did you feel that the person who wanted something was likely to get what he wanted?
- How did you feel about watching someone behave in an aggressive manner? Have you ever been in a similar situation? If so, how did you choose to work it out?
- How did you feel about watching the assertive behavior?

If there is time, repeat the role play that illustrated aggressive behavior; however, this time use an assertive approach instead. Younger boys may need assistance in differentiating the two approaches.

Practicing and rehearsing assertiveness and seeing it modeled teaches abused boys that their needs can be met, and problems solved, without aggression.

The following are some sample role-play situations (note that some apply more to younger boys or to older ones):

- An older child grabs a younger child's lunch and starts to eat it (can be an example of either assertion or aggression).
- One teenager sees a second teenager bothering his girlfriend and approaches him about it.
- A young boy (or girl) has been going in and out of an older brother's bedroom without permission. (The older sibling confronts the younger.)
- A sibling is having a rough time and is taking it out on everyone in the family. (Another sibling confronts the first.)
- Your dad tells you he does not like your friend John and restricts you from seeing him.
- A supervisor keeps forgetting to pay a subordinate overtime for work done more than a month ago.
- A child has repeatedly asked a math teacher for some extra help; the teacher always promises to get back to the child but never does.

Common Responses

Boys of all ages will benefit from having a simple way to remember how to respond assertively. You may want to make and display an assertiveness poster that includes the following information as a reminder.

> When you want to be assertive, you say
> "I *think*" (state what the facts are)
> "I *feel*" (state how the facts affect you emotionally)
> "I *want*" (ask for a change)
> An assertive statement deals with one thing at a time
> and is specific and focused.

Boys may disclose that aggression is expected and encouraged in their homes. They may report that they hear such messages as "Boys always fight; otherwise you're a sissy." If a child tells you something like this, request a meeting with the parent to assess how much support, if any, there would be to help the child change his aggressive behavior.

With certain families or living situations, giving up aggression is not a realistic goal. You will then have to help the boy differentiate between expectations at home and expectations in other places (at school, in sports, and in therapy). If he can replace aggression with assertive behavior in one of these other areas, he may at least get some exposure to positive outcomes.

◆ ACTIVITY 30: Recognizing What's Always OK and What's Never OK

Target Ages
- Seven through ten

Abuse Issues Addressed
- Clarifying what constitutes abusive behavior
- Developing awareness of feelings

Objective
- To teach each boy to recognize situations or circumstances that can make him vulnerable to remolestation

Rationale
Prevention of additional abuse is an important aspect of treatment. Children need to be able to recognize risk situations early, and one way to do this is for them to recognize uncomfortable emotions and then act on them.

Procedure
On index cards, write descriptions of a variety of situations involving different examples of touching (one situation per card). Some situations need to depict inappropriate touching; others need to depict appropriate touching; still others need to be ambiguous or dependent on circumstances not known. Incorporate opposite-sex and same-sex situations as well as a mixture of children and adults.

Give each boy a card and ask the boys to take turns reading the situations aloud; after each is read, ask the group to decide together whether the touching described is always OK, sometimes OK (depending on the circumstances), or never OK. Point out that many situations involve a gray area—the behavior may be OK in some circumstances but not in others—then ask the boys to discuss how they would make a decision about what to do in an ambiguous situation.

Incorporate discussion of feelings as very important tools in decision making. For some situations, for example, you might ask the boys how they think a child (rather than an adult) might feel under those circumstances. If the boys are younger, you might want to display a poster of "feelings" faces (happy, sad, uncertain); the illustrations can help them correctly label a wide range of emotions.

The following are some sample situations:

- Taking a shower together (child and adult)
- Receiving a body massage or back rub
- Tickling
- Hugging

- Punching so that a bruise or cut is left
- Being asked to undress so that pictures can be taken
- Touching someone else's private parts
- Touching your own private parts
- Insisting that a child sleep in the same bed with a parent or older child
- Spanking with a hand
- Spanking with a belt or other item
- Parents being naked in front of their children
- Parents being sexual with each other in front of their children
- Someone coming into the bathroom when you are using the toilet or bathing
- An aunt or uncle wanting to hug and kiss you, but you do not want to
- Watching someone else change clothes
- Hitting someone in the face

Common Responses

You may hear disclosure of additional physical or sexual abuse. If this is the case, inform the boy in question that you must contact his parent and report the abuse to authorities.

You also may hear about current situations that appear to be high risk. In such a case you will need to intervene with the parent, suggest alternatives, and clearly explain the reasons for your recommendations.

◆ ACTIVITY 31: Fear Mural

Target Ages
- All

Abuse Issues Addressed
- Fears
- Anxiety

Objective
- To encourage each boy to develop at least one behavioral or cognitive coping skill to use when he experiences fear

Rationale

Molested boys often have fears that are extremely difficult for them to acknowledge. It is important for them to identify and discuss these fears so that misinformation can be corrected and coping skills developed or enhanced. Sometimes the fear is greatly lessened just by hearing someone else voice it.

Procedure

Provide a piece of newsprint or butcher paper that is large enough to allow all group members to work on it simultaneously (to create a mural). With a large group, you may want to tape the paper to a table or to the floor. If your group has good impulse control and you have adequate time for preparation and cleanup, you can have the children use paints. Otherwise, have them use felt-tipped markers, crayons, and colored pencils.

Instruct the boys either to sit in a relaxed position or to lie down; then ask them to close their eyes. Encourage deep breathing to assist with both physical and mental relaxation. Ask each boy to remember a time when he felt afraid and to recall who was there, what was being said, what happened, and what other feelings he had in addition to fear. Do not make this a prolonged visualization, as your purpose is only to focus on a memory in order to allow feelings to surface. *Caution:* Do not suggest specifically that each boy remember a time when he was molested.

Encourage the boys to relax and continue deep breathing throughout, reminding them they are in a safe place. Use words such as the following to end the imagery: "Before you open your eyes, imagine yourself back in our room together. You're sitting with the other group members, and your counselors [or 'leaders' or 'therapists,' depending on how you refer to yourself and your cotherapist] are also here. Take another deep breath and feel your body sitting comfortably on the chair or on the floor. You are in a safe place. When you are ready, slowly open your eyes."

Explain that the boys are to use the paper and other supplies to create a mural illustrating the things they fear. Ask each boy to draw as many feared things as he can remember. As the boys work on the mural, encourage them to talk about what they fear. (They may find it easier to discuss and deal with their fears in general before they go on to specific things—situations, people, objects, and so on— that scare them.) When they hear they are not alone in feeling afraid, and when those fears are acknowledged and normalized, they may find it easier to explore specific fears having to do with their abuse.

Point out that fears become more exaggerated and intense if a person avoids discussing them until it is impossible to ignore them. Try to keep the discussion focused on one fear at a time and on how each boy is affected now by that fear. Some examples of fears that abused boys commonly experience include fear that the perpetrator might harm him, fear that someone might walk in and discover what was happening, fear of getting a sexually transmitted disease, fear of dying, and fear of being perceived as gay. This activity commonly identifies fears that the boys may have never before been able to verbalize.

Common Responses

Be sure to allow plenty of time for both discussion and deescalation, as even a short visualization can trigger powerful memories and related emotions. Also, one or more boys may report having flashbacks, or you may observe dissociative behaviors. Use such responses to educate the boys about flashbacks and dissociative symptoms. Let them know that many things can trigger flashbacks, such as sights, sounds, smells, or touches. Explain that one way to lessen the impact of flashbacks is to identify possible triggers and then to try to change the circumstances associated with the triggers.

Discuss dissociative behaviors as a response to trauma that serves to protect a child from pain or hurt. Explain that there might be changes in memory (such as memory gaps), in perception (such as persistent feelings of detachment), in identity, and even in consciousness. Give concrete age-appropriate examples. For example, you might state that a boy with dissociative symptoms might appear to be lying (because he cannot remember things that others have witnessed and, therefore, denies that these things happened). A boy with dissociative symptoms might also engage in fantasy play; have imaginary friends; appear absentminded or inattentive; or exhibit erratic moods, behavior, and appearance. A detailed assessment is recommended for any child who exhibits dissociation, as it is frequently missed in children. Treatment recommendations will vary, depending on the severity of symptoms.

◆ ACTIVITY 32: Conquering Nightmares

Target Ages

- Seven through eleven

Abuse Issues Addressed

- Sleep disturbance
- Fear
- Anxiety

Objectives

- To encourage each child and his parent to monitor and record the child's nightmares over a one-month period
- To help lessen the frequency and severity of nightmares and sleep disturbances

Rationale

Nightmares are common in young abused children and are related to ongoing stress, fears, anxiety, depression, or a combination of these. Learning skills to master nightmares gives the child a sense of control. Sleep disturbances require prompt intervention, as ongoing fatigue will impair the child's ability to cope with everyday life.

Procedure

Begin by reading aloud a book about nightmares or scary feelings, such as Mercer Mayer's *There's a Nightmare in My Closet*. Then distribute paper, pencils, and felt-tipped markers and ask each boy to draw a nightmare that he has experienced recently. (If a child says that he has not had nightmares, ask him to draw a fear.)

If you find resistance to doing this, you can offer to assist a boy in drawing his nightmare or ask him to describe it as you draw. When each boy has a visual representation in front of him, you will then work with each boy individually as peers listen. Have the child close his eyes and in his imagination carry out the things that you suggest to him to conquer the nightmare (or the fear). You want to use description and simple action techniques to empower him with a sense of control over his fears. The following are some suggestions:

- Exaggerate one part of your picture so it becomes silly instead of scary.
- Imagine you have a powerful eraser to "wipe out" whatever part of the picture you want.
- Pretend the picture is on a television screen; simply reach out and change the channel to a picture you want to see.
- Scribble out the picture with a dark-colored felt-tipped marker.
- Take a deep breath and see the picture fading completely as you blow it out.
- Imagine a bomb blast that destroys the scary dream.
- Pretend that you have a magic item that can protect you against anything scary, and use it.

Note: Another group activity for younger boys is to create that magic object, such as a wand or a hat, which can be a symbol for self-protection.

Younger boys may need help in visualizing and practicing these ideas so that they will be able to use these skills when nightmares or fears occur.

Parents may not understand how imagination can be used in a self-empowering way, so be sure they are informed about the purpose of using the visualization skills. Explain that their sons will not be likely to continue trying these ideas if they are discouraged from doing so at home.

Common Responses

Group members may be reluctant to talk about nightmares because of high levels of fear about the dream content. As an intervention, choose a less scary dream to practice with instead. Contact the child's parent to establish whether there is any pattern to the nightmares. Consider, for example, whether they might be triggered by such factors as illness, fatigue, family stress, or events (anticipated visitation with a noncustodial parent, for instance). Discuss whether any of these triggers can be avoided in order to decrease the frequency of nightmares.

◆ ACTIVITY 33: Practicing the Problem-Solving Process

Target Ages
- All

Abuse Issues Addressed
- Powerlessness
- Helplessness

Objectives
- To acquaint the boys with an effective process for solving problems
- To encourage each boy to practice this process using a problem of his choice

Rationale

Most abused boys enter therapy lacking the knowledge they need to solve problems and make decisions effectively. Learning an effective process for solving problems and practicing the steps involved help alleviate feelings of helplessness and build a sense of empowerment.

Procedure: Part 1

This activity requires a minimum of two group sessions. During the first session, introduce and explain the steps involved in the problem-solving process, using age-appropriate language:

1. Define the problem (the *current* situation—things as they are right now) as clearly and specifically as possible. Break it down into its separate components or manageable pieces. What is happening right now?
2. Describe the resolution (the *desired* situation—things as you would like them to be). What would you like to be happening?

3. Identify the factors that are contributing to the problem (behaviors, events, circumstances, and so on, that are causing things to stay as they are, instead of as you would like them to be). What is keeping you from creating the desired situation?

4. Brainstorm ways to overcome the barriers and turn the desired situation into reality. (*Brainstorming* refers to a group process in which the members generate as many ideas as possible as quickly as they can. All ideas are listed on a chalkboard or a poster; no one is allowed to evaluate them until everyone has run out of ideas. You can brainstorm by yourself by listing all your ideas, one after another and as quickly as possible until you do not have any more. Do not stop to consider whether your ideas will work.)

5. Evaluate the ideas listed. Choose one to try—something that might change the current situation into the desired situation and something that you can actually do.

6. Figure out what you need in order to act on your choice. Decide who or what can help you; then get the necessary resources.

7. Examine the potential consequences of your choice, in terms of both positive and negative outcomes.

8. Rehearse (practice) the option you selected.

9. Carry out the selected option.

10. Evaluate the outcome: How have things changed? Has the problem been resolved? Have you created the desired situation? If not, start again with step 5.

Explain that by learning this process and following these steps, the boys are more likely to solve or resolve their problems. As you explain each step, record it on a large poster that can be displayed prominently during this and subsequent sessions. If you want, you can also create a handout for distribution.

To help members follow the process from beginning to end, ask for a volunteer to share a current problem. As an alternative, if you have a cotherapist, you and your cotherapist can demonstrate the process using a role play.

Procedure: Part 2

During the next session, have the boys take turns selecting problems and going through the problem-solving steps, approaching each problem as a group task. Depending on the problems selected, this process could take as much as one group session per child.

The boys' current inability to cope with problems may be due to lack of motivation, resources, opportunity, or skills. Therefore, this process with each boy might address issues such as how to motivate oneself, how to develop and practice the skills necessary to solve problems, and how to obtain resources.

Distribute pencils and index cards or paper. Ask each boy to choose a current problem that he would like to resolve and to complete step 1 of the problem-solving process. Remind the boys that this is an opportunity to practice trusting others by giving and receiving help from one another. Younger children may need examples, such as fighting, nightmares, getting poor grades at school, or not seeing a parent enough. Monitor the process of problem selection and check each child's problem. If a boy identifies a problem situation over which he has no control (such as the divorce of his parents), make this point in the group and have him choose either some aspect of the problem that he can control or another problem.

Collect the cards, choose one, and walk the group through each step of the problem-solving process. Involve all the members in brainstorming, encouraging questions and clearly announcing each step as you progress. If you prefer, you may have the boys role play the entire sequence of steps, with you, your cotherapist, and volunteers playing the various roles. Make sure that you, your cotherapist, or a volunteer from the group records all of the members' ideas accurately on a chalkboard or poster.

During step 8 (rehearsal), encourage the boys to support one another. Practicing can feel very risky, so give each child as much control as possible. If you are resolving a boy's problem in a role play, for example, let him decide who will play his father. Does he want to practice today or during the next session? Does he want the other members to observe or just listen with their eyes closed?

Ensure that each boy decides on a realistic time for carrying out his selected option. Later you need to follow up with each child: Did he try the solution? Was the solution effective? If not, the child needs to return to the problem-solving process to develop a second alternative. The boys need to see that first choices do not always work, yet this does not mean the problem cannot be solved.

Common Responses

You may see overt expressions of anger, because this activity can trigger feelings of powerlessness. Emphasize that learning and practicing both problem-solving and decision-making skills counteracts powerlessness. Also stress that although the boys cannot always control certain situations, they can control their responses to those situations.

If a boy consistently demonstrates poor decision making, accompanied by irrational or distorted thinking, his interactions with other children require close monitoring. These two areas are potential risk factors for development of perpetrating behavior.

When following up with your group members about their decisions, you may discover that lack of support at home led to a lack of follow-through. If you can, arrange to meet with the parent in question to explain why practice in solving problems is so important for abused boys, and request cooperation. Point out the benefits to the parent when a boy is less angry and takes more responsibility.

◆ ACTIVITY 34: What If?

Target Ages
- Seven through twelve

Abuse Issues Addressed
- Powerlessness
- Helplessness
- Low self-esteem

Objectives
- To help the boys recognize potentially problematic or dangerous situations
- To assist each boy in identifying self-protective actions available to him

Rationale

Increased knowledge and practice with prevention, self-protection, and problem-solving skills help a child regain a sense of mastery and competence. The better prepared he is to cope with potential problems—especially another attempted abuse—the more empowered he will feel.

Procedure

Lead the boys in brainstorming potentially problematic or dangerous situations that require using problem-solving skills, determining appropriate responses, and behaving assertively. On index cards, write down each situation in the form of a question starting with "What if . . . ?" The following are some examples:

- What if a teacher repeatedly asked you to stay after school to help, and you felt weird about being alone with her?
- What if your dad's girlfriend gave you a kiss on the mouth and told you not to tell anyone?
- What if your older brother had friends over to the house when your parents were not home, let them use alcohol or drugs, and joined them in looking at magazine pictures of naked women?
- What if your best friend told you he had a secret that made him feel awful, but someone had told him not to tell?

Divide the group into two teams and give each team a flip chart and a felt-tipped marker. (Using the flip chart and marker, the boys can see their ideas recorded and recognize the value of brainstorming as well as see the progress they are making. If these materials are not available, however, you may give each team a large pad of paper and a pencil.) Appoint one member of each team as the recorder of ideas. Explain that the members are to take turns picking "What if?" cards at random and reading them aloud to the team; then the team will brainstorm ideas for solving the problem, and the recorder will list all ideas.

Allow the generation of ideas for at least twenty minutes, then instruct the teams to stop. Collect each team's lists. State that after the session you will transfer their ideas to a single index card for each boy. The card will not include the problems, only the solutions provided by the entire group. Explain that each boy can keep his card in a place where he can see it and use it whenever necessary (for example, in a wallet, on a bedside table, in a favorite book). Stress that they can use their cards to remind them of all the possible ways in which they can take care of themselves.

Make sure that the cards include the following instructions in some form:

1. Be alert, aware, and careful at all times.
2. Avoid dangerous situations.
3. If someone attempts to approach or abuse you, you can do the following things:
   • Get away.
   • Yell "Fire!"
   • Say no.
   • Tell the person you will tell.
   • Find an adult immediately and ask for help; if the first adult does not respond, find another.
   • Pay attention to how the person looks in case you are asked questions later.

Next lead a discussion on responsibility. Emphasize that abuse is never the child's fault and explain that often it cannot be prevented no matter what a boy does. Stress that when this is the case, the boy can tell one or more adults until the abuser is stopped; this option restores some degree of control to the child.

Common Responses

It is common to hear from boys that they are certain they will never be abused again. If you hear such a comment, encourage the boy's peers to respond to it. Explain that this type of thinking needs to be replaced with a different thought that is based in reality and that improves the boy's ability to take preventive action. Some alternative thoughts are "It's good to be prepared" or "Thinking ahead keeps me on top of things."

Try using earthquake preparedness (or preparedness for tornado or hurricane or whatever disaster, depending on possibilities in your area) as an analogy: "There's a chance that I will never have to use my disaster kit, but there is also a chance that I will. Being prepared can mean the difference between surviving or not, losing my home or not, and being able to help others or not." I point out that I will do everything possible to control those potential negative consequences.

You may also see passivity, with such responses as "There's nothing I can do to keep bad things from happening." Such a comment indicates that the boy feels powerless—that he has no sense of control over the future and no belief in his ability to affect his life. Check in with his parents and with school personnel who see the boy regularly to see if there are any other circumstances that are contributing to powerlessness or depression. Assess for additional depressive symptoms and obtain a medication evaluation if indicated.

◆ ACTIVITY 35: Making Life Choices

Target Ages
- All

Abuse Issues Addressed
- Powerlessness
- Helplessness

Objective
- To help each boy identify areas of his life in which he does have control, areas in which he does not have control, and one area in which he would like more control

Rationale
When boys are victimized, they often see themselves as powerless over all aspects of their lives. To increase their sense of empowerment, they need to know that they do control some areas. It is also important for them to differentiate these areas from the areas they do not control and to plan ways to have greater control where possible.

Procedure

One of the most potentially damaging consequences of sexual abuse is the feeling of powerlessness, helplessness, and being unable to control. If this dynamic is not effectively resolved, it can develop into an identification with the offender and possible offending behavior. You must help boys recognize feelings of helplessness, identify their typical responses to this feeling, and replace those responses with empowering ones.

Begin by reviewing some areas in which the boys may currently have choices. Examples might include the following:

- Whether and to what extent they will participate in the group
- The people they choose as friends
- The snacks they eat
- What they do in response to boredom, anger, and excitement

Emphasize that choices generally depend on the circumstances. Offer examples: the boys may not have a choice about the topics covered in school or about the degree of freedom that a parent allows.

Distribute pencils and copies of the Choices Worksheet. Ask each boy to answer each question as honestly as possible. With younger boys, you might want them to form pairs, with the partners taking turns interviewing each other and recording answers.

When all members have completed the task, invite them to share their responses. Ask such questions as the following:

- Who feels he has many choices in his life?
- Who feels he has very little control over day-to-day decisions? If you do not make the choices, who does?
- Is the situation different for your older brothers or sisters? Why or why not?
- How does it feel to be allowed and encouraged to make choices? How does it feel when you do not have choices?

Encourage each boy to select one area in his life in which he would like to have choices and to make changing that area a priority. Offer suggestions of ways to implement changes and ask the other boys to make suggestions as well.

Common Responses

A child whose responses to the Choices Worksheet are predominantly "Never" or "Sometimes" needs immediate help in the home and school arenas. Ask the parent to come in and complete the same worksheet, but with different instructions: for example, "As a child, how often did you get to make your own choices about . . .?"

This can assist the parent in seeing many areas where it is safe and beneficial to allow the boy to make his own decisions. Explain that being in control of one's choices also means accepting responsibility for the consequences of one's choices—an important aspect of keeping the child from becoming an offender.

If a boy responds to this activity with noncompliant behavior, it may be because the discussion of powerlessness has exacerbated these feelings for him. Confront the behavior and label it as noncompliance. Then suggest alternative behaviors that the boy can use to regain control on his own. If he persists in the noncompliant behavior, be sure to carry out consequences.

You may hear some members express resentment or envy about the life, home, or family situations described by others. To intervene, ask how they can use these feelings to their benefit. Ask them to think about what they can do to change their circumstances. Point out that resentment with passivity only reinforces the victim role.

Choices Worksheet

Instructions: For each of the following areas of life, think about whether you *never* have a choice, you *sometimes* have a choice, or you *always* have a choice; then place an *X* in the appropriate box.

	Never (✔)	Sometimes (✔)	Always (✔)
1. What friends to play with	( )	( )	( )
2. Fighting back if a kid picks on you	( )	( )	( )
3. What to eat at meals	( )	( )	( )
4. What television show to watch	( )	( )	( )
5. Selecting clothes for school	( )	( )	( )
6. Showing angry feelings	( )	( )	( )
7. How to work out a problem with a brother or sister	( )	( )	( )
8. Going to church	( )	( )	( )
9. Your bedtime	( )	( )	( )
10. How to spend your free time	( )	( )	( )
11. What household chores you do	( )	( )	( )
12. What to eat for dessert	( )	( )	( )
13. Going to school every day	( )	( )	( )
14. Hugging or kissing a relative	( )	( )	( )
15. How to spend your allowance	( )	( )	( )
16. Obeying grownups	( )	( )	( )

◆ ACTIVITY 36: Clarifying the Connection Between Abuse and Arousal

Target Ages
- Twelve through eighteen

Abuse Issues Addressed
- Confusion about sexuality
- Homophobia

Objective
- To clear up confusion and alleviate anxiety concerning sexual arousal during abuse

Rationale
When sexual abuse is accompanied by physical arousal on the boy's part, he may feel guilty, confused, or afraid, depending on the meaning he attributes to his physical response. There are common, unspoken fears about physical arousal.

Procedure
Caution: Before you conduct this activity, make sure the boys have received and understood basic information on the following subjects:

- Male physiology
- Male sexual responses; how and why erections occur
- The variety of situations in which stimulation can result in a physical response

Read the following story aloud:

David was molested by his stepfather from the age of seven until he was twelve. Six months after his stepfather abandoned the family, David finally felt safe enough to tell his mother what happened. He was lucky that his mom believed him, told him it was not his fault, and said her husband had to be held responsible for what he did. The police were called, and a detective came to David's school to interview him. The questions were embarrassing, but he was feeling OK until the detective asked the following questions:

- Did his penis change when he made you suck it?
- Did your stepfather come in your mouth? .
- What happened to your penis when your stepdad sucked it?
- Did it feel good?
- Did you like it when he touched your penis?

David answered honestly even though he felt really embarrassed. He told the detective that both his penis and his stepdad's got larger and stiff during the sucking, and that his body felt really good when some stuff came out of his penis. Immediately after this, the detective ended the interview and left. David felt very confused and wondered if he had done or said something wrong. Two weeks later his mom got a letter in the mail, saying that there was not enough evidence to file charges against his stepfather. David thought it was his fault and that something must be wrong with him because of the way his body reacted. He felt so awful he could not tell anyone. All he knew was that something must be wrong with him. He wondered if he was gay.

Ask for comments, feedback, and reactions; use these to guide the discussion. Explain that a boy's arousal during molestation is a physiological response; in and of itself, it says nothing about the boy's sexual orientation or his emotional reaction to the sexual activity. Ask the boys if they have any questions about sexual responses. If you do not know the answer to a specific question, tell the boy that you will research it and get back to him. (Be sure to obtain the answer quickly so that you can talk with him the next time you see him.)

Common Responses

The youngest boys in this age range may exhibit disruptive behavior in response to their anxiety and embarrassment about the topic. Encourage as much open discussion as possible so that you can point out incorrect or inaccurate beliefs, such as the following:

"If I got an erection, that must mean I'm gay" (when offender is male).

"If I did not enjoy it, that must mean I'm gay" (when offender is female).

Ask directly whether the abuse felt good physically and, if so, whether the boys feel guilty about this fact. Continue to use age-appropriate education to clarify sexuality-related concerns.

If one or more boys disclose that they experienced erections during the abuse, peers may attempt to scapegoat. Confront this immediately and be very clear in expressing the need for consideration and respect for everyone in the group. Acknowledge all questions and individual sharing. Make the following points:

- It is a risk to talk about difficult things.
- Taking this risk can have a positive result: those boys who do so are likely to experience the most benefit from their therapy.

◆ ACTIVITY 37: Identifying Your Red Flags

Target Ages
- All

Abuse Issues Addressed
- Powerlessness
- Helplessness

Objective
- To help each boy identify two situations that trigger a feeling of powerlessness and subsequent problematic behaviors

Rationale
In order to implement effective coping mechanisms, each boy needs to recognize what situations (involving people, behaviors, comments, thoughts, feelings, memories, objects, sights, sounds, or whatever) generate a feeling of powerlessness to which he responds negatively

Procedure
Ask the boys to think about situations in which they felt powerless to control their emotions or behavior or both. Cover situations in each of the following environments separately.

- At group sessions
- At home
- At school

As each boy shares, record his responses in a separate column headed with his name. Explain your reasons for recording the members' responses separately: (1) you need this information to help you provide the most effective therapy for each boy, and (2) you plan to make each boy a list of his own triggers so that he can refer to it from time to time. After recording responses related to the group environment, briefly discuss the situations and offer your own observations regarding those occasions.

Ask the boys what kinds of things they usually do when they feel powerless or out of control. Then discuss their responses. Next ask them to compare the lists and point out any similarities or patterns. Give some examples of triggers that molested boys commonly cite: being told what to do, feeling threatened, being criticized, and anticipating criticism or rejection. (These triggers or similar ones will probably appear on more than one list; pointing out commonalities will help the boys feel less isolated.)

Explain that awareness of personal "red flags" can help a boy avoid as many such situations as possible, ask for help before responding with problematic behaviors, or plan alternative responses in advance. With older boys, recommend keeping a journal of feelings of powerlessness, subsequent behaviors, and outcomes. Suggest that they bring their journals to group sessions to discuss the contents.

This session requires follow-up:

- Inform each boy's parent about the child's red flags. Ask the parent to support the boy in his efforts to control his responses to feelings of powerlessness.
- Make each boy a list of his own triggers; distribute the lists at the beginning of the next session.

Common Responses

Some boys may resist changing problematic behaviors. If so, help them recognize what they achieve by using those behaviors—what rewards they gain for being out of control. If the rewards are significant, they may have little or no motivation to change. When this is the case, encourage each boy to consider the long-term consequences of using problematic behaviors (or acting out) to get what he wants. Encourage his peers to give him feedback about their own experiences in trying to deal with people who act out.

Sometimes a boy is unable or unwilling to see his own behavior as problematic. If so, you must confront him. Be sure to discuss the choices he has and emphasize his right to make his own decisions. Remind him that accepting the right to make decisions means that he also must accept responsibility for the consequences that follow from those decisions.

◆ ACTIVITY 38: Taking Preventive Action

Target Ages
- Eleven through eighteen

Abuse Issue Addressed
- Sexually abusive behavior

Objectives
- To make sure each boy understands that being abused does not inevitably mean that he will become an abuser

- To promote the boys' awareness of the potential of becoming abusers and the need to take preventive action

Rationale

Many molested boys and their parents believe that being abused leads a boy to become an abuser himself. Accurate information is essential, in terms of both alleviating their anxiety and encouraging them to take steps to prevent offending behavior.

Procedure

Read the following letter aloud, explaining that it was written by therapists who put together thoughts and feelings they had heard expressed by sexually abused boys:

To all the kids in group:

I've been thinking about writing this letter for a long time. It's a really hard letter to write, but I've decided it might help some kids. There's no easy way to say it— my dad molested me. Even now as I say it, it's hard to believe. Dads aren't supposed to abuse kids. They are supposed to take care of you and help you grow up feeling good about yourself.

Since I first told about being molested, it's taken a long time to feel OK again. In counseling I talked about the feelings I've had about being molested—the fear, anger, guilt, sadness, loneliness, and confusion. Talking about these has helped me feel better.

The hardest thing was feeling that I couldn't do anything about the abuse. I tried to tell my mom, but she didn't seem to listen. I was really afraid of what would happen if I told: people might not believe me, I might get into trouble, or I might even get taken away from my family. Looking back, I think being abused made me feel helpless about lots of different things.

I was trying to find ways not to feel so helpless, and I found out I could control younger kids sometimes. It felt great to be in charge, especially after feeling helpless for so long. I found out I could tell little kids what to do and they did it. I told them to steal money for me, and they did. I told one boy to lie for me, and he did. I told another one to take his clothes off so we could play a game. When he did, I wanted to touch his penis, but I stopped. I was so confused. At the time it felt good to be able to make other kids do what I wanted, but later I felt awful. I worried that maybe I hurt or scared that kid who took his clothes off.

Later I talked about this with my counselor, even though I was scared, and it helped me sort things out. I know it was wrong for my dad to molest me, and it's also wrong for me to touch other kids' private parts. I found out I could get in trouble with the law. I realized that I could have hurt kids in the same way that I was hurt when my dad molested me.

Now I have better ways to feel good about myself and to feel in control, like talking about my feelings with my family. I try to help other kids and spend time with my friends, and I work hard at things I like to do.

I used to feel that there was something wrong with me for all of this to have happened, but now I know that it's not true. It wasn't my fault that my dad sexually abused me, and it wasn't your fault that you were abused either. Thanks for listening.

This letter frequently encourages members to express their own concerns about becoming offenders. After you have finished reading, ask for comments and questions. Emphasize that being abused does not mean that a boy will inevitably abuse others, but it does mean that each of them must take steps to avoid that possibility.

Common Responses

One potential problem is that the group may respond to the letter with anxiety and disruptive behavior. If this happens, divide the boys into two groups to discuss the letter content. Reinforce their ability to talk rather than act out. State that the purpose of reading the letter was to introduce accurate information on the issue of abusing others—an important issue for boys who have been abused themselves.

Explain that therapy gives boys the option to identify and express their feelings in ways that do not hurt anyone. Remind them that they can always make the choice to control both their thinking and their behavior.

Another potential problem is that some boys may drop out as a result of introducing the topic of preventing offending behavior. Although the initial assessment calls for informing boys and their parents that therapy will address this topic, you may find that either the boys or their parents cannot handle it. If someone drops out, you need to talk openly with the group, as the remaining members may be feeling both angry and abandoned.

It is very important to talk through the decision to leave with the boy and his parent. Make sure they have adequate information, they understand the ramifications of dropping out, and they are firm in this decision. Suggest that they take some time to think it over, and set a time limit of no longer than one week. It is not recommended that you tell the boy he can return to the same group later if things change. However, you can let him know that you would accept him into the next group formed for boys his age.

◆ ACTIVITY 39: Changing Erroneous Thinking

Target Ages
- Eleven through eighteen

Abuse Issue Addressed
- Sexually abusive behavior

Objective

- To assist each boy in identifying an error in personal thinking that generates feelings of anger or retaliation

Rationale

Cognitive distortions are a major factor in the development of sexually abusive behavior. Helping boys recognize, verbalize, and then correct these thoughts is one important aspect of preventing victimizing behavior.

Procedure: Part 1

Provide an overview of cognitive restructuring: explain that there are numerous ways to interpret any experience. How a person interprets an experience influences that person's feelings about it and behavioral response to it. To change a behavioral response to an experience, a person must change the way he or she interprets that experience. Post the steps of the process in a place where the boys can readily refer to them during this and subsequent sessions.

Tell the boys that when they want to change their behavioral response to an experience, they can use the following process, which consists of answering a series of questions about the experience:

1. What happened?
2. How did you interpret/perceive/view what happened?
3. How did you feel about what happened? What did you do in response to what happened?
4. How can you challenge your interpretation of the experience so that you feel differently about it and respond with a different behavior?

With your cotherapist, carry out a role play that demonstrates a thinking error. One of you plays a teenager who had asked his mother to run an errand for him, and the other plays his mother, who forgot due to a hectic day at work. The son comes in, asks about the errand, and blows up at his mother when she says she forgot. He refuses to listen to her explanation and storms out of the room.

Lead the boys through the four steps, exploring in particular the possible ways in which the teenager interpreted his mother's failure to run the errand. List all of the boys' suggestions. Review each item on the list, offering an alternative interpretation to show how the experience can be looked at differently. Also explain that cognitive errors are often based on ascribing particular motives to another person's actions; this is a mistake in thinking, because we cannot know why another person acts as he or she does. Then invite the boys to share examples of ways in which their perceptions of experiences resulted in negative feelings or behaviors.

Procedure: Part 2

Introduce common thinking errors that can play a part in developing offending behavior and explain that these thinking errors are often used to rationalize or justify abuse. Some examples follow:

- I have to be in control in order to feel OK, and that includes controlling others.
- What I did is OK because everyone does it.
- She liked what I did to her.
- It is not a problem, because I did not get caught.
- I am OK, because she will not say anything.

Lead a discussion of what is wrong with the thinking in each of these cases and how to correct it.

Common Responses

Many sexually abused boys are impulsive; they pay little attention to their thoughts prior to acting on them. They may have a lot of trouble slowing down enough to identify what they are thinking. When you notice an example of erroneous thinking during a group experience, stop and call attention to it and ask the boy in question to verbalize what he is thinking; then have the group members brainstorm different interpretations that would lead to different feelings and different, more positive behavior. Try to do this at least two or three times per session so that the boys can practice making cognitive changes. Remind them that managing impulsive behavior is accomplished through self-control and thinking before acting.

◆ ACTIVITY 40: Understanding the Sexual Assault Cycle

Target Ages
- Twelve through eighteen

Abuse Issue Addressed
- Sexually abusive behavior

Objectives
- To develop each boy's understanding of the connection between feelings of powerlessness and sexually abusive behavior
- To help each boy identify current situations in which he feels powerless
- To encourage each boy to recognize and acknowledge any personal involvement in abuse toward another person

Rationale

Learning how and why offending behavior occurs develops the boys' awareness of potential risk factors. With this knowledge and awareness, the boys can learn how to control and manage these factors. The boys need to understand that offending behavior is not an inevitable outcome following molestation; instead, it is a choice and is, therefore, under one's control.

Procedure

This activity is actually a collection of exercises aimed at building the boys' understanding of the sexual assault cycle and preventing offending behavior. To begin, post the chart shown here that depicts the cycle—a progression of thoughts, feelings, and behaviors that typically precedes a sexual assault; leave it on display through this and any subsequent sessions dealing with prevention.

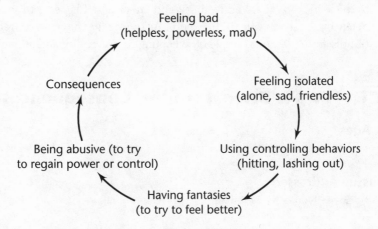

Feeling bad
(helpless, powerless, mad)

Feeling isolated
(alone, sad, friendless)

Consequences

Using controlling behaviors
(hitting, lashing out)

Being abusive (to try
to regain power or control)

Having fantasies
(to try to feel better)

Explain the cycle and lead the boys through any or all of the following exercises, depending on the group's specific needs:

• Identify red-flag feelings and behaviors. Help the boys recognize stressors that trigger the feelings and behaviors that lead to sexual assault. Ask these questions: What things make you feel helpless, powerless, or out of control? What other feelings do you have in connection with your anger? What negative behaviors do you use in an effort to regain a sense of control?

• Have boys share their own experiences at each stage of the sexual assault cycle. This sharing develops their capacity to examine their own behavior and motives as well as their sense of responsibility for involvement in the therapeutic process.

- Educate the boys about the consequences of offending behavior.
- Have the boys generate healthy alternatives that serve to interrupt each stage of the cycle. Ask such questions as these: How can you avoid high-risk situations? What thinking errors are you making at each stage of the sexual assault cycle? What are some positive, rational thoughts that you could use instead? How can you manage your personal triggers? What has to happen in order for you to make a positive choice instead of a negative one?
- Discuss options to control negative behaviors. Reinforce personal responsibility and choices.

Common Responses

If one boy acknowledges offending behavior, you may encounter high anxiety, scapegoating, and antagonistic behavior from the other members. Do not allow his peers to engage in angry confrontation with him. Instead, encourage the boy to share his thoughts and feelings, and encourage his peers to share how such behavior negatively affects the victim. Acknowledge the boy's courage in sharing this disclosure, as an example of accepting responsibility and asking for help.

◆ ACTIVITY 41: Brainstorming Consequences

Target Ages
- Twelve through eighteen

Abuse Issue Addressed
- Sexually abusive behavior

Objective
- To develop each boy's understanding that the responsibility for abusive behavior rests only with the offender

Rationale

Accepting responsibility for one's own behavior involves considering potential consequences before making a conscious decision to act. Unfortunately, many perpetrators escape significant consequences for their acts, and sometimes this fact leads a boy to minimize the potential consequences for his own behavior.

Procedure

Note: This activity is intended to be used only after thoroughly discussing the sexual assault cycle and ways to interrupt it.

Ask the boys to brainstorm the potential consequences if they were to molest other children. Encourage them to consider the issue from various perspectives (legal, physical, emotional, behavioral, and so on). Record their responses on a chalkboard or a poster.

Looking at the reality of potential consequences is sobering for group members, and this activity is intended to have this impact. However, it is important to keep the tone of the discussion nonthreatening; otherwise, the boys experience too much anxiety to benefit from this information. They are more likely to retain awareness of the seriousness of abusing others if they identify the consequences as part of an effort to prevent offending behavior.

Common Responses

You can expect to be challenged at times during this discussion, as members point out that their own offenders did not incur serious consequences. Most commonly, boys tend to concentrate on the failure of the legal system to convict offenders. You need to point out that many potential consequences have nothing to do with legal issues.

Encourage the boys to explore what a perpetrator ought to be required to do, in addition to paying any legal debt:

- Admit to abusive acts
- Acknowledge that such behavior was wrong
- Assure others that the abuse will not be repeated

If you choose, discussion of this topic can lead into a discussion of risk taking and considering potential consequences when weighing the risk. Ask the boys to consider risk taking when it is associated with other potentially harmful behaviors, such as smoking. Do a comparative list of risks and benefits to show the boys one way to evaluate an act before taking action.

◆ ACTIVITY 42: Establishing a Prevention Plan

Target Ages
- Twelve through eighteen

Abuse Issues Addressed
- Sexually abusive behavior
- Powerlessness

Objectives

- To enable each boy to recognize behaviors that enhance his sense of personal control
- To assist each boy in establishing a plan for preventing abusive behavior

Rationale

Boys need to develop skills in controlling any impulse for abusive behavior toward others. These skills include coping with stress or uncomfortable feelings in positive ways. As the feeling of powerlessness often triggers offending behavior, the boys also need to develop skills in reestablishing personal control.

Procedure

In order for this activity to be helpful, all members need to have some understanding of how and why sexual abuse victims can develop offending behavior. In addition, they must be able to recognize and deal appropriately with feelings of anger and powerlessness, which have the potential to lead to abusive acts. Consequently, you need to review the definition of molestation, the fact that everyone has choices about expressing sexual desires, and the feelings related to the decision to become sexually active.

Distribute pencils and copies of My Prevention Plan and ask the boys to complete the form. After everyone has finished, encourage the boys to share all or parts of their plans. Be sure to congratulate the boys for creative ideas. Also point out the need to change any unrealistic or unworkable ideas (for example, planning to "go visit a girlfriend" when the boy does not have a girlfriend).

Requiring that the boys sign their plans is important. It emphasizes that their awareness of prevention needs to extend beyond the setting of therapy and that they need to remember their plans and use them if necessary. Stress that although the boys cannot change the fact that they were molested, they do have the choice not to act out abusive behavior toward others.

Make a copy of each boy's plan; keep the copy and return the original. Explain that the copies are for reference in future sessions. Encourage the boys to keep their copies readily accessible and to review their plans from time to time.

Common Responses

Boys who present with an attitude of thinking they know everything may resist this activity in the belief that molesting others would never be a problem for them. If you find such resistance, assure the group that most molested boys never do carry out abusive behavior. Then explain that it is nevertheless important to be prepared with an action plan if the situation ever does arise. State that planning in advance is one way to prevent any type of impulsive behavior.

My Prevention Plan

1. The first thing I will do when I feel helpless or powerless is . . .
2. I will ask for help from . . .
3. If I have sexual feelings and am around younger children, I will regain control by doing the following:

I understand that I am responsible for my actions and their consequences. [signature]

◆ ACTIVITY 43: Taking Action to Avoid Offending Behavior

Target Ages
- Twelve through eighteen

Abuse Issues Addressed
- Sexually abusive behavior
- Powerlessness

Objective
- To have each boy establish a plan for using peer and adult support in avoiding abusive behavior

Rationale

A boy's powerlessness is minimized when he can recognize alternatives and is able to implement an alternative of his choosing. Consequently, having a prevention plan before abusive behavior occurs enhances self-control.

Procedure

Note: Complete Activity 42 before you conduct this one.

Ask the boys to review their prevention plans. Remind them why taking personal responsibility is empowering: the way to feel in control is to take responsibility for oneself; blaming others only keeps a person in the role of helpless victim.

Distribute pencils and paper. Instruct the boys to relax and close their eyes if they choose. Ask each boy to recall a time when he felt powerful and in control by using a positive behavior. Then ask the boys to open their eyes. Instruct each boy to write down a minimum of five actions he can take if he ever encounters a potential trigger for offending behavior. After everyone has completed the task,

ask the boys to share the actions they listed; as they share, record their responses on a chalkboard or poster.

As patterns of coping become apparent, lead the discussion into a consideration of whether the boys' coping mechanisms are working well currently. For example, if a boy volunteers the coping action "Don't think about it," you might point out to him that whenever he encounters a problem during a group session, he tends not to think about it by denying, ignoring, or withdrawing. Then you can ask him whether that strategy is successful in achieving what he wants. Your objective is to encourage recognition of ineffective patterns that the boys need to consider changing.

Common Responses

Boys frequently list "commit suicide" as an action to take if they ever have thoughts about molesting. If so, address this problem immediately. You may find that thoughts of suicide arise regularly in response to feelings of helplessness and hopelessness.

Point out that there are always choices, that there is a huge difference between thinking about suicide and acting on it, and that one can choose not to act on suicidal thoughts. Emphasize personal coping strategies: talking with someone instead of trying to cope alone, exercising, being around people, writing in a journal. Discuss the importance of avoiding substance abuse. The consequences of suicide also need to be explored.

Arrange to meet alone with any boy who mentions suicidal thoughts. You must assess his risk and work with him to create an individual safety plan. Hospitalization, crisis intervention on an individual basis, and a medication evaluation are potential interventions.

◆ ACTIVITY 44: Writing a Letter to the Offender

Target Ages

- All

Abuse Issue Addressed

- Confusion about or ambivalence toward offender

Objectives

- To assist each boy in writing a letter to the person(s) who molested him
- To invite the boys to share all or part of their letters
- To encourage the boys to demonstrate acceptance when others have different feelings or opinions

Rationale

Often a boy questions whether something is wrong with him if does not hate or feel anger toward the offender. This exercise clarifies that all feelings are normal and that having certain feelings does not make a person "bad" or "weird."

Procedure

Remind the boys that thoughts and feelings are neither right nor wrong. Also stress that no one has a right to tell them what or how to feel.

Distribute pencils and copies of My Letter to the Offender and ask the boys to fill in the blanks with anything they want. Tell them that there are no right or wrong ways to complete the letter; encourage them to be as blunt as they possibly can. Explain that later you will be asking for volunteers to share their letters but that they are free to choose whether and how much they share.

The fill-in statements are suggested as one possibility to help the boys begin to write. If you are working with younger boys and they are having difficulty, you might suggest that they dictate their letters to you or your cotherapist. Also make it clear that if a boy prefers to write a letter of his own instead of using the format provided, he is free to do so.

When all the boys have completed their letters, ask if anyone would like to share all or part of his letter. Once several boys have shared, point out similarities and differences, validate all feelings expressed, and use the opportunity to continue any needed education (for example, explaining that ambivalence toward the offender is normal and common).

Ask whether anyone has confronted his offender and what the outcome was. State that after participating in this activity, boys sometimes feel safe enough to send their letters.

Common Responses

Any child who shares feelings that are different from those of others in the group may be a target for verbal attack. If this happens, ask the boys to remember times when someone told them they *should* or *should not* do something and how they felt as a result. Explain that these words communicate judgment rather than acceptance of a boy's choices.

Ask the boys which feels better: to be judged or to be accepted? State that the purpose of discussing feelings is not to judge or compare them but to help clarify and understand them.

My Letter to the Offender

To:

The way I feel about you right now is . . .

I feel so angry that you . . .

From you I expected . . . but what I got instead was . . .

It hurts me when . . .

What I deserve from you is . . .

I hope that you will . . .

I wish . . . would happen to you.

What I want most to say to you is . . .

What makes me the saddest is . . .

What I need from you right now is . . .

◆ ACTIVITY 45: Introducing the Grieving Process

Target Ages
- All

Abuse Issues Addressed
- Depression
- Isolation

Objectives
- To acquaint the boys with the grieving process
- To help the boys understand the necessity of going through this process in order to resolve loss

Rationale

The boys need to be educated about grief, its various stages, the length of time it takes, and the level of energy necessary to grieve. When they understand that grief is a normal and natural response to loss, their feelings and behaviors often make more sense to them. This cognitive understanding is one important step toward enhanced self-control.

Procedure

With younger boys you may want to begin this activity by reading them a book about some type of loss. With older boys you may skip the reading and begin by presenting some basic information about grief. Regardless of the boys' ages, you need to share these facts, using age-appropriate language:

- The only effective way to resolve grief is to go through it. It will not go away if you try to deny it or go around it.
- The process of grieving is hard work; it is never easy.
- You can't resolve grief effectively alone or in isolation; the support of others is essential.

Explain that everyone goes through significant losses in life: the death of a loved one, losing a parent through divorce, moving, changing schools, losing a pet because it dies or runs away, suffering through a serious illness. Then describe the stages of grief, explaining that everyone progresses through them in their own individual process and time frame (Kübler-Ross, 1969; Jewett, 1982).

1. Denial (which can include shock, numbness, and withdrawal)
2. Anger
3. Bargaining
4. Depression (which occurs as the person acknowledges the pain and sense of loss)
5. Acceptance (which involves adapting to the loss and moving on)

Ask for volunteers to share any personal experiences with these stages. The more examples the boys hear, the better they will understand the concept of grieving.

Common Responses

Younger boys often believe that grief is experienced only after death of a loved one. You will need to expand their understanding by explaining the loss that accompanies many other significant events that they can relate to, such as leaving one school and transferring to another or losing a friend who moves far away.

Older boys often express frustration when they hear that grieving requires time and work. They also may argue with the notion that while grieving they will need the support of others; the idea of sharing sadness or tears may seem too threatening. Point out that they will encounter many obstacles to grieving but that it is important they do not omit any of the five stages. Acknowledge, too, that despite the universality of the stages of grieving, each person's losses and subsequent reactions are unique; consequently, there is no right or wrong way to experience grief.

◆ ACTIVITY 46: Identifying Your Sadness Triggers

Target Ages
- All

Abuse Issues Addressed
- Depression
- Anger
- Powerlessness

Objectives
- To help each boy identify situations and events that may generate grief
- To encourage each boy to create a ritual for grieving to help him cope with difficult situations and events related to his abuse

Rationale
Children feel enhanced control when they are prepared ahead of time for occasions that will generate grief or possible periods of increased sadness. As they learn to be aware of potentially difficult times, they can plan appropriate coping strategies.

Procedure
Invite the boys to share their most significant losses. Ask each boy to identify when the loss occurred (such as "the summer after fourth grade" or "the year we went to Grandma's for Christmas"). An adolescent may be able to name the exact day when a loss occurred, whereas a younger boy may only be able to designate the time in a general sense.

Explore if any of the boys remember having difficulty each year around the time of the loss. Let them know it is common to have some kind of reaction or exacerbated feelings whenever an anniversary period rolls around. Explain that when the loss involves a person, additional stress can be expected with the anniversary (for example, the "first Christmas without Dad").

Suggest that the boys can make anniversaries less difficult by planning and carrying out some kind of ritual to use at such times. Rituals can be soothing as well as healing. Ask the boys to brainstorm ideas for rituals, and record their contributions. To get them started, you might want to offer such examples as the following:

- Visit a place that was important to you and your loved one.
- Visit the grave of the person you lost.
- Go to church and say a prayer.

- Write in your journal about how you remember the person.
- Write a good-bye letter if you have not already done so.
- Make a phone call or write a letter to anyone who has helped you cope with the loss.
- Plan to spend time with a person who is supportive and knows about your loss.
- Buy some flowers or plant something living in remembrance.
- Talk to other people close to you who were also affected by the loss.
- Spend the day with someone—not alone.

Note that parents may need to be involved in some rituals, so contact them in advance and ask if they would be willing to help with follow-through.

Common Responses

This activity may trigger tears, which some boys will not tolerate. They may try to focus the group's attention on a peer or become frustrated with themselves for expressing their sadness in front of other people. Remind the group that sharing honest feelings is a sign of strength and progress, not weakness.

◆ ACTIVITY 47: Meeting with an Adult Survivor

Target Ages

- Twelve through eighteen

Abuse Issues Addressed

- Feeling different or damaged
- Hopelessness

Objective

- To offer the boys an opportunity to meet with an adult male survivor of child sexual abuse for the purpose of gaining information and insight

Rationale

Meeting with an adult male survivor who has effectively resolved the problems stemming from sexual abuse shows the boys that they are not "different" or "damaged."

Procedure

Participation in group therapy can help address the overwhelming isolation that many sexually abused boys experience. Most boys would also benefit from contact with a positive adult male role model who can demonstrate that recovery from childhood sexual abuse is possible; however, most do not have the opportunity. Consequently, one very powerful group activity involves inviting an adult male survivor to join the boys for a group session and to answer questions from the members, you, and your cotherapist.

You must carefully screen potential visitors. You may consider a man who has been recommended by his therapist, if you know that therapist well enough to trust his or her recommendation. You could also contact a survivor whom you hear present at a conference, who is interviewed in the newspaper, or who has written about his experiences. Be sure to ask any candidate whether he would be comfortable answering the boys' questions. You might want to give him some examples of the questions he might hear. Despite a recommendation, do not consider an individual if he has any history of offending behavior or if you know that others suspect that he committed such behavior.

Inform the boys at least three weeks before the scheduled visit and explain the purpose of having the man come to the group. State that the man's visit is intended to be informative and empowering. Two weeks ahead of time, encourage the boys to begin thinking about some of the questions they would like to ask this person.

One week before the survivor's visit, give each boy five index cards and ask him to write a single question on each of the cards. If a boy cannot come up with five questions, encourage him to write three. Clarify that each question ought to reflect something that is important for the boy to learn or hear about. Stress that the visitor may have been able to cope successfully with some of the problems the boys are currently experiencing: for example, bed-wetting, nightmares, fears about becoming a perpetrator, difficulty with anger management, or parents' rejection. Inform the boys that the questions will be read randomly, so no one will know who wrote what.

After the boys have finished writing, collect all the completed index cards. After the group session, review the cards and then include your own questions to address any uncovered areas that you know are of interest to the boys. (The boys often overlook certain issues, and they avoid others that are of interest but too embarrassing to write down.) Make sure to include questions about the impact of abuse on the man's sexual identity and behavior, how he has dealt with the issues of guilt and responsibility, and his honest feelings about therapy.

Common Responses
The boys may initially be very uncomfortable with a stranger in the group, especially one who knows they have all been molested. You can begin the group with

the usual opening ritual, including the survivor in the ritual. If you plan to serve snacks, do so at the beginning, so the boys have some time to share information about the past week before hearing the survivor's presentation.

You may need to be more directive in facilitating this meeting than you usually are, directing questions to the boys or asking them for specific feedback. A more directive approach will allow you to point out similarities between the survivor's situation and the boys' individual situations; however, keep in mind it is each boy's choice how much he wants to share about himself with this new person.

◆ ACTIVITY 48: Saying Good-Bye

Target Ages

- All

Abuse Issues Addressed

- Depression
- Anger

Objectives

- To help each boy identify at least one important loss caused by molestation
- To encourage each boy to let go of that loss

Rationale

Sexually abused boys experience many losses that can cause or exacerbate depression. Feelings of hopelessness and powerlessness are common. As the boys identify their losses and grieve over them, they ultimately let go of those losses; then their depression, hopelessness, and powerlessness become less intense.

Procedure

Child sexual abuse, like all traumatic life events, involves losses. Some of these losses are obvious to the child. For example, a boy who has been molested by his father may be removed from his home and placed in foster care; his immediate losses include leaving his parents for an uncertain period, moving to a temporary family and new parental figures, changing schools, and leaving his friends. Other losses may be less obvious but are just as potentially damaging: loss of self-esteem, a positive body image, normal childhood experiences, appropriate peer relationships, and control over his body.

Jewett (1982) identifies phases that children need to go through and understand when they have experienced a loss. These include sadness, anger and aggression, making sense of what has happened, impaired self-esteem and self-control, and ultimately letting go and moving on. She stresses that "[l]oss is a cumulative experience; unless the child is helped to resolve a major loss, even trivial subsequent losses will provoke similar stress" (p. xiii).

This activity helps each boy determine which abuse-related loss is most significant for him and let go of that loss so that he can move on. Explain that each boy will create a symbol of his loss; share any feelings, thoughts, or wishes about that loss, if he wants; and then say good-bye to the loss by doing whatever he wishes with the symbol.

Here are some of the alternatives you might suggest for the boys' creations:

- Write a letter.
- Draw a picture.
- Make a book.
- Make an audiotape or videotape.
- Stage a role play.
- Dictate thoughts and feelings to you so that you can write them down.

Provide as many options as you can think of and allow plenty of time. Have a large supply of materials and equipment on hand for the boys to use.

After the boys have completed their work, ask them to share whatever they want about their creations. After the sharing, stress that whatever the boys do with their creations is up to them; they may want to rip them up, burn them, send them to other people, ask you to keep them safe, or take them home.

Common Responses

If you observe significant anger, expressed either verbally or behaviorally, encourage the boy involved to explore his feelings. If he is unable to let go of the anger, tell him that he needs further time to resolve his feelings before making the symbolic creation. In this case you may encourage him to work with another loss that he has already resolved.

Some boys become very sad during this activity. Reinforce that fully experiencing the sadness is a necessary part of grieving. Remind them that they have experienced multiple losses and need to be patient with the time it takes to resolve those losses fully.

◆ ACTIVITY 49: Reviewing Goals

Target Ages
- All

Abuse Issue Addressed
- Taking appropriate responsibility for oneself

Objectives
- To encourage each child to give feedback to adults in an assertive way
- To offer each child a chance to practice giving feedback

Rationale

An important part of therapy is encouraging boys to take responsibility for themselves and for meeting their own needs. For them to do so, they need to learn to give feedback to adults on what they want and need. This activity gives them an opportunity to practice giving feedback. In addition, boys find it empowering to be asked for feedback, to be listened to, and to know that their opinions will be carefully considered.

Procedure

It is useful to conduct this activity twice: once at the halfway point of the group cycle, and then again as a termination exercise sometime during the final four weeks of the group. At the midway point, this review can identify important issues that the boys still need to work on as well as issues that you and your cotherapist need to address more strongly. At the conclusion of the group, the activity can help you evaluate the effectiveness of therapy.

Procedure: Mid-Session Evaluation

Either post the group's original goals or distribute them to the boys in handout form. Explain the purpose of the activity. Ask the boys to discuss the goals one by one. As each goal is stated, ask, "How well do you think we're doing so far with this goal?" Make sure that each boy responds, explaining why he feels the way he does and how he would like the goal to be approached in the future. Help each boy clarify his feedback by summarizing his comments. Make notes as the boys share comments, so that you will be able to plan in accordance with the feedback.

After this mid-session evaluation, set a time to meet with your cotherapist to review the feedback; decide what changes are necessary and how these changes will be implemented. For example, you may decide to decrease unstructured sharing time, to contact parents for a session involving evaluation and feedback, to provide more individualized attention to a particular boy who needs it, or to set up a meeting with school personnel who appear to be unintentionally interfering with therapy.

Procedure: Final Evaluation

The session involving the final evaluation works about the same way. If it is determined that more work is still needed on any of the goals, you need to discuss ways in which the boys can continue that work on their own or in conjunction with some other kind of treatment. Again make notes and incorporate the feedback into your planning for future groups.

Common Responses

When your group is in the middle of treatment, you can expect the boys to express discomfort with some of the more challenging treatment goals that have not yet been worked on fully. Frequently there will be denial or minimization of the need for those goals to be addressed. If this happens, point out that the boys have already done a lot of work together and that continued progress requires building on their earlier work. State that exploring their discomfort and learning how to cope with it lead to effective resolution of issues rather than avoidance.

If your group is in the process of ending, it is possible that the boys will be angry with you and your cotherapist and will use this activity to criticize or verbally attack you. If so, respond by acknowledging that it is permissible for people to have different opinions, and share your own perception of whatever issue is being discussed.

Explore how the boys are feeling about the end of group therapy. Ask what they would have liked to have done differently. Explore for other concerns they may have, such as worries about a report you must make to the court or a contact with parents.

◆ ACTIVITY 50: Listing "Wins"

Target Ages
- All

Abuse Issues Addressed
- Self-esteem
- Impaired relationships

Objective

- To help each boy recognize the positive changes he has made during therapy

Rationale

Most boys who attend group therapy find it difficult to face the end of the group and say good-bye. This activity allows them to recognize and process their feelings, to share the benefits they have received from the experience, and to acknowledge their own hard work and accomplishments.

Procedure

If your group is time limited, everyone knows the scheduled ending date well ahead of time. You can begin discussing the group's termination a minimum of four weeks before the ending date. Some examples of different good-bye activities are described in the sections that follow.

Group Progress Review. One way to address termination is to review the group's progress, including significant events (such as outings) or especially powerful sessions (such as watching a movie about molested boys). Ask the boys to contribute examples of such milestones. Although the emphasis is on the boys' recollections of events and feelings, you and your cotherapist may also add your observations of change and growth within the group as a whole.

In a time-limited group, the boys begin as strangers and are often antagonistic to one another, yet they are able to develop a sense of cohesiveness and trust by the time the group ends. Pointing out important changes such as this can add to the members' hope and optimism about the future.

Record all contributions on a chalkboard or a flip chart. Later, if you wish, you can create a handout listing the contributions and give each boy a copy.

Individual Progress Review. Another method is to ask the group members to assemble into pairs. Each boy shares his memories about what his partner was like at the beginning of the group, the changes the partner has gone through during the group, and what the partner is like now. Encourage the group members to give honest and specific feedback about any areas they feel would be important to their peers. Explain that the emphasis is to be on giving positive feedback about each boy's participation and improvement. Give each boy a pencil and paper and encourage him to record his own achievements.

Younger boys may require some assistance with this activity. You may need to give them specific questions to ask or partial statements to complete. For example, you can instruct a boy to ask his partner such questions as these: "Do

you remember when you used to . . . during group sessions? How were you feeling then? Have you noticed that you don't do that anymore? How do you feel now
during group sessions?"

Success Sharing. Another way to say good-bye is to have the boys help one another make lists of successes or "wins" that they achieved during treatment, either
in or outside the group (one list per boy). You and your cotherapist may help in
developing these lists. Here are some examples of the kinds of comments the boys
might be encouraged to make to one another:

- You got angry at another person in the group and showed your feelings with-
  out getting violent.
- You said no to your mom when she wanted you to visit your dad and you really
  didn't want to.
- You do not fight as much with your sister.
- You made two new friends.
- You allow yourself to feel sad and let yourself cry in the group, and it is OK
  with you.
- You shared a secret that you had been keeping inside.
- You testified in court even though you felt afraid.
- You stayed in the group and stuck with it even though it made you uncom-
  fortable.
- You no longer blame other people for your problems.

  If you are working with younger boys, you may want to give each a tangible
symbol of what he has achieved in the form of a certificate listing his "wins." Or
the collective group wins may be put on a certificate and reproduced for each
member.

Common Responses

Members who have attended consistently may start missing group sessions as soon
as you announce termination. It is important to provide some general education
about common reactions to the loss of the group, and to normalize these feelings.
Prepare the boys for possible regression or recurrence of some symptoms, and be
sure it is understood that this does not indicate more therapy is needed. Encourage as much discussion as possible of feelings and thoughts about the ending of
the group.

APPENDIX: NINE THERAPEUTIC INTERVENTIONS

This appendix describes nine interventions you can use at any time during therapy. They are particularly useful in group therapy, but several can be adapted for use in individual therapy as well. Using these interventions helps in developing skills and knowledge, exploring feelings, expressing thoughts and feelings, practicing effective decision making, and enhancing communication.

1. Art therapy
2. Books
3. Celebrations and outings
4. Games
5. Guest speakers
6. Journal writing
7. Play therapy
8. Puppets
9. Tension busters

Art Therapy

Art therapy is expressive, relaxing, creative, and revealing. The variety of media you can work with is almost unlimited: crayons, colored pencils, paint, clay, finger painting, and collage are only a few possibilities. When facilitated by a therapist, art activities can help boys communicate things they may not be able to express verbally. Experiencing success through artwork is empowering to a child, as it increases his sense of mastery to see something he has created (Naitove, 1982). Rubin (1984) is one resource for therapists who would like additional information about art therapy.

Books

Books are effective tools in both group and individual settings, especially as a starting point for discussions with younger boys. The books listed in the Resources (under the heading "Books to Read with Children") are especially useful with boys ages eleven or younger. *Note:* Although there are many books about abuse for children, relatively few are specifically written for boys.

It is a good idea to start a library of books kept in the therapy setting so that boys can take them home to read (generally for one week at a time) on their own or with parents. Discussion with parents reinforces the material and demonstrates parental support. The only book listed in the Resources that is not appropriate for parents to read with their boys is the activity guide that accompanies *So What's It to Me? Sexual Assault Information for Guys* (Stringer & Rants-Rodriguez, 1987).

Celebrations and Outings

Celebrations of important occasions (such as birthdays) and outings are important for all molested boys, regardless of age. Abused children frequently miss many normal childhood experiences. Providing a birthday celebration for a child and letting him decide how he wants to celebrate can be a corrective experience and gives him practice in making assertive requests.

Also, when the boys in a group do things together with you and your cotherapist, these experiences build cohesiveness. Give the boys a range of options, if possible, taking into consideration time, money, and transportation limitations. Going out might include the video arcade, a pizza parlor or fast-food restaurant, batting cages, or a picnic at the park. Staying in to celebrate might involve playing a favorite game, watching video games, watching a videotaped movie, making ice cream sundaes, or decorating cupcakes.

Games

The following therapeutic games cover a wide range of topics appropriate for abused boys, including safety, feelings, exploration of abuse, decision making, and communication. They are an entertaining approach to introducing information and exploring various problem areas. You are likely to find less resistance to certain topics when you combine them with games. It may also be easier for boys to remember new skills and then practice them at home when learning is attached to a game activity. The games listed here are to be used in therapy sessions only, rather than at home with family or friends. Companies that provide materials specific for therapy include games like the ones listed. Some suggestions are Creative Therapy Store (800-648-8857), Childswork Childsplay (800-962-1141), and Kidsrights (800-892-KIDS).

- The Anger Control Game
- The Anger Solution Game
- The Angry Monster Machine
- Be Safe, Be Aware
- Breakaway
- A Case for Conflict Resolution
- Communicate
- Communicate Junior
- The Conduct Management Game
- Consequences of Choice
- Coping and Decisions
- The Coping with Anger Target Game
- Dealing with Feelings Card Game
- The Dinosaur's Journey to High Self-Esteem
- Face It! Card Deck
- Family Happenings
- Feeling Good Card Game
- The Feelings Game
- The Great Feelings Game
- In Control: A Book of Games to Teach Children Self-Control Skills
- Let's Talk About Touching
- One Dozen Feeling Games
- Our Game
- Play It Safe with SASA
- The Positive Thinking Game
- POW! Personal Power!
- Problem-Solver
- Right or Wrong: A Decision-Making Game
- The Road to Problem Mastery
- The Self-Control Patrol Game

- The Self-Esteem Game
- The Stamp Game
- Stop, Relax and Think
- Story Telling Card Game
- Stress Attack
- Talking-Feeling-Doing Game
- The Ungame

Guest Speakers

With careful selection and preparation, you can use guest speakers as a powerful presence for your group. All must be screened ahead of time to assess their comfort level in discussing sexual abuse, role playing their answers to possible questions, and determining any potential concerns. Group members also need to be notified well ahead of the planned presentation and to have the opportunity to prepare questions (see also Activity 47).

The following are some types of speakers to consider:

- An adolescent or adult male who was sexually abused, has completed therapy successfully, and is recommended by his therapist
- A health educator who can provide sex education for adolescents
- A safety educator who emphasizes self-help skills and empowerment for children to act when they are threatened in any way
- A therapist who has extensive experience working with sex offenders
- A representative of the court who can answer questions about child protective services or the criminal justice process

Journal Writing

Using a home journal can be therapeutic for older boys. It can help relieve feelings that boys often express through acting-out behaviors. Journal writing can also increase self-understanding, as the child can be helped to recognize patterns, problems, and alternatives for improved coping.

Journal writing can also be useful for reinforcement of learning between sessions. You can give the boys guided writing tasks. If writing is difficult for a child, he can use the journal for other means of creative expression, such as artwork.

Play Therapy

Play therapy is a nonthreatening way to observe boys and intervene with patterns of problematic behavior. For younger abused boys, play may be the only way they are able to communicate what has happened to them. Playtime can also be tension reducing at the end of a therapy session. Play therapy allows the abused child to work through his victimization using play and fantasy, allowing him to experience a sense of mastery and control.

When play is used in a group, you need to interact with the boys in a nondirective way. Gently reinforce effective and empowering strategies with the boys as they play, and assist them in practicing more effective resolution of past experiences and traumas. A playroom should offer a wide range of toys as well as a sandbox, dollhouse, puppets, dolls and assorted family figures, art materials, foam bats, and punching bags.

Puppets

Puppet play for younger boys is an effective way to give them some distance from the topic of sexual abuse or from their feelings, which makes it less threatening for them to disclose. Again, this kind of activity may be the only way a young boy is able to share what has happened to him. To name a few examples, puppets can be used to facilitate disclosure of molestation details, to act out confronting the offender, or to create scenes in which each child acts out some kind of family interaction.

Tension Busters

If you are working with a group, include the boys in developing tension or stress busters that they will use at the end of stressful group sessions and during crisis periods. Certain therapeutic activities typically result in increased anxiety, tension, or stress. For example, role playing a confrontation with the offender or sharing all the details of the molestation is typically very difficult. Similarly, stressors outside the group, such as a recurrence of molestation or having to testify in court, can also trigger an escalation of emotions.

The following options for physical and emotional release of tension can allow therapeutic work to continue. They can be adapted or varied depending on the age range in your group.

- Have each boy draw the silliest thing he can think of.
- Have each boy draw the "grossest" thing he can think of.
- Rent a video that is an action-adventure or fantasy.
- Play board games.
- Have a picnic in the park.

- Go on an outing to the ice cream store.
- Play any outdoor sport or physical game.
- Make and bake your own pizza.
- Have a water balloon or squirt gun fight.
- Paint ceramics.
- Play video games.
- Take a nature walk where boys can also run to release pent-up energy.
- Have a "pillow day" during which boys decorate pillowcases and are instructed in how to use the pillows to release stress.

REFERENCES AND RESOURCES

T he following references and additional resources have been arranged by topic. The topics are as follows:

Historical Perspective

Literature Review

Characteristics of Male Sexual Abuse

Effects of Sexual Abuse: Childhood Impact

Empowerment in Therapy
Treatment Activities

Treatment Issues and Modalities

Understanding and Treating Sexually Abusive Behavior by Abused Boys

Sexual Identity and Sexual Abuse

Specific Populations

Adult Survivors

Female Offenders

Books to Read with Children

Historical Perspective

Burgess, A., Groth, A. N., Holmstrom, L., & Sgroi, S. (1978). *Sexual assault of children and adolescents.* San Francisco: New Lexington Press.

Literature Review

DePanfilis, D. (1986). *Literature review of sexual abuse.* Washington, DC: U.S. Department of Health and Human Services, Office of Human Development Services, National Center on Child Abuse and Neglect.

Finkelhor, D. (1984). *Child sexual abuse: New theory and research.* New York: Free Press.

Grayson, J. (1989). Sexually victimized boys. *Virginia Child Protection Newsletter, 2,* 1–1b.

VanderMey, B. J. (1988). The sexual victimization of male children: A review of previous research. *Child Abuse and Neglect, 12,* 61–72.

Watkins, B., & Bentovim, A. (1992). The sexual abuse of male children and adolescents: A review of current research. *Journal of Child Psychology and Psychiatry, 33,* 197–248.

Characteristics of Male Sexual Abuse

Bagley, C., Wood, M., & Young, L. (1994). Victim to abuser: Mental health and behavioral sequels of child sexual abuse in a community survey of young adult males. *Child Abuse and Neglect, 18,* 683–697.

DeJong, A. R., Emmett, G. A., & Hervada, A. A. (1982). Epidemiologic factors in sexual abuse of boys. *American Journal of Diseases of Children, 136,* 990–993.

DeJong, A. R., Emmett, G. A., & Hervada, A. R. (1982). Sexual abuse of children: Sex, race and age-dependent variations. *American Journal of Diseases of Children, 136,* 129–134.

DeJong, A. R., Hervada, A. R., & Emmett, G. A. (1983). Epidemiologic variations in child-hood sexual abuse. *Child Abuse and Neglect, 7,* 155–162.

Ellerstein, N. S., & Canavan, J. W. (1980). Sexual abuse of boys. *American Journal of Diseases of Children, 134,* 255–257.

Faller, K. C. (1989). Characteristics of a clinical sample of sexually abused children: How boy and girl victims differ. *Child Abuse and Neglect, 13,* 281–291.

Farber, E. D., Showers, J., Johnson, C. F., Joseph, J. A., & Oshins, L. (1984). The sexual abuse of children: A comparison of male and female victims. *Journal of Clinical Child Psychology, 13,* 294–297.

Finkelhor, D. (1981). The sexual abuse of boys. *Victimology, 6,* 76–84.

Fritz, G. S., Stoll, K., & Wagner, N. N. (1981). A comparison of males and females who were sexually molested as children. *Journal of Sex and Marital Therapy, 7,* 54–59.

Johnson, R. L., & Shrier, D. K. (1985). Sexual victimization of boys: Experience at an adolescent medicine clinic. *Journal of Adolescent Health Care, 6,* 372–376.

Johnson, R. L., & Shrier, D. K. (1987). Past sexual victimization by females of male patients in an adolescent medicine clinic population. *American Journal of Psychiatry, 144,* 650–652.

Kaufman, A., DiVasto, P., Jackson, R., Voorhees, D., & Christy, J. (1980). Male rape victims: Noninstitutionalized assault. *American Journal of Psychiatry, 137,* 221–223.

Levesque, R.J.R. (1994). Sex differences in the experience of child sexual victimization. *Journal of Family Violence, 9,* 357–369.

Pierce, R., & Pierce, L. H. (1985). The sexually abused child: A comparison of male and female victims. *Child Abuse and Neglect, 9,* 191–199.

Reinhart, M. A. (1987). Sexually abused boys. *Child Abuse and Neglect, 11,* 229–235.

Rimsza, M. E., & Niggeman, E. H. (1982). Medical evaluation of sexually abused children: A review. *Pediatrics, 69,* 8–14.

Risin, L. I., & Koss, M. P. (1987). The sexual abuse of boys. *American Journal of Interpersonal Violence, 2,* 309–323.

Roane, T. H. (1992). Male victims of sexual abuse: A case review within a child protective team. *Child Welfare, 71,* 231–239.

Spencer, M. J., & Dunklee, P. (1986). Sexual abuse of boys. *Pediatrics, 78,* 133–138.

Woods, S. C., & Dean, K. S. (May 14, 1985). *Implications of the findings of the sexual abuse of males research.* Workshop presented at the southern regional conference of the Child Welfare League of America, Gatlinburg, TN.

Effects of Sexual Abuse: Childhood Impact

Adams-Tucker, C. (1982). Proximate effects of sexual abuse in childhood: A report on twenty-eight children. *American Journal of Psychiatry, 139,* 1252–1256.

Bolton, F., Morris, L., & MacEachron, A. (1989). *Males at risk: The other side of child sexual abuse.* Thousand Oaks, CA: Sage.

Browne, A., & Finkelhor, D. (1986). Impact of child sexual abuse: A review of the research. *Psychological Bulletin, 99,* 66–77.

Everstein, D., & Everstein, L. (1989). *Sexual trauma in children and adolescents: Dynamics and treatment.* New York: Brunner/Mazel.

Finkelhor, D. (1981). The sexual abuse of boys. *Victimology, 6,* 76–84.

Finkelhor, D., & Browne, A. (1985). The traumatic impact of child sexual abuse: A conceptualization. *American Journal of Orthopsychiatry, 55,* 530–541.

Freeman-Longo, R. E. (1986). The impact of sexual victimization on males. *Child Abuse and Neglect, 10,* 411–414.

Friedrich, W. N. (1995). *Psychotherapy with sexually abused boys: An integrated approach.* Thousand Oaks, CA: Sage.

Friedrich, W. N., Beilke, R. L., & Urquiza, A. J. (1988). Behavior problems in young sexually abused boys: A comparison study. *Journal of Interpersonal Violence, 3,* 21–28.

Friedrich, W. N., & Luecke, W. J. (1988). Young school-age sexually aggressive children. *Professional Psychology: Research and Practice, 19,* 155–164.

Gilgun, J. F. (1990). Factors mediating the effects of childhood maltreatment. In M. Hunter (Ed.), *The sexually abused male: Vol. 1. Prevalence, impact, and treatment* (pp. 177–190). San Francisco: New Lexington Press.

Goldman, R. L., & Wheeler, V. R. (1986). *Silent shame: The sexual abuse of children and youth.* Danville, IL: Interstate Printers and Publishers.

Grayson, J. (1989). Sexually victimized boys. *Virginia Child Protection Newsletter, 29,* 1–1b.

Hunter, R. S., Kilstrom, N., & Loda, F. (1985). Sexually abused children: Identifying masked presentations in a medical setting. *Child Abuse and Neglect, 9,* 17–25.

James, B. (1989). *Treating traumatized children: New insights and creative interventions.* San Francisco: New Lexington Press.

James, B., & Nasjleti, M. (1983). *Treating sexually abused children and their families.* Palo Alto, CA: Consulting Psychologists Press.

Johnson, R. L. (1988). Long-term effects of sexual abuse in boys. *Medical Aspects of Human Sexuality, 22,* 34–38.

Kluft, R. (Ed.). (1985). *Childhood antecedents of multiple personality.* Washington, DC: American Psychiatric Press.

Lew, M. (1988). *Victims no longer: Men recovering from incest and other sexual child abuse.* New York: Nevraumont.

Nielsen, T. (1983). Sexual abuse of boys: Current perspectives. *Personnel and Guidance Journal, 62,* 139–142.

Porter, E. (1986). *Treating the young male victim of sexual assault: Issues and intervention strategies.* Brandon, VT: Safer Society Press.

Ryan, G. (1989). Victim to victimizer: Rethinking victim treatment. *Journal of Interpersonal Violence, 4,* 325–341.

Sebold, J. (1987). Indicators of child sexual abuse in males. *Social Casework, 68,* 75–80.

Summit, R. C. (1983). Child sexual abuse accommodation syndrome. *Child Abuse and Neglect, 7,* 177–193.

Tong, L., Oates, K., & McDowell, M. (1987). Personality development following sexual abuse. *Child Abuse and Neglect, 11,* 371–383.

Urquiza, A. J., & Capra, M. (1990). The impact of sexual abuse: Initial and long-term effects. In M. Hunter (Ed.), *The sexually abused male: Vol. 1. Prevalence, impact, and treatment* (pp. 105–135). San Francisco: New Lexington Press.

Waterman, C. K., & Foss-Goodman, D. (1984). Child molesting: Variables relating to attribution of fault to victims, offenders, and nonparticipating parents. *Journal of Sex Research, 20,* 329–349.

Young, R. E., Bergandi, T. A., & Titus, T. G. (1994). Comparison of the effects of sexual abuse on male and female latency-aged children. *Journal of Interpersonal Violence, 9,* 291–306.

Empowerment in Therapy

Carlson, S. (1990). The victim/perpetrator: Turning points in therapy. In M. Hunter (Ed.), *The sexually abused male: Vol. 2. Application of treatment strategies* (pp. 249–266). San Francisco: New Lexington Press.

Finkelhor, D., & Browne, A. (1985). The traumatic impact of child sexual abuse: A conceptualization. *American Journal of Orthopsychiatry, 55,* 530–541.

Friedrich, W. N. (1995). Managing disorders of self-regulation in sexually abused boys. In M. Hunter (Ed.), *Child survivors and perpetrators of sexual abuse* (pp. 3–23). Thousand Oaks, CA: Sage.

Froning, M. L., & Mayman, S. B. (1990). Identification and treatment of child and adolescent male victims of sexual abuse. In M. Hunter (Ed.), *The sexually abused male: Vol. 2. Application of treatment strategies* (pp. 199–224). San Francisco: New Lexington Press.

Gerber, P. N. (1990). Victims becoming offenders: A study of ambiguities. In M. Hunter (Ed.), *The sexually abused male: Vol. 1. Prevalence, impact, and treatment* (pp. 153–175). San Francisco: New Lexington Press.

James, B. (1989). *Treating traumatized children: New insights and creative interventions.* San Francisco: New Lexington Press.

Lew, M. (1988). *Victims no longer: Men recovering from incest and other sexual child abuse.* New York: Nevraumont.

Mandell, J. G., & Damon, L. (1989). *Group treatment for sexually abused children.* New York: Guilford Press.

Pescosolido, F. J. (1989). Sexual abuse of boys by males: Theoretical and treatment implications. In S. M. Sgroi (Ed.), *Vulnerable populations: Vol. 2. Sexual abuse treatment for children, adult survivors, offenders, and persons with mental retardation* (pp. 85–109). San Francisco: New Lexington Press.

Porter, E. (1986). *Treating the young male victim of sexual assault: Issues and intervention strategies.* Brandon, VT: Safer Society Press.

Porter, F. S., Blick, L. C., & Sgroi, S. M. (1982). Treatment of the sexually abused child. In S. M. Sgroi (Ed.), *Handbook of clinical intervention in child sexual abuse* (pp. 109–145). San Francisco: New Lexington Press.

Rogers, C. M., & Terry, T. (1984). Clinical intervention with boy victims of sexual abuse. In I. R. Stuart & J. G. Greer (Eds.), *Victims of sexual aggression: Treatment of children, women and men* (pp. 91–104). New York: Van Nostrand Reinhold.

Ryan, G. (1989). Victim to victimizer: Rethinking victim treatment. *Journal of Interpersonal Violence, 4,* 325–341.

Sgroi, S. M., Bunk, B. S., & Wabrek, C. J. (1988). Children's sexual behaviors and their relationship to sexual abuse. In S. M. Sgroi (Ed.), *Vulnerable populations: Vol. 1. Evaluation and treatment of sexually abused children and adult survivors* (pp. 1–24). San Francisco: New Lexington Press.

Urquiza, A. J., & Capra, M. (1990). The impact of sexual abuse: Initial and long-term effects. In M. Hunter (Ed.), *The sexually abused male: Vol. 1. Prevalence, impact, and treatment* (pp. 105–135). San Francisco: New Lexington Press.

Vasington, M. C. (1989). Sexual offenders as victims: Implications for treatment and the therapeutic relationship. In S. M. Sgroi (Ed.), *Vulnerable populations: Vol. 2. Sexual abuse treatment for children, adult survivors, offenders, and persons with mental retardation* (pp. 329–350). San Francisco: New Lexington Press.

Treatment Activities

Gil, E., & Johnson, T. C. (1993). *Sexualized children: Assessment and treatment of sexualized children and children who molest.* Rockville, MD: Launch Press.

James, B. (1989). *Treating traumatized children: New insights and creative interventions.* San Francisco: New Lexington Press.

James, B., & Nasjleti, M. (1983). *Treating sexually abused children and their families.* Palo Alto, CA: Consulting Psychologists Press.

Mayer, A. (1983). *Incest: A treatment manual for therapy with victims, spouses and offenders.* Holmes Beach, FL: Learning Publications.

Treatment Issues and Modalities

Berliner, L., & Ernst, E. (1984). Group work with preadolescent sexual assault victims. In I. R. Stuart and J. G. Greer (Eds.), *Victims of sexual aggression: Treatment of children, women and men* (pp. 105–124). New York: Van Nostrand Reinhold.

Breer, W. (1992). *Diagnosis and treatment of the young male victim of sexual abuse.* Springfield, IL: Thomas.

Friedrich, W. N. (1995). *Psychotherapy with sexually abused boys: An integrated approach.* Thousand Oaks, CA: Sage.

Friedrich, W. N., Berliner, L., Urquiza, A. J., & Beilke, R. L. (1988). Brief diagnostic group treatment of sexually abused boys. *Journal of Interpersonal Violence, 3,* 331–343.

Friedrich, W. N., Luecke, W. J., Beilke, R. L., & Place, V. (1992). Psychotherapy outcome of sexually abused boys. *Journal of Interpersonal Violence, 7,* 396–409.

Gil, E., & Johnson, T. C. (1993). *Sexualized children: Assessment and treatment of sexualized children and children who molest.* Rockville, MD: Launch Press.

Gonsiorek, J. C. (1994). Diagnosis and treatment of young adult and adolescent male victims: An individual psychotherapy model. In J. C. Gonsiorek, W. H. Bera, & D. LeTourneau, *Male sexual abuse: A trilogy of intervention strategies* (pp. 56–110). Thousand Oaks, CA: Sage.

Grayson, J. (1989). Sexually victimized boys. *Virginia Child Protection Newsletter, 29,* 1–16.

Hack, T. F., Osachuk, T.A.G., & DeLuca, R. V. (1994). Group treatment for sexually abused preadolescent boys. *Families in Society, 75,* 217–228.

Halpern, J. (1987). Family therapy in father-son incest: A case study. *Social Casework, 68,* 88–93.

James, B. (1989). *Treating traumatized children: New insights and creative interventions.* San Francisco: New Lexington Press.

James, B. (1994). *Handbook for treatment of attachment-trauma problems in children.* New York: Free Press.

Jewett, C. (1982). *Helping children cope with separation and loss.* Boston, MA: Harvard Common Press.

Kübler-Ross, E. (1969). *On death and dying.* New York: Collier Books.

Lamb, S. (1986). Treating sexually abused children: Issues of blame and responsibility. *American Journal of Orthopsychiatry, 56,* 303–307.

Mandell, J. G., & Damon, L. (1989). *Group treatment for sexually abused children.* New York: Guilford Press.

Naitove, C. E. (1982). Arts therapy with sexually abused children. In S. M. Sgroi (Ed.), *Handbook of clinical intervention in child sexual abuse* (pp. 269–308). San Francisco: Lexington Books.

Nelki, J. S., & Watters, J. (1989). A group for sexually abused young children: Unravelling the web. *Child Abuse and Neglect, 13,* 369–377.

Oaklander, V. (1978). *Windows to our children.* Moab UT: Real People Press.

Pescosolido, F. J. (1989). Sexual abuse of boys by males: Theoretical and treatment implications. In S. M. Sgroi (Ed.), *Vulnerable populations: Vol. 2. Sexual abuse treatment for children, adult survivors, offenders, and persons with mental retardation* (pp. 85–109). San Francisco: New Lexington Press.

Porter, E. (1986). *Treating the young male victim of sexual assault: Issues and intervention strategies.* Brandon, VT: Safer Society Press.

Porter, F. S., Blick, L. C., & Sgroi, S. M. (1982). Treatment of the sexually abused child. In S. M. Sgroi (Ed.), *Handbook of clinical intervention in child sexual abuse* (pp. 109–145). San Francisco: New Lexington Press.

Rogers, C. M., & Terry, T. (1984). Clinical intervention with boy victims of sexual abuse. In I. R. Stuart & J. G. Greer (Eds.), *Victims of sexual aggression: Treatment of children, women and men* (pp. 91–104). New York: Van Nostrand Reinhold.

Rubin, J. A. (1984). *The art of art therapy.* New York: Brunner-Mazel.

Schacht, A. J., Kerlinsky, D., & Carlson, C. (1990). Group therapy with sexually abused boys: Leadership, projective identification, and countertransference issues. *International Journal of Group Psychotherapy, 40,* 401–417.

Smith, S. (1985). *Children's story: Sexually molested children in criminal court.* Rockville, MD: Launch Press.

Whitfield, C. L. (1995). *Memory and abuse: Remembering and healing the effects of trauma.* Deerfield Beach, FL: Health Communications.

Yalom, I. D. (1985). *The theory and practice of group psychotherapy.* New York: Basic Books.

Understanding and Treating Sexually Abusive Behavior by Abused Boys

Bagley, C., Wood, M., & Young, L. (1994). Victim to abuser: Mental health and behavioral sequels of child sexual abuse in a community survey of young adult males. *Child Abuse and Neglect, 18,* 683–697.

Ballester, S., & Pierre, F. (1995). Monster therapy: The use of a metaphor in psychotherapy with abuse reactive children. In M. Hunter (Ed.), *Child survivors and perpetrators of sexual abuse* (pp. 125–146). Thousand Oaks, CA: Sage.

Benoit, J. L., & Kennedy, W. A. (1992). The abuse history of male adolescent sex offenders. *Journal of Interpersonal Violence, 7,* 543–548.

Berliner, L. (1993). Identification and treatment of children with sexual behavior problems. *National Resource Center on Child Sexual Abuse News, 2,* 4–7.

Bolton, F., Morris, L., & MacEachron, A. (1989). *Males at risk: The other side of child sexual abuse.* Thousand Oaks, CA: Sage.

Breer, W. (1992). *Diagnosis and treatment of the young male victim of sexual abuse.* Springfield, IL: Thomas.

Browne, A., & Finkelhor, D. (1986). Impact of child sexual abuse: A review of the research. *Psychological Bulletin, 99,* 66–77.

Cantwell, H. B. (1995). Sexually aggressive children and societal response. In M. Hunter (Ed.), *Child survivors and perpetrators of sexual abuse* (pp. 79–107). Thousand Oaks, CA: Sage.

Finkelhor, D. (1986). *A sourcebook on child sexual abuse.* Thousand Oaks, CA: Sage.

Finkelhor, D., & Browne, A. (1985). The traumatic impact of child sexual abuse: A conceptualization. *American Journal of Orthopsychiatry, 55,* 530–541.

Friedrich, W. N., & Luecke, W. J. (1988). Young school-age sexually aggressive children. *Professional Psychology: Research and Practice, 19,* 155–164.

Froning, M. L., & Mayman, S. B. (1990). Identification and treatment of child and adolescent male victims of sexual abuse. In M. Hunter (Ed.), *The sexually abused male: Vol. 2. Application of treatment strategies* (pp. 199–224). San Francisco: New Lexington Press.

Gerber, P. N. (1990). Victims becoming offenders: A study of ambiguities. In M. Hunter (Ed.), *The sexually abused male: Vol. 1. Prevalence, impact, and treatment* (pp. 153–175). San Francisco: New Lexington Press.

Gil, E. (1987). *Children who molest: A guide for parents of young sex offenders.* Rockville, MD: Launch Press.

Gil, E., & Johnson, T. C. (1993). *Sexualized children: Assessment and treatment of sexualized children and children who molest.* Rockville, MD: Launch Press.

Groth, A. N. (1979). Sexual trauma in the life histories of rapists and child molesters. *Victimology, 4,* 10–16.

Groth, A. N., & Burgess, A. W. (1980). Male rape: Offenders and victims. *American Journal of Psychiatry, 137,* 806–810.

Groth, A. N., & Oliveri, F. J. (1989). Understanding sexual offense behavior and differentiating among sexual abusers: Basic conceptual issues. In S. M. Sgroi (Ed.), *Vulnerable populations: Vol. 2. Sexual abuse treatment for children, adult survivors, offenders, and persons with mental retardation* (pp. 309–327). San Francisco: New Lexington Press.

Johanek, M. F. (1988). Treatment of male victims of child sexual abuse in military service. In S. M. Sgroi (Ed.), *Vulnerable populations: Vol. 1. Evaluation and treatment of sexually abused children and adult survivors* (pp. 103–113). San Francisco: New Lexington Press.

Johnson, T. C. (1989). Female child perpetrators: Children who molest other children. *Child Abuse and Neglect, 13,* 571–585.

Johnson, T. C., & Berry, C. (1989). Children who molest: A treatment program. *Journal of Interpersonal Violence, 4,* 185–203.

Kaufman, A., DiVasto, P., Jackson, R., Voorhees, D., & Christy, J. (1980). Male rape victims: Noninstitutionalized assault. *American Journal of Psychiatry, 137,* 221–223.

Kikucki, J. J. (1995). When the offender is a child: Identifying and responding to juvenile sexual abuse offenders. In M. Hunter (Ed.), *Child survivors and perpetrators of sexual abuse* (pp. 108–124). Thousand Oaks, CA: Sage.

Knopp, F. (1985). *The youthful sex offender: The rationale and goals of early intervention and treatment.* Brandon, VT: Safer Society Press.

Lew, M. (1988). *Victims no longer: Men recovering from incest and other sexual child abuse.* New York: Nevraumont.

Pfafflin, F. (1992). What is in a symptom? A conservative approach in the therapy of sex offenders. In E. Coleman, S. M. Dwyer, & N. J. Pallone (Eds.), *Sex offender treatment: Psychological and medical approaches* (pp. 5–17). New York: Haworth Press.

Porter, E. (1986). *Treating the young male victim of sexual assault: Issues and intervention strategies.* Brandon, VT: Safer Society Press.

Rogers, C. M., & Terry, T. (1984). Clinical intervention with boy victims of sexual abuse. In I. R. Stuart & J. G. Greer (Eds.), *Victims of sexual aggression: Treatment of children, women and men* (pp. 91–104). New York: Van Nostrand Reinhold.

Ryan, G. (1989). Victim to victimizer: Rethinking victim treatment. *Journal of Interpersonal Violence, 4,* 325–341.

Seghorn, T. K., Boucher, R. J., & Prentky, R. A. (1987). Childhood sexual abuse in the lives of sexually aggressive offenders. *Journal of the American Academy of Child and Adolescent Psychiatry, 26,* 262–267.

Sgroi, S. M. (Ed.). (1988). *Vulnerable populations: Vol. 1. Evaluation and treatment of sexually abused children and adult survivors.* San Francisco: New Lexington Press.

Sgroi, S. M., Bunk, B. S., & Wabrek, C. J. (1988). Children's sexual behaviors and their relationship to sexual abuse. In S. M. Sgroi (Ed.), *Vulnerable populations: Vol. 1. Evaluation and treatment of sexually abused children and adult survivors* (pp. 1–24). San Francisco: New Lexington Press.

Summit, R. C. (1983). Child sexual abuse accommodation syndrome. *Child Abuse and Neglect, 7,* 177–193.

Williams, L. M., Siegel, J. A., Banyard, V. L., Jasinski, J. L., & Gartner, K. L. (1995). *Juvenile and adult offending behavior and other outcomes in a cohort of sexually abused boys: Twenty years later.* Durham: University of New Hampshire, Family Research Laboratory.

Sexual Identity and Sexual Abuse

Blumenfeld, W., & Raymond, D. (1988). *Looking at gay and lesbian life.* Boston: Beacon Press.

Breer, W. (1992). *Diagnosis and treatment of the young male victim of sexual abuse.* Springfield, IL: Thomas.

Doll, L. S., Joy, D., Bartholow, B. N., Harrison, J. S., Bolan, G., Douglas, J. M., Saltzman, L. E., Moss, P. M., & Delgado, W. (1992). Self-reported childhood and adolescent sexual abuse among adult homosexual and bisexual men. *Child Abuse and Neglect, 16,* 855–864.

Finkelhor, D. (1981). The sexual abuse of boys. *Victimology, 6,* 76–84.

Finkelhor, D. (1986). *A sourcebook on child sexual abuse.* Thousand Oaks, CA: Sage.

Froning, M. L., & Mayman, S. B. (1990). Identification and treatment of child and adolescent male victims of sexual abuse. In M. Hunter (Ed.), *The sexually abused male: Vol. 2. Application of treatment strategies* (pp. 199–224). San Francisco: New Lexington Press.

Gilgun, J. F., & Reiser, E. (1990). The development of sexual identity among men sexually abused as children. *Families in Society, 71,* 515–523.

Isay, R. (1989). *Being homosexual: Gay men and their development.* New York: Farrar, Straus & Giroux.

Lew, M. (1988). *Victims no longer: Men recovering from incest and other sexual child abuse.* New York: Nevraumont.

Planned Parenthood. (1986). *How to talk with your child about sexuality: A parent's guide.* New York: Doubleday.

Specific Populations

Allen, D. M. (1980). Young male prostitutes: A psychosocial study. *Archives of Sexual Behavior, 9,* 399–426.

Janus, M., Burgess, A. W., & McCormack, A. (1987). Histories of sexual abuse in adolescent male runaways. *Adolescence, 22,* 405–417.

McCormack, A., Janus, M., & Burgess, A. W. (1986). Runaway youths and sexual victimization: Gender differences in an adolescent runaway population. *Child Abuse and Neglect, 10,* 387–395.

Adult Survivors

Bear, E., & Dimock, P. T. (1988). *Adults molested as children: A survivor's manual for women and men.* Brandon, VT: Safer Society Press.

Briere, J., Evans, D., Runtz, M., & Wall, T. (1988). Symptomatology in men who were molested as children: A comparison study. *American Journal of Orthopsychiatry, 58,* 457–461.

Bruckner, D. F., & Johnson, P. E. (1987). Treatment for adult male victims of childhood sexual abuse. *Social Casework, 68,* 81–87.

Dimock, P. T. (1988). Adult males sexually abused as children: Characteristics and implications for treatment. *Journal of Interpersonal Violence, 3,* 203–221.

Hunter, M. (1990). *Abused boys: The neglected victims of sexual abuse.* San Francisco: New Lexington Press.

Kelly, R. J., MacDonald, V. M., & Waterman, J. M. (1987, January). *Psychological symptomatology in adult male victims of child sexual abuse: A preliminary report.* Paper presented at the joint conference of the American Psychological Association Division 12 and the Hawaii Psychological Association, Honolulu.

Lew, M. (1988). *Victims no longer: Men recovering from incest and other sexual child abuse.* New York: Nevraumont.

Singer, K. I. (1989). Group work with men who experienced incest in childhood. *American Journal of Orthopsychiatry, 59,* 468–472.

Female Offenders

Banning, A. (1989). Mother-son incest: Confronting a prejudice. *Child Abuse and Neglect, 13,* 563–570.

Harper, J. (1993). Prepuberal male victims of incest: A clinical study. *Child Abuse and Neglect, 17,* 419–421.

Johnson, T. C. (1989). Female child perpetrators: Children who molest other children. *Child Abuse and Neglect, 13,* 571–585.

Krug, R. S. (1989). Adult male report of childhood sexual abuse by mothers: Case descriptions, motivations and long-term consequences. *Child Abuse and Neglect, 13,* 111—119.

Peluso, E., & Putnam, N. (1996). Case study: Sexual abuse of boys by females. *Journal of the American Academy of Child and Adolescent Psychiatry, 35,* 51–54.

Books to Read with Children

Chamberlin, N. (1985). *My day at the courthouse.* West Linn, OR: Trials and Smiles.

Dayee, F. (1982). *Private zone.* New York: Warner Books.

Drake, E., Gilroy, A., & Roane, T. (1990). *Working together: A team effort.* Gainesville, FL: Child Care Publications.

Fay, J. (1979). *He told me not to tell.* Renton, WA: King County Rape Relief.

Flynn, K. (n.d.). *Some questions you may ask about going to court.* Minneapolis, MN: Hennepin County Public Affairs Department.

Freeman, L. (1983). *It's my body.* Seattle: Parenting Press.

Gil, E. (1986). *I told my secret: A book for kids who were abused.* Rockville, MD: Launch Press.

Gordon, S., & Gordon, J. (1984). *A better safe than sorry book.* Fayetteville, NY: Ed-U Press.

Haddad, J., & Martin, L. H. (1984). *What if I say no!* Bakersfield, CA: M. H. Cap and Company.

Hindman, J. (1985). *A very touching book.* Durkee, OR: McClure-Hindman Associates.

Lankton, S. R. (1988). *The blammo-surprise! book: A story to help children overcome fears.* New York: Magination Press.

MacFarlane, K., & Cunningham, C. (1988). *Steps to healthy touching.* Mount Dora, FL: Kidsrights.

Madaras, L. (1987). *The what's happening to my body? book for boys.* New York: Newmarket Press.

Marcus, I. W., & Marcus, P. (1990). *Scary night visitors: A story for children with bedtime fears.* New York: Magination Press.

Mayer, M. (1968). *There's a nightmare in my closet.* New York: Dial Books for Young Readers.

Mayle, P. (1973). *Where did I come from?* Secaucus, NJ: Lyle Stuart.

Mayle, P. (1975). *What's happening to me?* Secaucus, NJ: Lyle Stuart.

Mills, J. C., & Crowley, R. J. (1988). *Sammy the elephant and Mr. Camel: A story to help children overcome enuresis while discovering self-appreciation.* New York: Magination Press.

Narimanian, R. (1990). *Secret feelings and thoughts: A book about male sexual abuse.* Philadelphia: Healing Hearts Series.

National Committee for Prevention of Child Abuse. (1987). *Spiderman Comics: Spiderman, Spiderman and Power Pack, Special Editions.* New York: Marvel Comic Group.

Rape and Abuse Crisis Center of Fargo-Moorhead. (1992). *Andy.* Fargo, ND: Red Flag Green Flag Resources.

Russell, P., & Stone, B. (1986). *Do you have a secret?* Minneapolis, MN: CompCare.

Ruzicka, J. (n.d.). *Kids go to court, too.* Minneapolis, MN: Hennepin County Public Affairs Department.

Sanford, L. (1982). *Come tell me right away.* Fayetteville, NY: Ed-U Press.

Satullo, J., Russell, R., & Bradway, P. (1987). *It happens to boys too.* Pittsfield, MA: Rape Crisis Center of the Berkshires Press.

Stowell, J., & Dietzel, M. (1982). *My very own book about me!* Spokane: Lutheran Social Services of Washington.

Stringer, G., & Rants-Rodriguez, D. (1987). *So what's it to me? Sexual assault information for guys.* Renton, WA: King County Rape Relief.

Stringer, G., & Rants-Rodriguez, D. (1987). *So what's it to me? activity guide: Sexual assault information for guys.* Renton, WA: King County Rape Relief.

Wachter, O. (1983). *No more secrets for me.* New York: Little, Brown.

Williams, J. (1983). *Red flag green flag people.* Fargo, ND: Rape and Abuse Crisis Center.

THE AUTHOR

LISA CAMINO is a licensed clinical social worker in the Aspen Community Services Post-Traumatic Stress Disorder Program in Orange County, California. She received her B.A. degree (1979) in psychology and social welfare from the University of California-Berkeley, and her M.S.W. degree (1983) at San Diego State University. She has sixteen years of experience working with sexually abused children.

Camino is a member of the National Association of Social Workers, Phi Beta Kappa, Author's Guild, and the American Professional Society on the Abuse of Children. She wrote the pamphlet, "You Can Help: Assisting Your Son After Sexual Abuse" (1988).

INDEX

A

Absences: in group therapy, 68, 69; in individual therapy, 110–111

Abusive behavior, clarifying, 200–201

Acceptance of help: evaluating, for discharge from group, 85; facilitating, 16–17

Acceptance, unconditional, 12–13

Accountability: addressing, for prevention of sexually abusive behavior, 11; group goals related to, 76, 77; strategies for promoting, 9

Achenbach Child Behavior Checklist, 130

Achenbach Teacher Rating Scale, 130

Acting-out behaviors. *See* Aggressive behaviors; Problem behaviors

Activities. *See* Structured activities

Administrative challenges, 129–131

Adult Survivor, Meeting with an (Activity 47), 231–233

Affirmations (Activity 8), 154–157

Age ranges: group goal setting by, 76–77; listed, 66; organizing groups around, 66–67

Agency referrals for groups, 73–74

Aggressive behaviors, 8; addressing anger and, 59–61; assertive behaviors versus, 197–199; in groups, 71, 115–116; structured activities for, 193–199. *See also* Anger; Problem behaviors

Anatomically correct dolls, 172

Anger: addressing, for prevention of sexually abusive behavior, 11; addressing, in group therapy, 76, 77, 115–116; addressing, in individual therapy, 59–61; affirmations for repressed, 155; case examples of, 61; depression and, 55; educating parent about therapy for, 92–93; group goals related to, 76, 77; healthiness of, 60; identifying contributing factors in, 60; issues to address for, 59–61;

parental support for child's managing, 102–104; of parents, 103–104; payoffs of, 59; as response to abuse, 53; role models for handling, 103; structured activities for, 151–154, 192–199, 230–231, 233–236; symptoms related to, 27, 102; techniques for releasing, 55, 60, 95, 115; worsening of, at beginning of therapy, 36

Anger, Releasing and Resolving (Activity 28), 195–197

Anger Zone, Identifying Your (Activity 27), 193–194

Anxiety: structured activities for, 147–149, 151–154, 168–169, 171–174, 201–205; symptoms related to, 26–27

Apology, offender, 24

Art therapy, 239–240

Artwork, 55, 60, 110, 239–240; structured activities with, 169–171, 172, 190–191, 201–203

Assertive communication, 121, 197–199